Under One Roof

Under One Roof

Retail Banking and the International Mortgage Finance Revolution

Michael Ball
Department of Economics, Birkbeck College, University of London

St. Martin's Press
New York

First published in the United States of America in 1990

Printed in Great Britain

ISBN 0-312- 05566-8

Library of Congress Cataloging-in-Publication Data
Applied for.

Contents

Contents

Figures

Tables

Acknowledgements

This book has been developed from a series of research projects undertaken in the 1980s. A number of them were undertaken with Michael Harloe and Maartje Martens and are summarised in Ball *et al*. (1990). Maartje Martens' specific contribution to the work on West Germany is acknowledged in the joint authorship of that chapter, but more generally I should like to thank both of them for an enjoyable series of collaborations and their advice and encouragement to me during the writing of this book. In addition, I should like to thank Jerry Coakley and Lucia Hanmer for their comments on earlier drafts of specific chapters.

Finally, I should like to thank the following bodies for funding aspects of the research on which the book is based: the Economic and Social Research Council, the Leverhulme Trust, the Anglo—German Foundation for the Study of Industrial Society and the Joseph Rowntree Memorial Trust.

None of the above bears responsibility for the analysis, conclusions and any remaining errors.

1

The international mortgage finance revolution

If someone in an advanced economy wanted a mortgage to buy a house in the post-war years up to the mid-1970s they would go to one or more of specialist institutions dealing in mortgage finance. The mortgage terms offered would generally be far more attractive than could be achieved by raising any other form of funding. Plentiful, low cost mortgage finance was an aim of all governments. There was a consensus that this could be achieved only through explicit state intervention: into financial markets — by giving mortgage institutions privileges to encourage investors to deposit funds with them — and by subsidising mortgage borrowers through a variety of tax relief, savings and subsidy schemes.

Tax relief and subsidies to homeowners still remain, but in some countries the privileges of the mortgage institutions have been substantially eroded and elsewhere previously independent institutions have been taken over by banks and insurance companies. New institutions have muscled into mortgage markets, sometimes threatening the very existence of the traditional lenders. From being relatively isolated from the mainstream of the financial world, house mortgages have become one of the keystones of the much talked about financial supermarkets of the future. Even the flow of funds into housing finance is being internationalised, with mortgage-backed securities and bonds increasingly traded on and between the major financial centres and large-scale loans raised on the Euromarkets. The world of mortgage finance has been irrevocably changed.

At the same time, retail banking too has undergone major change. Until the 1970s, many commercial banks put little emphasis on their personal customers. The banks were often encouraged in this approach by government restrictions on their activities and/or by cartel arrangements amongst the banks. Bank customers had little choice but to accept the services and charges banks offered them. The two decades that followed changed all that. The depositor base of the banks came under threat from new savings mediums and from the deposit interest rates offered by mortgage institutions. Technology and deregulation opened up new potential areas of retail business. The banks went 'personal'. By the late 1980s, for instance, US and British bank customers enjoyed interest on most of their deposit accounts (including their current/checking accounts).

Everywhere the mortgage market came to be one of the most important retail areas for general financial institutions. Well over half of consumer debt is usually tied up in house mortgages and a number of other financial products are bought by consumers at the same time as the mortgage is taken out. More firms also want to become general retail banks. The traditional mortgage institutions in Britain and the USA have increasingly taken on banking functions, whilst in western Europe may previously independent mortgage banks have been absorbed by large commercial banks. Severe crises hit the US mortgage industry twice during the 1980s and it is likely that many of the institutions that survive into the 1990s will be subsidiaries of larger groups. The British building societies have also begun to shed the mutual status that formally distinguishes them from banks. From being an independent sphere, mortgage finance is now firmly part of retail banking, so the two have to be considered together.

Many banks that are not already so are keen to become 'universal banks' offering to clients the whole range of wholesale and retail banking services. Non-banking financial services, such as insurance and pensions, are also being increasingly drawn into the net. This could eventually lead to widespread integration between banks and insurance companies. So a future can be envisaged when all financial services are obtained from 'under one roof'. Integration may not stop there, as some have suggested that electronic payment systems will encourage firms involved in retail shopping to take advantage of their customer base and extend their activities into the financial services sphere. Whether or not such scenarios actually come into being, the wide variety of options under discussion indicates the extent of the changes currently taking place and the uncertainty over what they will ultimately lead to.

Change in retail financial services between countries is not taking a standardised form. So, whilst transformations in retail banking and mortgage finance have occurred in many countries, generalisations must be made with care. The financial systems of individual countries are still structurally very different despite widespread deregulation. Mortgage finance and its institutional frameworks are no exception. Housing markets also vary considerably between countries. This means that there is little likelihood of standardised systems of mortgage finance arising internationally within the foreseeable future.

It is important not to see developments in mortgage finance as arising simply from external events which have imposed themselves on the mortgage market. What stands out most clearly from a historical analysis of housing markets and mortgage finance is that a static, sleepy world did not exist before the mortgage finance revolution. Considerable developments were always occurring and institutions were continually adjusting their strategies and roles to new circumstances. Much of the impetus for the mortgage finance revolution arose as a result of growing problems in previous systems. Those problems were brought to a head in the tumultuous years of economic crisis and rapid inflation during the late 1970s and early 1980s and they have still not been fully resolved.

This book describes in some detail the changes in mortgage finance that are taking place and how mortgage finance has merged into and affected retail banking. Detailed examination is made of developments in three countries: Britain, West Germany and the USA. The aim is not just to map out the changes but to explain why they are occurring, and who benefits or loses from them.

1.1 Approaches to understanding the mortgage finance revolution

A wide variety of explanations of the transformation of retail banking and mortgage finance have been suggested: some place emphasis on macroeconomic trends, others concentrate on the impact of information technology, and yet others focus on competition and the quest for efficiency. Three broad empirical concerns can be distinguished in the analytical approaches used to explain the changes: their attitude to the operation of financial markets and the institutions active there; their treatment of structural change and other contemporary economic phenomena; and, lastly, the weight that they give to the role of housing markets. Not all approaches cover all three aspects. In fact, many ignore the housing market altogether because of the overriding role given to other features of contemporary economic change. The analysis in this book emphasises the interrelationship between developments in housing and financial markets when they examine the processes through which retail banking and mortgage markets have become integrated.

Explanation requires a theory within which to evaluate change, and distinct theoretical frameworks exist with respect to the analysis of retail banking. To an extent, those frameworks are formulated on the basis of divergent beliefs about the operation of financial markets and the behaviour of agents active within them. A major schism in the literature is between those who believe that financial markets are fundamentally stable and efficient and those who see them as unstable and crisis prone.

These issues have influenced the structure of this book. After the scene has been set in Chapter 2, Chapter 3 elaborates the major theoretical approaches to financial markets and assesses their relevance for understanding the transformation of mortgage finance. Differences between these theories revolve partly around distinct views on the role of institutions and incentives and on the formation of expectations. Thus these issues are considered in detail. A division arises here between the US and European literature. Following the extraordinary excesses and crooked dealing in the activities of parts of the US savings and loans industry that have come to light in recent years, it is perhaps not surprising that principal/agent incentives and moral hazard have been central to US debates over the savings and loan deregulation debacle; yet in western Europe such issues have received scant attention. One major absence in the general literature is any theoretical examination of the nature of competition in retail banking. Chapter 4 highlights the issues involved and suggests that market profiles rather than producer economies are the basis of competition. Chapters 5 to 8 consider actual developments over the past thirty years in the USA, Britain and West Germany. Chapter 9 draws out some of the implications of these empirical findings for general theoretical discussion and policy debate.

1.2 Is the extra mortgage competition good for everyone?

It was widely held in the late 1980s that parables about the efficiency of unrestrained competitive markets can be easily transposed to actual markets and the operations of the agencies within them. The means of achieving this is as simple as the parables themselves — all possible market relations should be opened up to the powerful forces of private enterprise, and government interference should be reduced to a minimum. In some situations it is accepted that market competition is impractical or infeasible. Then it is argued the agents involved should be given incentives or constraints to operate in the desired ways (ones that are usually attempts to replicate atomistic markets). An example in financial services is the regulatory insistence on 'Chinese walls' or 'firebreaks' within some multi-function firms, so that one activity does not gain from privileged information available in another. Deposit-insurance, as practised in the USA, has also been highlighted as an area for market-related reform to avoid excessive risk-taking by participant banks (see Chapter 6).

In general, the deregulation of mortgage markets receives strong and unquestioning approval on the basis of these parables. The development of new mortgage instruments, the greater range of mortgage lenders and heightened competition between them are obviously good things when viewed through such ideological light. The nub of the competitive argument is that previous legislative and institutional arrangements gave privileged mortgage lenders a cosy life which made them inefficient, unresponsive to innovation, and high cost intermediaries. Everyone benefits from the reduced costs forced by competition and the searching out of new sources of funds and ways of lending them to prospective homeowners.

Two quotes illustrate the unqualified acceptance of the universal benefits of the changes. They represent by far the dominant view in the financial press and academic literature. The first is a quote from the 1988 chairman of the Building Societies Association in Britain. After having reviewed the legislative and competitive changes that had occurred in the 1980s, he concluded:

> For the consumer all this is very encouraging. Anything which increases the range of choice, whether it be in the financial services market, the banking market, or the housing finance market, must be beneficial, and there has been a marked improvement in the quality of service, particularly in respect of banking and mortgage finance. (Stoughton-Harris, 1988, p. 6)

One academic comparing developments in the mortgage markets in the USA and Britain concluded that, 'on the whole, changes in the housing finance sectors in Britain and the United States offer a fairer and more efficient mortgage market' (Roistacher, 1987). Even in the USA, after the thrift catastrophe in the deregulated 1980s which is likely to cost the US government over $170 billion in the next decade, most commentators would still not question the benefits of unrestrained competition but criticise only the market distortions generated through flat-rate deposit insurance, inadequate capital/asset ratios and lax regulatory supervision.

Yet, is the bracing world of financial competition as comforting in its outcomes as free market protagonists would have us believe? This is the key question addressed in this book. One possible outcome of the revolution in mortgage finance is particularly worrying. Rather than moving from a situation where certain mortgage institutions were given quasi-monopolistic privileges by the state to one of beneficial atomistic competition, is not the world of mortgage finance moving rapidly towards a situation of monopolistic competition? In it, the strategy of a limited number of institutions can influence strongly the terms and availability of mortgage and other retail finance products in a framework where chronic excess capacity is an ever-present threat; whilst the lending policies of 'rogue' institutions can threaten the viability of mortgage markets and even national financial systems themselves. There is some evidence from a number of countries that such negative consequences do arise and that the problems they pose may grow in the future. The outcomes of the mortgage finance revolution, in other words, may foreshadow unpredicted structural problems and lead to market inefficiency and undesirable redistributions of income and wealth. This does not mean that the past situation was necessarily better. The old mortgage finance and retail banking structures have gone forever, but what has replaced them should still be subject to critical enquiry and new ground rules may need to be devised.

It will be argued here that the simple parable of a contrast between efficient competition in an unrestrained marketplace and distortions and resistance to change with strong state regulation of those markets is a false one which does not accurately portray the current transformation of financial services. Instead, more subtle recognition is required of the behaviour of financial institutions in specific market structures and historical contexts. If this is undertaken and acted upon then governments may have greater success in formulating rules that bring out the benefits of competition in retail financial services rather than inadvertently encouraging the excesses.

2

Setting the scene

When looking at processes of change it is necessary to know what is being changed and some of the general pressures encouraging the developments. This chapter serves a number of functions in order to facilitate the subsequent analysis. First, it provides some basic information on mortgage finance and housing markets and their transformation. Next, it considers the relation of mortgage credit to overall consumer debt, followed by a brief examination of the relevance, if any, of the decline in the savings ratio experienced in a number of countries during the 1980s and the impact of the institutional structure of the savings market. Then it evaluates two underlying processes of change in financial markets, internationalisation and new technology, and assesses their relevance in explaining contemporary transformations of mortgage finance.

The general functions of retail banking and deposit-taking are well-known and are common across countries. No broad overview of retail banking consequently is required here. There are considerable variations in precise institutional practice and regulatory controls between countries. But the relevant aspects of the frameworks within which each country's banking system operates will be described in the specific chapters dealing with the three case-study countries. What is less well-known are the wide differences in countries' traditional systems of mortgage finance, the impact on them of the growth of owner occupation and adverse effects on them of inflation, interest rate volatility and mass unemployment in the 1980s. These issues are now addressed in broad terms.

2.1 Traditional systems of mortgage finance

The capital cost of adequate housing is generally too high to be financed directly out of current household income, so recourse to borrowing is necessary. Public and private landlords also borrow to fund their housing investments. Housing provision has as a result been closely associated with savings and capital markets since the advent of large-scale urbanisation at the end of the eighteenth century. Yet the need to borrow funds for housing obviously does not determine the form in which they are made available. For a variety of reasons, distinct mortgage finance systems evolved in specific countries, and mortgages as they are known today became prevalent in the late nineteenth and early twentieth centuries.

It is a sign of the development of a sophisticated financial system that institutions are able to channel funds into the small-scale and potentially risky sphere of lending to individual households to buy their homes. The difficulties that have to be overcome are considerable. Large volumes of funds have to be drawn in from a variety of sources and disseminated to millions of borrowers. The creditworthiness has to be ascertained of what to the ultimate investors are unknown borrowers. Those investors have to be persuaded to deposit money or purchase bonds at rates of interest and repayment terms that reflect widespread belief in the security of mortgage debt and the soundness of mortgage lending enterprises.

Prior to the evolution of institutional mortgages, funds for house purchase were often scarce because they were limited to informal local lending networks through which borrowers would be put in direct touch with investors by some intermediary (such as a family lawyer or accountant). Investors also acquired a highly illiquid asset as no general market existed on which mortgage obligations could be traded. Because of such a fragmented structure, the risk of individual default could not be spread across a pool of outstanding mortgage debt. Modern mass homeownership, therefore, needed as a precondition for its existence some form of large-scale mortgage finance institution.

In practice, most countries have for many years had an almost bewildering variety of means through which to obtain mortgage finance, but generally one type of mortgage institution and its mortgage instruments became the linchpin around which others operated. Two main forms of mortgage finance can be identified. One relies on medium- to long-term, fixed interest investments from capital markets; the other depends on short-term savings deposits from the personal sector.

The state played a key role in the setting up of mortgage institutions associated with capital markets. Legislation was necessary to permit the floating of mortgage bonds on what were often primitive capital markets, and intervention was sometimes necessary in the formation of the mortgage institutions themselves. With personal sector short-term deposits, conversely, governments did not have to take a direct role in the initial creation of small-scale 'self-help' mortgage institutions, but quite quickly they had to intervene to protect savers from unscrupulous institutions or bankruptcy. State intervention via regulation and initiation, therefore, is as old as mortgage finance itself.

In some countries — including most of western Europe — a tradition of *mortgage bonds* exists as the prime form of mortgage finance. They are generally issued by specialist mortgage banks. Mortgage banks issue tradeable bonds on the basis of pools of mortgages. They are required to match the terms on which mortgages are lent with those of the bonds sold to finance them, both with regard to repayment periods and the fixed rate of interest. In this way the mortgage bank is not exposed to the risks associated with interest rate movements and differences in the repayment profiles of assets and liabilities. With mortgage bonds, investors have a well-defined financial asset with clear interest and repayment profiles and an ability to assess the soundness of the institution issuing them. Mortgage bonds are major elements of the capital markets of those countries where they have been in widespread use for long periods. They are most important in places where the corporate sector issues few equities or bonds, as in West Germany and Denmark.

In other countries, notably Britain, its ex-dominions and the USA, funding systems for housing arose in other ways. For large-scale rental housing, capital markets are still the prime source of funds. A rental institution issues equities or debt in its name to be traded on the general equities and bond markets. Council housing in Britain, for example, is indirectly funded in this way via general local-authority borrowing — with the added advantage of the bonds being implicitly guaranteed by the state. For small-scale rental housing and owner occupation, however, mortgages increasingly came to be issued by institutions relying on deposits in households' savings accounts.

The savings account as a source of finance for mortgages began in a small way in eighteenth century Britain with the formation of the first building society. The institutional form was subsequently exported to countries that at one time or another formed part of the British Empire. Similar building and loans associations were founded in the USA in the nineteenth century — whether they were a British or German import is under dispute (Daunton, 1988). Britain and the USA now have the largest number of this type of institution, and British building societies are some of the biggest financial institutions in the country. In the USA, the savings and loans associations (S&Ls) as a whole are similarly a central component of the financial system, although the sector is more fragmented. Along with general US savings banks and credit unions, S&Ls have for generations been known as thrifts.

Outside the UK, western European countries do not have building societies as such, yet all have general savings banks which are active in mortgage lending. Indeed, West Germany and Austria have contractual savings institutions whose prime function is to lend for house purchase. Savings banks differ considerably from specialist retail finance mortgage institutions yet, like them, they traditionally invested in long-term (and generally fixed-interest) assets because they were the banks of the mass of the population who, excluded from such facilities as pension schemes, would use the services of savings banks as a means of covering long-term contingencies like income in old age.

Specialist housing-related savings institutions pool individual deposits to provide sufficient funds for mortgage lending. No attempt is made to match the terms of mortgages issued with those given to depositors. Mortgages are long term whilst savings deposits may be withdrawn at short notice. The setting of interest rates varies from country to country. In the USA, with an anti-usury tradition and a distrust of financial institutions, fixed-term interest rates for borrowers (but not for savers) rapidly became the norm until the 1980s. Over time, repayment terms lengthened from five years or less (common at the time of the massive mortgage defaults of the early 1930s) to twenty years or more. In Britain, its more pliant housing consumers have had to bear all of the potential interest rate risk as mortgages developed on which interest charges could be varied whenever the lender wanted to revise them. Here, too, repayment periods gradually lengthened to twenty to thirty years.

Some of the prime distinctions in mortgage finance consequently arose for historical reasons associated with the evolution of a particular country's financial system and the role of mortgage finance within it. Reliance on capital markets is frequently termed *wholesale funding*. Financing via individuals' deposits in savings and other accounts is commonly called *retail funding*. Mortgages themselves are of varying length in terms of repayment periods. Generally, repayments are spread over what remains of the high earning years of a typical borrower, which is a period of between twenty and thirty years. Mortgage interest can be either *fixed* at a rate determined at the beginning of a loan, *variable*, or some hybrid of the two.

Neither the wholesale nor the retail systems emerged smoothly. In the USA the early 1930s witnessed one of the most dramatic periods of mortgage default and a widespread collapse of thrifts and banks. In Germany, periodic mortgage market panics and hyperinflation wreaked havoc with the value of mortgage bonds in the late nineteenth century, the 1920s and 1940s. The history of mortgage finance in most countries is littered with the collapse of reckless mortgage finance institutions. Most regulatory legislation emerged in response to financial excesses. Legislation generally evolved in a piecemeal, damage limitation fashion, and its implementation often did not take much account of the consequences for the competitive structure of mortgage provision.

Although different countries can be categorised on the basis of their traditional dominant system of mortgage finance, virtually all have for many years had a mix of the wholesale and retail systems. Sometimes access to one or other source was delineated by housing tenure. Evolution has continually occurred in mortgage finance, and strictly what is being described here as the traditional form of mortgage finance is often really only that which existed in the 1950s and 1960s. Since then, however, there has been a noticeable shift in the balance between retail and wholesale funding. Capital markets have come to play more important roles in mortgage finance in Britain and the USA, whilst retail financial institutions and insurance companies have expanded their mortgage business in bond dominated countries.

2.2 Pressures on the traditional mortgage institutions

Much of the impetus for change since the early 1970s came from institutions muscling into the house mortgage market with innovatory packages, as happened with investment banks in the USA and clearing banks and others in the UK. Yet it would be wrong to see this competition as a sudden change in the environment faced by the traditional mortgage institutions. Prime facilitators of the conditions encouraging new entrants in the late 1970s and early 1980s, in particular, were the severe contemporary difficulties faced by traditional lenders. In part, those difficulties were beyond the traditional lenders' control, but analysis of their responses to changed circumstances offers a key to understanding the restructuring of mortgage finance in specific countries.

Some traditional lenders saw their old markets slowly decline, whilst for others one problem was the sheer buoyancy of demand for owner-occupied mortgages during much of the 1970s and 1980s. In markets dominated by retail savings, the flow of mortgage funds had to be increased — even though other savings media were concurrently becoming more attractive.

The rise of inflation in the 1970s was a major element in the demise of traditional mortgage finance systems. All traditional forms of mortgage finance were devised to operate within economic environments characterised by stable prices and interest rates. The onset of rapid inflation, rising nominal interest rates and volatility in financial markets led to fundamental strains. Problems existed for borrowers as well as lenders. Mortgage debt is generally calibrated at historic cost — the price level existing at the time the loan was made. Real interest rates can be sustained through rises in nominal rates, but uncertainty and distributional problems still arise. With long-term, fixed-interest mortgages the task of accurately forecasting inflation over the period of the loan is impossible, so both lender and borrower are threatened (in opposite ways) by unforeseen changes in inflation. Inflation and high nominal rates also lead to the phenomenon of 'front-loading' whereby the real value of interest and principal repayments are considerably higher in the early repayment years than later, in contrast to the annuity principle which aims to spread repayments evenly over the loan period. Changed real repayment profiles create problems for lenders and force borrowers in real terms to pay back far more of the loan in the early years.

Associated with inflation from 1973 onwards were economic crises and rising unemployment. Unemployment has been a particularly severe problem in western Europe. It excludes households from entering new mortgage commitments and greatly increases the threat of default. Mortgage lending became a more risky activity in many countries from the late 1970s onwards.

The impact of the altered interest rate framework proved disastrous for the previously developed financing principles of many mortgage institutions. As a result they also faced periodic interest rate crises. The most spectacular were the enormous losses faced by US thrifts caught in the early 1980s holding large pools of low fixed-interest rate mortgages. Interest rate volatility again played a role in exacerbating the late-1980s thrift crisis. British building societies faced interest rate problems when they could no longer maintain their mortgage rates below levels which made wholesale market funding attractive, thereby enabling other institutions to enter what had often previously been an unprofitable market for them. Western European mortgage banks began to encounter difficulties in matching the terms demanded by bond investors and mortgage clients in the late 1970s. Rising interest rates imposed large-scale capital losses on bond holders and discouraged households from borrowing. In addition, many mortgage banks faced unprecedented collapses in their countries' housing markets — most spectacularly in the Netherlands, where within the space of a few years all of the previously independent mortgage banking institutions disappeared as separate entities through insolvency and/or takeover (Martens, 1988).

Housing markets were affected by the general economic pattern of inflation, higher interest rates, recession and then upturn. No country has been immune from housing market problems at some time during the 1980s. The demand for capital finance for council housing in Britain and social housing in the rest of Europe dried up in the early 1980s as housebuilding programmes were slashed, and in the case of Britain because council housing sales receipts outstripped new expenditure. From the early 1970s onwards, owner-occupied housing markets — like interest rates — began to exhibit increased volatility, both in the level of transactions and the rate of house price change. House price falls virtually unheard of in the twenty years prior to 1974 became a depressing occurrence in all countries at one time or another. The worst problems in most countries have been localised to areas of severe economic collapse. Yet everywhere there have been signs of periodic strain with housing costs rising at a greater rate than average incomes (although with cyclical variations) and extra mortgage default — as the individual country chapters below show.

2.3 The growth of mortgage debt in different types of housing market

Housing finance differs from other forms of consumer credit not only because of the scale and longevity of the debt that households and landlords incur but also because of the nature of housing provision itself. Two factors are of particular contemporary importance: the tax benefits and subsidies uniquely available when borrowing (and sometimes saving) for housing purposes, and the expansion of owner-occupation at the expense of rental tenures. Countries' housing systems vary considerably, both in their tenure structure and in the ways in which housing is subsidised. They have also been changing in different ways, so not surprisingly some of the reasons for current variations between countries in the nature of mortgage provision and its integration into the broader structure of retail finance is to be found in housing provision.

Benefits to mortgage financiers of housing subsidies

In most countries, housing has a privileged tax status. The greatest privileges are conferred on owner-occupiers. Many commentators have criticised the distorting effects of such subsidies. They are said to increase demand and over-stimulate investment in housing as a whole, and to distort the allocation of housing and households between the different types of tenure. Problems arise over the extent to which these effects occur as much of the subsidy may be capitalised in the price of housing and in increases in the cost of the services offered by agencies in the system of provision. Supply elasticities in housing provision vary considerably and are generally unknown. (For discussion of the issue in the context of the USA, see Aaron, 1972 and Downs, 1980; for the UK see Nevitt, 1966 and the Duke of Edinburgh Report, 1985; although none of these references consider capitalisation and supply effects.)

As far as the provision of mortgage finance is concerned, housing subsidies make housing an attractive sphere in which to lend. Not only is it likely that housing demand in general is encouraged by such fiscal benefits, but also the forms of some of the key subsidies have particular advantages for mortgage credit institutions. One of the principal fiscal dispensations given to owner-occupiers in many countries is income tax relief on mortgage interest. The financial product sold by mortgage finance institutions, in other words, is specifically subsidised. Subsidies, therefore, not only induce more housing demand as a whole but also create a substantial bias towards mortgage borrowing. Homeowners are encouraged to take out larger mortgages to maximise their tax benefits; possibly to the detriment of using more own wealth in house purchase or at the expense of other forms of consumer credit in countries where only housing debt incurs tax relief.

Apart from its stimulus to the demand for mortgages, another effect of mortgage interest tax relief is that mortgage consumers are less sensitive to interest rate costs, as tax reliefs are generally proportional to the level of interest charged. As a result consumers are shielded from bearing the full brunt of the pricing policies of mortgage finance institutions. Mortgage institutions, therefore, have greater freedom in their mortgage pricing strategies than would be the case in an unsubsidised market. Part of the tax relief on mortgage interest, therefore, frequently ends up subsidising the profits or the inefficiencies of mortgage credit institutions rather than helping owner-occupiers to buy their homes.

Impact of the shift towards homeownership

Owner-occupation has been growing relative to other tenures in many countries. The USA was an exception in the 1980s — its homeownership rate even fell by a few percentage points. The expansion of owner-occupation has been particularly strong in western Europe, where many countries have abandoned large-scale social housebuilding programmes and rental housing stocks have been substantially reduced through sales to owner-occupiers. The scale of the shift varies from country to country, being greatest in Britain (Ball *et al.*, 1988).

Despite the growth of homeownership in the 1980s, significant differences in the scale of owner-occupation still exist between countries, variations which have important effects on the nature and need for mortgage finance. Continental western European countries have much lower owner-occupation rates than Britain and the USA. In West Germany, for example, only 40 per cent of households were owner-occupiers in the mid-1980s, and the percentage was far less in most urban areas. The growth of mass homeownership in Britain and the USA was intimately associated with the expansion of building societies and thrifts. Mortgage banks in western Europe, conversely, traditionally lent more funds to rental housing than to owner-occupation; they were an important conduit for public sector borrowing as well. The shift towards homeownership in the 1970s created new market contexts for the European mortgage banks to which not all institutions could successfully adjust. In West Germany the shift led to a relative decline of publicly-owned mortgage banks and in the Netherlands it led to badly judged property speculation.

Owner-occupied housing markets do not have uniform characteristics (Martens, 1988). There are several reasons for the differences, some of which are associated with the institutional structure of mortgage finance. Some of the consequences of the distinctive nature of their housing markets are discussed in the individual country studies in later chapters.

Particular housing tenures, furthermore, create specific demands for mortgage funds. Social housing either creates no demand for mortgage finance, as with the funding of council housing in Britain, or it creates a one-off demand to finance the cost of new dwellings or to renovate existing ones. Social housing institutions in western Europe have relied predominantly on mortgage finance, but mortgages fund only the historic costs of their housing stocks. Many social rental dwellings have an outstanding mortgage debt that is nil or very small.

Owner-occupation generates a much greater demand for mortgage finance. A dwelling in this tenure is brought to market many times throughout its life and sold at prevailing market prices. Much of the resale value each time is financed through a new mortgage, so in this tenure mortgage demand does not depend on the rate of new housebuilding. In addition, house prices tend to rise with general price inflation and increases in housing production costs relative to other commodities. Rising house prices and the spasmodic nature of the shift towards homeownership have periodically given major boosts to mortgage markets. New entrants to mortgage finance generally emerge during these booms.

Owner-occupied housing markets tend to be unstable, with periods of rapidly escalating prices followed by stagnation or slump. Decisions to purchase or move by households are closely tied to contemporary trends in income and wealth. Much household wealth itself for owner-occupiers is tied up in their homes, so even changes in their wealth are linked to the state of the housing market. Contemporary interest rate levels also influence the affordability of purchase. As a result owner-occupied housing markets are highly sensitive to changes in macroeconomic circumstances. The problems of mortgage institutions in the late 1970s and early 1980s, for instance, were closely associated with the depths of the economic recession then existing in most industrial countries. Conversely, the 1980s revolution in mortgage finance took place while most owner-occupied housing markets were booming; a situation which of course did not last forever.

2.4   The rise of mortgage and other consumer debt

During the 1970s and 1980s mortgage debt grew substantially in most countries, often as part of a general rise in consumer indebtedness. But its growth varied widely between countries. Some of the difference is associated with the nature of housing provision, particularly the extent of owner-occupation, how it is financed, and the level and movement of house prices. Household willingness to hold debt, and mortgage debt in particular, seems also to change — and some nations are debt averse whereas others are not.

The scale of mortgage holdings and their importance relative to total personal sector assets and liabilities is shown for the USA, UK, West Germany and Japan in Table 2.1. The data are expressed as ratios of total personal incomes to make international comparison easier, and are given for selected years from 1970 to 1987. It can be seen that they have all changed substantially, but in different ways.

The USA in 1970 was the most mortgaged country, which is not surprising given its high homeownership rate at the time relative to the other countries. Its mortgage to income ratio continued to rise throughout the next decade, after

Table 2.1 Mortgage to income and net worth to income ratios, 1970–87, selected countries

	1970	1975	1980	1982	1984	1986	1987
Mortgages/income							
USA	0.41	0.42	0.50	0.48	0.50	0.57	0.60
UK	n.a.	0.34	0.33	0.40	0.49	0.60	0.67
W. Germany	0.05	0.03	0.06	0.04	0.05	0.02	0.02
Japan	0.09	0.18	0.31	0.34	0.36	0.38	n.a.
Total liabilities/income							
USA	0.72	0.71	0.81	0.78	0.83	0.94	0.97
UK	n.a.	0.55	0.57	0.66	0.79	0.94	1.04
W. Germany	0.08	0.09	0.15	0.15	0.16	0.16	0.17
Japan	0.60	0.62	0.76	0.82	0.88	0.90	n.a.
Net worth/income							
USA	4.51	4.23	4.76	4.58	4.53	4.66	4.62
UK[a]	n.a.	1.30	1.28	1.45	1.71	1.97	2.06
W. Germany[a]	1.08	1.23	1.37	1.48	1.58	1.65	1.68
Japan	3.97	4.14	5.04	5.44	5.61	6.50	n.a.

[a] Net financial wealth.
Source: OECD (1988e).

which it stabilised during the high nominal interest years of 1980–4, and then grew by 20 per cent in only three years to stand at 0.60 of incomes in 1987. Overall, there was a substantial increase in the ratio between 1970 and 1987. In fact, all of the growth in the US personal indebtedness ratio since the early 1970s seems to have been associated with mortgage finance, as can be seen by comparing the ratios of total liabilities to income with mortgages to income alone in Table 2.1. In contrast to this growing personal indebtedness, the ratio of net worth to income was stable throughout the period so increases in personal wealth presumably counterbalanced the extra debt.

Britain shows the most spectacular growth in mortgage debt during the 1980s, and after 1985 it had the highest mortgage to income ratio of all the countries shown. Much of the growth was concentrated in a few years after 1983. Unlike the USA, other forms of personal sector debt increased as well. Rising house prices raised consumer wealth, as in the USA, offsetting the debt increase, but in the late 1980s house prices began to fall.

West Germany has a remarkably distinct pattern of mortgage debt. In relation to incomes, mortgage debt is insignificant with a ratio of only 0.02 in 1987, and there has even been a slight fall since 1980. Total liabilities did rise, however, although again the ratio was still comparatively low. So mortgages, contrary to the other countries, became a smaller source of total consumer debt in the 1980s. Part of the reason for the low recorded levels of mortgage debt, however, is the treatment of housing for tax purposes as an investment, so many personal sector mortgages do not appear in West German consumer data. The pattern in Japan again is different. The mortgage debt to income ratio rose rapidly during the 1970s, presumably because both homeownership and house prices increased. In the 1980s the rate of increase slowed, so that the mortgage debt to income ratio is still much lower than in the UK and USA.

There was much comment on both sides of the Atlantic throughout the 1980s over the high levels of debt that households seem prepared to bear, despite record real interest rates. Critical commentators have spoken moralistically of the 'live now, pay later' society. Concern was expressed in Britain during the period of rapid house price rise in southern England from 1986 to 1988, with worries not only about the scale of credit expansion but also of its effects in over-stimulating private demand and the distortions created in the economy as a whole. One distortion widely commented upon was the inability of workers to move to regions with buoyant labour markets because of high house prices (OECD, 1988a; Bover *et al.*, 1988).

A number of explanations have been put forward for the general rise in consumer debt in the 1980s, some of which are directly related to housing markets and the activities of credit agencies there. The rise in debt is claimed to be partly an artefact of new forms of transactions payment. Growing use of credit cards, in particular, leads to a greater recording of debt even when the outstanding sums on credit cards are paid off by their first billing date (FRB, 1987). Other explanations emphasise the formation of consumer preferences with respect to debt (e.g. Bank of England, 1989). They stress the greater certainty implied by the lower and more stable rates of inflation that existed in the 1980s as compared with the 1970s. Consumers, it is argued, felt more assured about their long-term real incomes and so were prepared to contemplate greater borrowings. Wealth effects have been suggested as well. In Britain it was argued that rising house prices and buoyant stock markets both augmented the net wealth of the personal sector offsetting the extra debt — enabling households to realise previously credit-constrained debt/asset ratios. One problem with the argument that net wealth offsets the extra debt is that the additional mortgage debt helped to fuel the house price rises that caused much of the increase in net wealth — which could be regarded as a classic property market speculative bubble rather than a prudent matching of assets and liabilities.

In US and UK housing markets, a process known as equity withdrawal became more marked in the 1980s. Equity refers to the difference between the current price of a house and the mortgage debt outstanding on it. It is the value the owner-occupied household would realise in selling the house, paying off all the debt and moving into a hotel. Equity withdrawal refers to a number of distinct processes. Consumers can increase their indebtedness either through remortgaging or by not using all of the net proceeds of a previous house sale when purchasing a new home. Use of such borrowings has advantages over other forms because of the lower rates of interest charged when debt is secured against real property and the tax exemptions of housing-related borrowing. Equity may also be withdrawn from owner-occupied housing through intergenerational transfer, by moving out of the tenure or abroad, or through the purchase of a cheaper dwelling, possibly in a lower priced locality.

Equity withdrawal has led to much adverse comment since the mid-1980s in Britain about the desirability of unrestrained mortgage credit expansion, particularly as owner-occupied mortgages are uniquely subject to mortgage tax relief. It is felt that tax reliefs aimed at housing costs have often been used to finance other consumer purchases; mortgage lenders in the late 1980s were required by the Bank of England to tighten up on vetting procedures to ensure that housing-related tax subsidies were not being misused. Lenders were also exhorted to ensure that households ploughed most of their housing equity back into their new home rather than increased their mortgages.

No such restrictions were adopted in the USA. The tax reforms of 1986 left housing-secured borrowings as the only personal interest costs available for tax relief, with reliefs on other interest payments being gradually phased out by 1991. The new tax privileged status of mortgage debt has led to rapid growth of home equity accounts (FRB, 1988). These accounts enable consumers to borrow against the equity in their houses, at variable rates of interest, subject to certain constraints. In 1987, only 4 per cent of homeowners had a home equity account so the market is expected to grow rapidly. The financial institutions pushed the accounts heavily: nearly half of all large financial institutions spent more on advertising home equity accounts in 1986 than any other loan product. Lenders like the accounts because of the low default risk, the automatic adjustment of interest rates in contrast to traditional mortgages and the potential to cross-sell other financial products. There has been some criticism of the way the accounts encourage consumption and the rundown of a consumer asset which could help finance longer-term needs such as retirement. The FRB (1988) report discounts the increased consumer spending argument, suggesting that the accounts lead to a switching of borrowings rather than to an overall increase. Interestingly, in contrast to Britain, no criticism is made of the use of house-related tax relief in this way. This is perhaps surprising because, if the accounts do increase substantially as anticipated, much of the extra tax revenue achieved by excluding non-housing interest payments from relief will be lost via the switch of consumer debt to home equity accounts.

2.5 Changes in savings

Retail deposits are obviously part of people's liquid savings. How much people save and in what forms they choose to hold their savings effect the supply of mortgage funds.

Overall, the savings ratio has declined during the 1980s in both Britain and the USA. In Britain the savings ratio fell from a peak of almost 16 per cent of personal disposable income in 1981 to only 4 per cent in 1987. The US 1987 figure was also only 4 per cent. In the rest of western Europe the pattern was more mixed. Denmark's fell to 7 per cent in 1987 from an exceptional high of 18 per cent in the early 1980s. In West Germany, conversely, the ratio rose slightly to stand at 12 per cent in 1987; while in the Netherlands, France and Italy savings ratios also remained high (13 per cent in 1986) (OECD, 1987 and 1988a—e). Part of the reason for falls in savings ratios is lower inflation. Inflation-adjusted savings ratios show less steep declines but even the inflation-adjusted ratios are still very low in the UK and USA (OECD, 1988e).

The large falls in the UK and US savings ratios at first glance would appear to reduce the availability of the funds for which building societies and thrifts compete. But the picture is complicated by transfers within the personal sector. The savings ratio calculated for the personal sector is a net figure: gross savings minus borrowings as a proportion of total personal disposable income. This means that most funds deposited with mortgage institutions and the mortgages borrowed from them by the personal sector are netted out in the overall ratio because they represent transfers solely within the personal sector — with some households' savings funding the borrowing of others. It is perfectly feasible, as a result, for deposits with savings institutions to rise as a proportion of total disposable income whilst the savings ratio itself declines.

Choice is not the only influence on consumers' allocation of their savings. A savings mode may be compulsory, as with pensions; or it may require large minimum sums or have high penalty costs of withdrawal. Some schemes commit savers to fixed sums over long periods with no possibility of switching to more competitive rates when they are offered elsewhere — as occurs, for example, with life policies, the Bausparkassen schemes in West Germany and some general savings schemes in France. Even mortgage debt itself can sometimes be in effect forced saving. With homeownership often the only feasible housing option, incurring a large mortgage debt might be the only means that lower income or younger households have of housing themselves.

Compulsory pension schemes have grown in importance in all countries over the past twenty years, as incomes have risen and an increasing proportion of the employed population is drawn into them. Even so, wide variations exist between countries. Denmark, for instance, has a relatively underdeveloped private pensions system, so that many Danes have to invest in bonds (a large part of which is mortgage bonds) in order to finance retirement. In a country like Britain, where compulsory pension schemes are virtually universal amongst full-time white collar employees and are spreading amongst manual workers, recourse to other savings media is less necessary for households. Most of the high Dutch savings ratio results from contractual savings with life insurance companies and pension funds. In 1986, only 2.8 per cent of the 13.3 per cent overall savings ratio was actually 'free' savings (OECD, 1987). Such institutional structures affect the flows of personal sector savings and whether they end up financing housing. One of the notable features of the British mortgage market, for example, is the virtual absence of pension funds from it, unlike in most other countries. Specific tax reliefs on certain savings media create similar channelling effects, as with special privileges to pension or life insurance contributions.

2.6 The internationalisation of money and capital markets

One of the most talked about features of the world financial system is its increased integration. National finance systems are now interdependent in ways inconceivable twenty years ago. The internationalisation of finance has had its impact on mortgage markets.

Technical change has been one spur to internationalisation. It is now possible to deal in a whole series of the world's financial markets from one location because of computerisation and the increased speed and capacity of telecommunications systems. Bonds, securities and other financial instruments are widely traded internationally. Investors for new issues can be looked for in many countries. Financial innovations developed in one country are rapidly transferred to others, often through the overseas branches of the innovating firms. The invention of mortgage-backed securities in the USA spread to Europe during the late 1980s; especially to Britain, with mixed, but growing, success. Similarly the US investment banks have been able to approach foreign investors, particularly the Japanese, to invest in US mortgage-backed securities. So what was solely a domestic US market in the 1970s became more international. Even in late 1988, however, the chief executive of Fannie Mae, the major US mortgage institution, was still saying that the international market for mortgage backed securities was very small (*Financial Times*, 7 October 1988). Foreign financial institutions can also buy up pools of mortgages, as with the sale of Chemical Bank's UK mortgage portfolio in 1988. (Chemical Bank itself was already a relatively recent US entrant to the British banking scene.)

The meteoric growth of the Eurodollar market has also had its effect on mortgage finance. Eurodollar loans and bonds are outside the regulatory scope of a particular national market or currency. Loans can be denominated in any currency and 'Euro' in reality simply denotes the international character of the market. Mortgage finance institutions have been able to tap this market in the 1980s. It has, for instance, provided one of the main sources of wholesale funds for the UK building societies in the 1980s. Rates of interest on the Eurodollar markets have become a benchmark against which to cost other sources of funds, such as retail savings.

Part of the reason for the internationalisation of finance is the large world trade imbalances of the 1980s. Some countries, the USA and Britain in particular, have large trade deficits; whilst others have equivalent surpluses, especially Japan and West Germany. Trade deficits have to be matched by inflows on capital accounts, and surpluses by outflows. Some of the financial inflows have found their way into mortgage markets. Along with the trade deficits, however, have gone high interest rates and exchange rate volatility, which have created problems in housing markets as much as elsewhere. But, at the same time they have encouraged non-traditional mortgage finance institutions to enter mortgage finance because of the national and international arbitrage possibilities that exist.

The need for risk assessment and rating has grown with internationalisation. The imperative for mortgage-backed securities to be insured has also increased, as international investors are generally unaware of the status of the issuing body. Mortgage institutions have sometimes found their credit-rating on international money markets relatively low because of international ignorance of the institution in question.

Internationalisation has been a competitive stimulus in a number of mortgage markets but so far only in limited ways. Partly because of the prior existence of mortgage-backed securities in the USA, there has been little direct impact on the structure of the US mortgage market. Yet, securitisation grew from around 7 per cent of outstanding mortgage debt in 1970 to almost 40 per cent in 1986 — and now accounts for 70 per cent of new mortgages (see Chapter 6). Ostensibly all that mortgage-backed paper could be traded internationally, although in practice most of it has to date been purchased by US institutions. American banking markets in general are dominated by domestic firms in a way that western European ones, apart from West Germany, are not. The extreme case of internationalisation is the UK (Table 2.2). To date, traditional mortgage lenders have not become part of international banking conglomerates but remain domestically owned. In western European countries with a strong mortgage bond tradition, internationalisation seems so far to have had little institutional effect on mortgage finance; although within the European Community the 1992 single market measures will mean that all financial

Table 2.2 The growth of foreign firms in domestic banking

| | Percentage of total assets of deposit money banks | | |
	1970	1980	1985
USA	2.9	12.1	9.1
UK	46.1	64.6	68.9
W. Germany	8.7	9.7	11.5
Netherlands	27.0	35.1	38.3
Denmark	6.7	24.5	39.6

Source: OECD (1988a).

institutions will be able to trade their products throughout the Community as long as at least one member state's regulatory authority has sanctioned them.

Internationalisation has been distinct in Britain. Firms there can enter the mortgage market knowing the advantages of London as a site for international financial transactions. It means that they do not have to rely on traditional UK sources of funds, and that mortgage portfolios once built up can easily be sold on, or securitised, if desirable. Consequently part of the new mortgage competition of the 1980s was foreign, either in its sources of funds or in the ownership of the new mortgage issuing institutions. Using their abilities to tap the international wholesale money markets these institutions have become a new third force in mortgage finance, alongside the building societies and the clearing banks. One of the most well-publicised new entrants is the National Home Loans Corporation, which by 1988 was one of the top mortage lenders, raising finance internationally as well as nationally. Some of its mortgages are packaged for the international market in mortgaged-backed securities.

2.7 The impact of technical change on mortgage finance

Computerisation has had a substantial effect on mortgage finance as it has in other parts of the financial services industry. The cost of handling transactions has fallen substantially. The range of information that can be quickly assembled has been transformed out of all recognition. The profile of repayment associated with different mortgage packages and assumptions about inflation and interest rates can be shown to prospective customers by pressing a few keys on a desktop computer rather than requiring laborious calculations of a limited number of options as was necessary in the mid-1970s and earlier. The ability to undertake such complex calculations quickly and present them in a way easily understandable to the lay-person has altered and widened the marketing options open to the sellers of mortgages land associated financial products. Mortgages can more easily be packaged to suit the individual needs of customers and firms can appear, and actually be, more responsive to the wishes of their customers. New savings products can also be offered, accounts updated quickly, and money transmission mechanisms upgraded. Automatic telling machines, especially when shared between a variety of institutions, vastly increase the effective branch network of even quite small savings institutions and extend the range of time during the day that customers have access to their savings and other accounts.

The costs of entry of institutions into specific financial services markets has been greatly reduced by the advent of widespread computerisation. This has enabled even small enterprises to become intermediary sellers of a wide range of financial services to the general public. It has been a major contributor, for example, to the growing importance of mortgage bankers in the USA. On a larger scale, it has enabled previously non-financial institutions to enter the financial services sector and mortgage finance in particular — a trend that is again most advanced in the USA. The financial supermarket, where people can obtain all of their financial needs, from mortgages to insurance to investment advice, is made possible (though not inevitable) by computerisation.

For many people it is the technical transformation of financial services that is a prime mover in breaking down barriers to competition and opening up new product markets. Technological change has been argued by many to be the dominant structural explanation for the long-term transformation of mortgage finance as part of a general decline it has created of specialist financial institutions (Kane, 1984; Carron, 1982a and 1983; Tucillo, 1983). Innovation in the context of financial services means new combinations and formulations of existing products. Much of the transformation of the retail financial sector, including mortgage finance can be interpreted as attempts by specific institutions to be ahead in the race towards the technically efficient financial supermarket of the future. Many see this race as leading to a small number of large institutions reaping economies of scale and scope through their financial supermarkets (cf. Fforde, 1983). The scenario of the financial supermarket, however, is one potential outcome of technological innovation. In chapter 4 it is argued that the technological superiority frequently suggested for the multi-product financial institution is questionable.

Computerisation has opened and transformed the competitive possibilities in financial services because information is central to the activities of a financial intermediary. The costs of its transmission, storage and presentation are major influences on profitability. But whilst it affects the potential range of competition, computerisation does not actually determine the competitive outcome. A wide variety of outcomes are feasible within its ambit. It is possible to hypothesise a centralisation of financial services into a few mega-institutions; or the opposite of widespread decentralisation resulting from the increased ease of access to general information systems and world markets. Or even to conceive of the total elimination of most financial intermediaries altogether as their skills and specialist knowledge are made redundant by the breadth of new computerised information systems.

Not all possible outcomes, however, are realisable. Competition in financial services is about more than the delivery of the most information at the lowest possible cost. Furthermore, greater information is not the same as perfect knowledge. It is the constraints on the span of knowledge available to individual parties in financial transactions, and the ways in which consumers and financial institutions react to the limits on their own information systems, that help to determine the actual outcome of any competitive market situation. The framework of competition in retail banking and mortgage markets is the concern of the next two chapters.

3

Economic theory and financial markets

Explanations of the changes taking place in retail financial markets are strongly influenced by the theoretical presuppositions on which they are formulated, even though those theories may only be implicit within the reasoning underlying the explanation. This chapter considers one aspect of the theoretical analysis of financial markets: the functioning of the financial system as a whole. Obviously such theories make assumptions about the behaviour of financial agents and have underlying theories about the ways in which those agents compete. Yet in many financial market theories, institutions and other agents are shadowy entities, behaving in ways specified by a few broad generalisations. Analysis that goes beyond those generalisations is left until the next chapter.

There are as many theories of financial systems as there are economic theories in general, but perspectives on the operation of the financial system can be broadly divided into three schools: efficient markets, chronic instability and institutional power. Mixes and compromises between these distinct views of the operation of the financial system are possible, but presented in their starkest form they help to indicate why different interpretations can be given of the international restructuring of retail banking and mortgage finance.

3.1 Efficient market theory

Many economists argue that financial markets are inherently efficient. Given the efficiency of market mechanisms, financial systems should predominantly be left to their own devices. But governments unfortunately are often tempted to interfere with financial markets to placate one or other special interest group. Efficient market theorists therefore have argued strongly for the deregulation of financial markets. American economists have been at the forefront of the efficient market view, and its popularity grew in the late 1970s and early 1980s with the increasing fashionability of rational expectations theory and new classical economics. (For an excellent introduction to the theory and policy prescriptions of the efficient market perspective see Kaufman and Kormendi, 1986. For more theoretical perspectives, see Fama, 1976 and Mishkin, 1986.)

Efficient market theory argues that competitive markets produce optimal outcomes because of the rapid and rational responses of agents to the available information and changes in it. Purchasers of financial services and instruments — such as bank and savings deposits, equities and bonds — make valuations of the worth of any instrument and, where necessary, the viability of the institution offering it. Their valuations are based on utilising all the information available on investment possibilities, including forecasts of future economic trends.

If an institution offers a financial asset or service, efficient market theory claims that its price has to reflect accurately the competitively determined costs of providing it. In the case of a bond, for example, its price is fixed in accordance with the flow of future income associated with it, valued in the light of contemporary market interest rates and information on factors such as default risk. Assessments of risk influence the price of the service and may determine the type of institution that can efficiently offer it. The latter occurs, for example, in cases where the pooling of risks across a wide variety of assets minimises the cost of provision, or where the additional payment of an insurance premium covers against risk. Through such processes financial intermediation costs are kept to a minimum. Any institution or asset not offering such competitive services will fall by the wayside.

What happens to a bank undertaking too many risky investments in this theory? Consumers, knowing of the risks associated with depositing money in the bank, will either demand a compensatingly higher rate of return or withdraw their funds. Collapse of the bank should not, however, threaten the stability of the financial system as other institutions knowing of the potential weakness of the bank would have refrained from investing in it or have limited their exposure to any threat of default that may arise. Poorly managed institutions either have to reform or go into liquidation. Failure is seen as an important stimulus to efficiency.

For efficient market theorists, state regulation is regarded unfavourably as it interferes with the effective operation of competitive market processes. Regulation limits the possibility of badly managed institutions failing, thereby weakening the discipline of the market. All major financial institutions know instead that governments ultimately will bail them out rather than face a perceived threat to the financial system as a whole (see Kaufman *et al.*, 1984). Federal deposit insurance in the USA has been subject to much criticism by efficient market theorists because the insurance premiums are flat rate. This encourages deposit-taking institutions to undertake excessively risky investments which distort the operation of the financial services sector and ultimately impose unsustainably large costs on the federal budget through insurance losses (see Chapter 6).

Central to efficient market perspectives is the view that individuals and institutions take all the available appropriate economic information and then use it as a basis to evaluate current market prices and risks. They operate, in other words, in terms of what has come to be known as the 'fundamentals' of the economy or market in question. Agents in this sense are rational, utilising the best information available and understanding that market economies rapidly adjust back to full capacity equilibrium after shocks, if governments let them. Because of the belief in the speed of adjustment of markets, individuals have little reason to be concerned over how other agencies are reacting to changing market circumstances. Others might judge events incorrectly, but there is little systematic possibility of profiting from their misjudgements.

Knowledge of the future is severely limited. Risk — which is formally defined as outcomes whose probability is calculable from a known variance — and uncertainty — outcomes whose probability is incalculable — are major features of financial markets. In relation to these inherent unknowns, efficient market theory (EMT) is making a number of strong assumptions about the formation of expectations with which other theories disagree. The assumptions are those associated with 'rational expectations' in which expectations are optimal predictions based on appropriate use of all the available relevant facts. Rational expectations theory does not suggest that individuals have perfect foresight, instead it claims that expectations are formed using the 'best possible' predictors of the future. Those predictions may turn out to be wrong, but given the available information no-one could systematically do better. The argument is similar to that of basing a strategy in a game of chance on knowledge of the probability of a six on a die — in individual games a six may not turn up as expected but over a large number of games it will, so systematic use can be made of the 'optimal prediction' that there is a one-in-six chance of a six. The real world, of course, is vastly more unpredictable which is one reason that the assumptions of rational expectations are questionable as will be argued below.

Rational expectations lead to a number of conclusions for the efficient market hypothesis. Perhaps the most important is that no-one has the ability or opportunity to profit systematically from guessing others' actions. Yet, such supernormal profits could exist in practice for a number of reasons. They will occur if the economy does not adjust quickly back to equilibrium as EMT assumes it does (or if the economy never reaches states approximating to equilibrium). Systematic opportunities for profit may, on the other hand, arise if the response of agents to a market 'shock' affects the subsequent path of adjustment. Being able to predict those responses, whilst others have failed to do so generates the possibility of profiting from those responses. Such interpretations of financial markets are held by many Keynesians. Keynes himself argued with regard to share prices that 'mass psychology' was a determinant: 'We have reached the third degree where we devote our intelligence to anticipating what average opinion expects the average opinion to be' (Keynes, 1936, p. 156). More recent Keynesians have re-emphasised the point (see Tobin, 1984).

The issue is not simply about how individuals formulate their expectations and behave in relation to them. Efficient market theory is also confounded if market agents are able to exercise oligopolistic practices because of their scale of operation or by being able to differentiate their product from competing financial services through devices such as advertising, locational convenience and other non-priced services.

What are the implications of the efficient market thesis for understanding mortgage finance and the operations of the institutions providing it? The answer is essentially that whatever exists in a situation with minimal government regulation is the best form of market and institutional structure. Efficient producers squeeze out the inefficient once regulatory barriers are dismantled. Kane, for example, asserts that 'the desegmentation of financial markets involves the expansion of low-cost producers at the expense of high-cost ones' (Kane, 1984, p. 760). This view would seem more reasonable when treated as a testable proposition rather than regarded as an axiomatic truth.

No clear-cut view emerges from EMT on what that market would actually look like. Large and small institutions could live side by side; the smaller ones benefiting from economies of specialisation (such as superior local knowledge) whilst the larger enterprises gain the risk spreading benefits of diversification. Mortgage instruments would be as varied as the profitable opportunities for providing them.

As no country's mortgage finance system has reached the levels of deregulation suggested by efficient market proponents, efficient market theorists have been major champions of deregulation and institutional restructuring. They have been at the forefront of arguments that regulatory régimes produce inefficient, bureaucratic, unresponsive mortgage finance institutions (a result achieved by deduction, as the empirical evidence is limited). For efficient market theorists, the beneficial competitive effects of deregulation overwhelm any potentially adverse consequences. In response to the threat of increasing monopolisation, efficient market theorists argue along the following lines: 'even if the number of firms in an industry declines following deregulation, the resulting churning of firms increases the competitive intensity of the industry, which is a major objective of deregulation' (Kaufman *et al.*, 1984).

What is meant by efficiency?

Efficiency tends to be used in unspecified ways in discussions associated with efficient market perspectives on the financial system. Some authors, such as Tobin (1984), have tried to break down the term into distinct types of efficiency.

The efficiency criteria suggested by Tobin that are relevant to retail banking and mortgage markets are fivefold and interlinked.

First, there is *arbitrage efficiency*. This occurs when no-one can gain from trading on the basis of publicly available information, as the market adjusts to it instantaneously. An example in the mortgage market is when no-one pays a mortgage interest rate greater than the cost of funds from the cheapest source plus a small mark-up for intermediation costs and risk. If any institution tried to issue mortgages at a higher rate they would find no takers as others would provide the service more cheaply.

The second suggested type is *fundamental valuation efficiency*. In general terms this implies that the valuation of a financial asset reflects accurately the expected value of the future payments to which the asset gives title. If fundamental valuation efficiency does exist continuously there will, of course, also be arbitrage efficiency. Translated into mortgage terms, the principle of fundamental valuation efficiency has a number of implications. It could be related to the market price of a mortgage bond or mortgage-backed security for an investor in the mortgage market. Alternatively, it could be related to the asset base of a mortgage credit institution — that their net worth reflects accurately current interest rates, inflation and assessments of asset risk. Alternatively, though perhaps more tentatively, mortgage contracts are usually a validation for a householder of the value of the property they purchased, a firm base on which to calculate the cost and benefits of house purchase. One of the keys to fundamental valuation efficiency in mortgage markets, therefore, is accurate assessment of current and expected house prices.

The third suggested efficiency criterion is *functional efficiency* where the resources devoted to financial services achieve some desired economic and social ends. Financial intermediaries, for instance, provide payments mechanisms, and mobilise and allocate savings. Functional efficiency for mortgage finance would relate to channelling funds into housing, although there is the caveat that mortgage finance might divert funds from other socially useful investments, a process which is frequently held to occur in practice (see Downs, 1980). Associated with functional efficiency is *operational efficiency*, that is whether mortgage credit institutions perform their roles at minimum cost.

The final criterion is *distributional efficiency* in the sense that there are no inherent biases in the financial system against specific groups. There could, for instance, be discrimination against small savers. British building societies and US savings and loans associations, for instance, were frequently said to pay small savers unreasonably low interest rates during the high inflation years of the 1970s, as later chapters show. Alternatively, particular types of location or household might be discriminated against by lending institutions on the bogus grounds of being too high a risk. A lack of particular mortgage instruments might also adversely affect certain types of household.

The empirical evidence for efficient markets

Efficient market theorists claim that their views are supported by extensive empirical evidence. Much of the empirical work refers to foreign exchange, equity and bond markets. The efficiency claims are based in part on studies which show that no-one can gain from generally known information. Early studies of share price movements have suggested that they are a 'random walk' rather than related to the relative profitabilities and payout ratios of specific companies (see Fama, 1965). Efficient market theorists argue that the randomness demonstrates their views because it shows that all relevant information affecting prices is rapidly discounted by the market, leaving only random factors to influence daily price movements (Fama, 1976; Mishkin, 1986). Furthermore, if all 'fundamental' information is instantly taken into account, leaving only random elements to influence the pattern of price change, professional investors have no advantages over novices. This belief corresponds to the results of studies showing that pension and other investment funds do not consistently outperform the market as a whole.

Stronger claims are also made that share prices reflect rational valuations of potential earnings. If stock markets do function in this way, the analysis can be extended to takeovers, where it is sometimes claimed that weak managements lead to share prices being lower than the true value of the business when efficiently run. This then encourages acquisition by firms with efficient managers. But the problem arises here of how do predators recognise such opportunities in a world where share prices are assumed to be accurate valuations of the expected future returns of a business. Would not that valuation already include an expectation of an early management shake-up?

In recent years, a growing body of empirical evidence suggests that stock prices do contain a predictable element based on their past performance. In particular it seems that to some extent stocks are 'mean-reverting' (see the survey in de Bondt and Thaler, 1989). Consistent with such evidence is the idea that investors systematically over-react to good or bad news about a company's current performance and that its share price then gradually reverts back to its longer-term performance as the market becomes aware of the over-reaction. By this interpretation trends can be predicted by looking at past performance, contrary to the random walk required of EMT, so that profits can be made by investing on the basis of that prediction. It appears that the share prices of firms that are contemporarily poor financial performers are especially prone to heavy share price falls and subsequent mean-reversion.

Interpretation of this evidence, and of more from the 1980s to be cited below, is controversial, however, as efficient market theorists like many other economic theorists are not necessarily prepared to reject their hypotheses simply because certain empirical evidence seems to confound them. Efficient markets theorists could contest the interpretation by saying that some rationally-based piece of information could be present but unspecified. What is being tested is a model of the formation of equilibrium prices and the efficiency hypothesis. The model rather than the hypothesis could be at fault, because, say, of the absence of some time varying influence on expected returns (Fama and French, 1988). Such 'missing links' are well-known didactic devices when formulating the defence of a theory under attack. But the critics of EMT may also suggest other interpretations of data. The randomness of changes in share prices, for example, could be argued to confirm the view that nebulous factors such as 'sentiment' rule stock markets rather than rational economic calculation. Data, moreover, may not provide the strong hypothesis confirmation suggested of it. There is no reason, for instance, why valuation errors (in the sense that they do not reflect fundamentals) should leave a statistically discernible trace in the pattern of returns, as Summers (1986) and others have argued. Summers' central point is that efficient market theorists have been persuaded into believing the fallacy that because empirical tests do not lead to rejection of efficient market postulates, the evidence actually demonstrates the theory's empirical truth. Summers suggests instead that the evidence is also compatible with other, arguably more plausible, hypotheses reliant on the existence of fads and the like.

Some empirical evidence would seem a clear example of behaviour contrary to EMT beliefs. The behaviour of investors in stock markets worldwide prior to and during the crash of October 1987 seems to confound even the most generous interpretations of investor rationality (Copeland, 1989). The overall level of share prices at the time seemed to be strongly influenced by their past levels — opening up the possibility of speculative bubbles existing contrary to efficient market predictions.

Less spectacular empirical results would similarly question the validity of the theory. There is substantial volatility in stock market price movements which does not auger well for investor rationality and the effective use of all available information (Shiller, 1981). Efficient market predictions on currency exchange rates in addition have not been successful predictors in a series of empirical tests (as the survey by Copeland (1989) indicates).

Little evidence on market efficiency is available specifically for mortgage markets. As has been noted, though, most commentators adopt an efficient markets perspective. However, one feature of the country by country evidence presented in later chapters is that it indicates a widespread non-correspondence of mortgage markets with one or more of the efficiency criteria outlined above. Theories other than EMT that might act as bases for examining recent developments in retail finance markets would seem to deserve greater prominence than the literature usually warrants.

Before reviewing other potentially attractive theories of financial markets, it is useful to consider one alternative to rational expectations formation that has been suggested in the efficient markets debate. De Bondt and Thaler (1989) cite substantial empirical evidence on individual expectations behaviour from the general psychology literature that to many interested in either property or financial markets has a familiar ring. First they note that psychological tests show individuals over-emphasising recent information when making forecasts. The implication when generalised to financial markets is that rather than corresponding to the EMT conclusion that such markets have no memory (i.e. future prices are unpredictable), actual markets contain many poor historians who exaggerate the longevity of the recent past whether good or bad. In property markets a common example of such expectations formation would be when house prices rise many purchasers treat them always as rising, or conversely that downturns are brief, so that housing is always a good medium- to long-term investment without looking at actual real trends which for many localities show housing frequently to be a relatively bad investment. The other feature raised by de Bondt and Thaler is that risk perceptions are faulty. Examples would include a tendency to exaggerate the risk (and hence the fear of) being killed in a plane or the likelihood of specific fatal illnesses. Again, if this behaviour were transferred to financial and property markets, it may explain some recent phenomena. Some investments, for instance, seem to require excessive risk premiums — for example, particular types of house, locality or household for mortgage lenders; whilst others encourage excessively low risk perceptions — for banks and mortgage institutions, examples could be Third World lending in the late 1970s, property lending at various times and the threat in the late 1980s/early 1990s of excess capacity in banking services. Obviously the two behavioural traits are interlinked because short memories encourage faulty risk evaluation. Arrow (1982) has also suggested an inherent tendency towards over-optimism in speculative markets. If investors, consumers, governments or managers/owners of financial institutions collectively or in isolation have such influences on their expectations formation a different type of financial theory from that of efficient markets would obviously be required.

3.2 Chronic instability thesis

Some economists and financial experts argue that financial markets are guided by investors' expectations of other investors' reactions to change. It is argued that what individual investors think are currently attractive investments and how they view future trends in share and other asset prices depend to a considerable extent on what everybody else is thinking at the time. If expectations are formulated in this way, and play the principal role in determining the contemporary characteristics of financial market dealings, fashion will exert an important role in the formation of market opinion. Sentiment is likely to be highly volatile, leading to periods of boom and bust as euphoria gives way to despondency. The financial system, therefore, is unstable because it depends on highly volatile expectations and herd-like behaviour by speculators.

Various commentators have formulated theories of financial markets on the basis of such views about investors'/speculators' expectations and their interaction. Keynes's chapter in his *General Theory* on the state of long-term expectations propounds such perspective, and it is widely held by modern economists. Minsky (1980, 1986) has developed theories about the operation of financial markets and their institutional structures in which there are inevitable periodic booms and busts. For him: 'the fundamental dilemma in economic organization is how to preserve the vitality and resilience of decentralized decisions without the instability accompanying decentralized financial markets' (Minsky, 1980, p. 520). Kindleberger (1978) has applied Minsky's approach in a historical analysis of financial markets in the western world since the seventeenth century. He emphasises the frequency of financial crises, their persistence throughout the development of modern capitalism, and their association with speculative manias where there is a loss of touch with reality or rationality. Others suggest that the growing international integration of financial markets has heightened instability. Strange (1986, p. 1) argues that 'the western financial system is rapidly coming to resemble nothing as much as a vast casino'. That casino needs cooling through sustained international actions by the world's major economic powers, otherwise crisis and long-term sluggish economic performance are unavoidable. Some financiers have also expressed scepticism about the ways financial markets operate, as in Soros's aptly titled book, *The Alchemy of Finance* (Soros, 1987).

A central policy conclusion of the instability theory is that governments need to regulate financial markets in order to limit the permanent threat of crisis associated with fragile expectations. The impact on the financial system as a whole of the collapse of a particular financial institution is far more important, they would argue, than the presumed loss of the coercive effect of bankrupcy on administrative efficiency and financial innovation. In addition, financial systems cannot be assumed to be efficient allocators of resources because of the way expectations are formed and the existence of oligopolistic practices by key institutions. So governments have justification for interfering with the flow of funds through the financial system.

Unstable market theories, however, cannot specify the form that regulation and intervention should take as that depends on historical curcumstances, the detailed operation of markets and on the institutional structures associated with them. In addition, the perspective has an ambiguous attitude to the operation of markets, and therefore to state intervention. On the one hand, competitive markets are seen as the only effective way of allocating resources in a complex modern economic society; on the other hand, it is claimed that the behaviour of agents within markets meant that they do not work efficiently. The ambiguity towards markets makes it difficult in practice to devise state policies that remove the bad whilst leaving the good. The ambiguity also creates problems for its proponents in defending state regulation and control against the criticisms of efficient market theorists. It is far easier to highlight the constraints on competition imposed by regulation than to demonstrate greater global efficiency resulting from the stabilising effects of systems of regulation.

Empirically chronic instability perspectives come to the fore at times of financial crisis. The way in which the world's banks encouraged the blossoming of Third World debt during the late 1970s is a strong candidate for the label of misplaced fashion. 'Bigger fool' theories, in which prices are determined only by the belief that there is someone else around who will buy the share for an even higher price, have great credibility during strong bull markets. The cumulative effect of panic and its threat to whole financial systems can also be seen during crashes. Cataclysmic events in specific financial markets occur infrequently, however, and even less often across the whole spectrum of financial activity. So chronic instability views have a policy influence that waxes and wanes in line with the overall state of the financial system. Theoretical ambiguity breeds inconstancy.

One feature of chronic instability theories which contributes to their ambiguity over the precise forms of intervention necessary to combat instability whilst maintaining market efficiency is their treatment of competition between institutions. Neither efficient market nor chronic instability theories feel it necessary to examine the behaviour of the agents active in markets in any great detail. For efficient market theory, the omission can be justified using a tautology. As markets are efficient, the institutions active there must be as well. Evolution under a régime of competition is the only process necessary under efficient market theory; although the assertion might to many seem unconvincing. Chronic instability theories assign destabilising roles to agents, which would imply a greater need to understand institutional behaviour. But in these theories institutions tend to have a plasticity that reveals only their general destabilising characteristics. Quite what the institutions are, their size and their competitive interaction are all regarded as irrelevant to the overriding importance of demonstrating destabilising tendencies. Yet the forms of intervention necessary to overcome instability if they are to succeed are predicated on understanding how the institutions to be regulated actually operate.

Credit crunches and financial regulation

A corollary of these theories that emphasise the instability of the financial system is that financial crises of varying degrees are likely to occur. Other theories would also suggest that financial markets are inherently crisis prone. Whatever the explanation given for them, crises have certain characteristics such as a rapid fall in asset values. Of particular interest for retail finance is the behaviour of interest rates and credit supply during a financial crisis. During them it is said that interest rates rise rapidly and/or the supply of credit is sharply curtailed. Eventually the crisis passes and interest rates and the supply of credit revert to 'normal' behaviour. If such crises can be identified they may be a powerful force in explaining the dynamics of change in financial markets and the regulatory rules governing them.

The concept of a financial crisis has been criticised for its qualitative rather than quantitative characteristics. 'Higher' interest rates and 'restricted' credit — or even defining a particular episode as a 'panic' — evoke terms whose meaning is relative. But the degree of the shift in each variable necessary to warrant the classification 'crisis' is impossible to measure accurately. Financial markets continually adjust and so do expectations with them, so the extent of the relative shifts in the assigned variables leading to the definition of a crisis is itself always changing. Such definitional and measurement problems have not stopped some analysts from attempting to specify such crises and from arguing that they play specific economic roles. Informed judgement, such investigations feel, can highlight approximately such phases, even if precise quantification of them is difficult. It could be added that exact measurement of many economic concepts is difficult, including some of the most basic. Many of the debates over competition face this problem, for example, especially as much depends on the threat of competition. How do you accurately measure a 'threat' that may never be implemented?

In the context of the mortgage market it is clear that some changes have been induced by crises affecting traditional mortgage institutions, and that those crises are related to developments occurring in wider financial markets. Of the three countries considered in later chapters this behaviour is more typical of the US mortgage market than of those in Britain and West Germany, but effects can still be seen in the two latter countries. It is consequently worthwile considering the arguments put forward for the existence of financial crises and their effects in greater detail.

Carron (1982b) suggests three broad definitions of financial crisis. The one associated with the work of Minsky can be termed 'catacyclismic' (my terminology not Carron's). Associated with a financial crisis of this type are widespread, forced liquidations of assets, sharp drops in asset prices and a general economic depression following from the effects of the crisis; all of which makes financial crises rare events. The second type can be termed 'cyclical'. At a certain stage in economic expansions liquidity becomes squeezed and monetary policy tight. The resulting high interest rates and credit shortages herald the recession phase of the cycle (see Sinai, 1976). This definition of crisis implies that one exists whenever money is tight. Carron himself proposes an intermediate definition ('heightened uncertainty') based on the idea that financial crises occur at times when borrowers face exceptionally high interest risk premia or severe credit constraints arising from general contemporary financial developments rather than their own prospects. The difficulties of defining a financial crisis can be seen in these three variants, as certain events are excluded by all. The stock market crash of October 1987 is a case in point, being short-lived and leading neither to widespread asset liquidations nor to severe credit shortages. A preferable definition of financial crisis might be to make crises more market-specific — a general financial crisis would only occur if all financial markets in an economy were affected, although it is still likely that crises in specific markets would have spillover effects in other financial and non-financial markets.

Wojnilower (1980) implicitly restricts the notion of financial crisis to specific markets by concentrating on the activities of the commercial banks in his discursive analysis of post-war financial developments in the USA. He adds the interesting thesis that each post-war financial crisis precipitated a reshaping of the US financial system, which he, in common with most other commentators, regards as most heavily regulated in the years following the Second World War. Credit growth, he argues, is essentially supply-determined and 'credit crunches' occur when there is an interruption somewhere in the supply process. The interruptions may be prompted by regulatory rigidities or by the advent of serious default problems in major institutions or markets. After each 'crunch' both the authorities — fearing recession and private institutions in the markets to protect future earnings — reshape the financial structure. Each crunch in the US financial system led to some deregulation, which progressively made it harder to control and consequently ever more prone to another crunch. The deregulation process is thus argued to be inexorably linked to the development of financial markets themselves rather than to be a policy measure based on particular economic ideologies.

The analogy of sandcastles in the face of an incoming tide perhaps illustrates Wojnilower's thesis most clearly. Regulatory controls are like sandcastles whose outer defences are undermined and circumvented by the flow of water seeking out the weakest spots, but as each outer defence is breached the whole structure becomes increasingly threatened and inevitably doomed. Without regulation, according to Wojnilower, far more dramatic financial crises are likely to occur, so credit crunches perform the useful effect of slowing down the economy before widespread bankruptcies ensue. Regulation, consequently, is a good thing, but government aversion to recession plus the pressures emanating from financial markets erode it away. Housing finance markets are especially frail. 'Freeing the thrift and mortgage markets from government subsidy and guarantee is like freeing family pets by abandoning them in the jungle' (Wojnilower, 1980, p.303).

The view that post-war financial regulation in the USA has generally changed as a result of political responses to financial turbulence in one form or another has strong empirical backing. But Wojnilower's specific arguments about the gradual weakening of beneficial regulatory controls by periodic financial crises contain unresolved difficulties.

It is not some generalised notion of regulation that was weakened in the USA during the post-war decades but a specific set of legislative measures enacted in the 1930s, the use of which varied over time depending on political expediency and the contemporary economic beliefs of successive governing bodies of the Federal Reserve and advisors to the government. It is far from clear whether either the regulatory framework or the different ways it was used were ideal for controlling the financial system to achieve the desired economic and social ends, especially as the economy and the financial system were undergoing continual change. Erosion of regulation could have arisen from the exposure of specific regulatory weaknesses rather than because no regulation could work effectively or be sustained. It would perhaps be better to see the history of post-war US financial regulation in terms of what went wrong and how the controls were and could have been reformed or adapted rather than of a no-regulation versus regulation dichotomy. The former approach, for example, has been adopted in most debates over the two savings and loans crises of the 1980s — even if the rhetoric within which they were conducted in the early 1980s tended to be of the 'how to deregulate' form.

Another criticism voiced of arguments about credit crunches is that they emphasise quantitative constraints on the supply of credit rather than price effects. Rather than a drying up of credit why do interest rates not rise instead, so that processes of adjustment are more continuous than crisis bound? As interest rates rise rapidly during periods classified as financial crises or credit crunches this claim is difficult to reject on empirical grounds — credit shortages cannot easily be measured but interest rates can. In reply it could be said that times may occur when the general risk of default is so great that no interest rate would compensate lenders for the risk. Again, for the financial system as a whole, such times may be rare but in specific markets they may be more common. Regulatory restrictions may also stop interest rates from playing that adjustment role in particular markets — like the existence in the USA for many years of interest rate ceilings on savings deposits. Alternatively, the operation of monopoly, oligopoly or cartel arrangements may have a similar effect of constraining the market clearing function of interest rates — as occurred in Britain for example during the operation of the building societies' cartel. A crisis may also not affect a financial market as a whole but specific institutions operating within it. Market conditions may move in ways to which some intitutions cannot adapt because of their mode of operation and/or the forms of regulation of those institutions. The West German mortgage banks are examples of financial institutions that could not cope independently with economic changes in the 1970s and 1980s.

The idea that financial crises can induce shifts in the operation of specific financial institutions and in their regulation is a useful analytical device when considering developments in mortgage finance. From the 1960s onwards mortgage finance institutions have been transformed as a result of the impact of general financial and economic events. Often the way in which change is generated arises because longer-term problems in the operation of particular mortgage institutions are brought to a head by general financial turbulence. This is especially true when such general turbulence leads to periods of sudden and sharp interest rate movements — which either make some institutions' mortgage business unprofitable or force mortgage providers to make major changes in their interest rate and wider business strategies.

The later analysis of developments in mortgage finance in Britain, West Germany and the USA illustrates the interrelationship between general financial and economic events and the mortgage market. But here it is interesting to note that many developments in mortgage finance received major stimuli during periods when the 'yield gap' between long- and short-term interest rates in general was negative. In 'normal' periods, the yield on long-term borrowing is generally higher than on short-term borrowing, as usually the risks and uncertainties for investors are greater the longer the investment. But at certain times the yields reverse and short-term rates rise above long-term ones. (Another common expression is that the yield curve flattens as short rates rise towards long ones.) Explanations of the causes of a sharp narrowing of the yield gap depend on the economic theory chosen, but all associate it with periods of impending recession, crisis or uncertainty, either within the financial sphere alone — as when a major borrower or bank unexpectedly collapses — or throughout the economy generally. Government monetary policy may be the initial stimulus pushing up short-term rates or holding down longer ones. Whatever the cause, prime victims of the narrowing spread are going to be those who lend long and borrow short. Use of the yield gap avoids having to define periods of general financial crisis whilst at the same time making it possible to refer to 'abnormal' states in general financial markets.

Table 3.1 highlights the periods between 1973 and 1988 when the yield gap was negative in Britain, Germany and the USA and comments on developments occurring in their respective mortgage markets at those times. No simple causality is meant to be implied, but interestingly some of the major changes in mortgage finance are associated with those periods. One reason that there can be no simple relationship is that the operation of mortgage markets changes over time. In the USA, for example, it is to be expected that the effects of a negative yield gap are different during the years when interest rate ceilings were imposed on savings deposits under Regulation Q and the following years in the 1980s when those controls no longer existed. Similarly, given the large number of financial institutions in the USA and the much smaller number in Britain, it is to be expected that periods with a negative yield gap will have distinct effects in each country. Markets with fewer and larger institutions create conditions where those institutions can more easily protect themselves from the adverse consequences of negative yield gaps, especially when they overtly or implicitly collude. Some of these differences will be drawn out at the relevant points in subsequent chapters.

Table 3.1 Negative yield gaps and difficulties faced by mortage finance institutions, 1973−88

	Approximate periods when yield gap was negative	Difficulties faced by mortgage finance institutions at the time
USA	1973−4	S&Ls — falling net income, severely squeezed margins on new mortgage business, declining profits (1974−5). Falls in housing starts (1973−5)
	1979, 1981	Major S&L crisis, 1980−2. Large losses, 1981−2. Widespread failures. Net income negative 1981−2. Declining housing market, 1979−82. Lowest levels of starts since early 1950s in 1982
	1988−	Renewed thrift crisis intensified. Problems in the secondary mortgage market
W. Germany	1973	Housing market boom brought to an end. Total completions fell sharply for the next decade. A downgrading of the role of the mortgage banks
	1979−82	Rapid shortening of mortgage bond maturities in 'matching crisis'. Sharp loss of business by the Bausparkassen. Housing market depression. End of 3-year price boom and start of substantial price falls for secondhand dwellings lasting until mid-1980s
UK	1973−4	Large fall in building society real net income and 'mortgage famine'. Collapse of a housing market boom. Onset of falling real house prices (dropped by a third between 1974 and 1977)
	1979−80	Sharply curtailed building society income and lending. Major weakening of building society cartel. Entry of banks into mortgage lending in 1981. Depressed housing market. Completions at lowest level since 1940s in 1981. Falling real house prices in 1981−2
	1985−6	Institutions shielded by relatively high mortgage rate. Declining building society real net income. Continued inroads in mortgage market by banks and other institutions. Building society mortgage share reached lowest ebb (50%) in 1987

Table 3.1 *continued*

Approximate periods when yield gap was negative	Difficulties faced by mortgage finance institutions at the time
1988—	Onset of severe housing market downturn. Building societies temporarily benefit from being able to keep mortgage interest below money market rates. New entrants' mortgage business made unprofitable

Sources: Yield gap — 6 month moving averages (OECD, 1988e); mortgage institution information from individual country chapters of this book

3.3 All-powerful institutions

The final approach to financial systems emphasises the overriding power of large institutions. They act as oligopolists with strategies that vary over time depending on macroeconomic circumstances. Their strategies, nonetheless, are the prime influence on the nature of specific financial sectors. The Marxist notion of finance capital is frequently used in this way (see Hilferding, 1981; Harvey, 1984). Much journalistic financial writing has all-powerful institutionalist leanings with their emphasis on the strategies of particular firms. In the mortgage finance literature, some commentators on the US scene have emphasised the ability of large institutions to break down legislative constraints on their operations (see Florida, 1986; Meyerson, 1986). In all countries there is a strong tendency to see changes in mortgage finance from the strategic perspective of a particular type of mortgage institution. In Britain, for example, analysis of mortgage finance is virtually synonymous with examining the perceived problems of and the constraints on the building society movement (Cleary, 1965; Gough, 1982).

Policy towards financial sectors from the all-powerful institutional approach heavily depends on understanding the aims of particular financial institutions and the extent to which they conflict with perceived social objectives. Where conflict arises the state should intervene with legislation to ensure the dominance of the social objectives (see Grebler, 1983). In practice, though, given the importance of large institutions in the formulation and enactment of much government legislation, there is only limited hope that legislation will actually achieve its corrective role.

Analysing changes in retail banking and mortgage finance from the perspective of institutional power can provide many insights. In particular, evaluation of business strategies can help elucidate potential conflicts of interest and explicit attempts by enterprises to use their market power. There are dangers, however, if institutions are seen as all-powerful which in some sense mirror those of the efficient markets perspective. Efficient markets argue implicitly that institutional strategies are unimportant because they are so heavily constrained by the operation of market forces. The all-powerful institution approach takes the opposite view and examines strategies on the assumption that market constraints on them are limited. Although external economic forces are never treated as an entirely absent influence on institutional behaviour, they can end up being only background justifications for the analysis of firms' strategy shifts (see Florida 1986). Similar criticisms have been voiced by economists over sociological approaches to industrial organisation theory where power exercised within organisations is treated analytically as though it has little market constraint (see Francis *et al.*, 1983).

Another problem for strong institutional power views is that the perspective may result in attempts to trace the causes of change solely to major institutions and their strategies. A belief in conspiracy is not necessary but may add conviction to the quest. Business strategies, however, can fail. Failure may not mean that the firm's actions had no effect on a market, especially if it is a large player there. The outcome of a particular strategy might be to change the context of market competition in unforeseen ways. Institutional power may exist, in other words, without being able to read back from a market outcome to a plan and a set of means used to implement it. Institutional power cannot be ignored, but a balance is needed between an emphasis on market forces and the market impact of specific institutions.

3.4 Competition, contestability and business strategies

Much theoretical work has been undertaken in recent years on the ways in which firms face and react to competition (Clarke and McGuiness, 1987). One strand of analysis, contestable market theory, has given greater emphasis than was common previously to the threat of new competition on the behaviour of existing producers. In this approach the key criterion for the degree of competition is whether firms can easily enter and leave a market and so contest it, rather than the actual number of firms active there. Another strand of theory accepts the persistence of markets with few players and examines the likely strategy of firms in specific circumstances using game theory. It emphasises the importance of firm's business strategies in evaluating the outcome of specific competitive situations.

Contestable market theory has been used in recent years to suggest that a deregulated banking system cannot lead to oligopolistic abuses as there is always a potential threat of competition in markets which are contestable (see Kane, 1984). There has been only limited use of game theory and business strategy perspectives to financial intermediation (Stiglitz and Weiss, 1981; Yanelle, 1989).

Contestable market theory

Contestable market theory argues that firms are forced to be efficient by the threat of entry of others into their markets (Baumol *et al.*, 1982). In particular it is suggested that the most important influence on a market is not the size and relative strengths of the current producers but the ease with which new firms can enter the market, whittle away monopoly profits and then leave it costlessly. It is argued that where free entry and exit of a market is possible, monopolistic abuses cannot occur — even if there is only one producer of a commodity — as the market is contestable. Government policy should, therefore, be less worried about firm size and more concerned with creating conditions which facilitate market entry and exit.

Contemporary retail financial service markets are being contested in the commonly accepted sense of the word, as new firms are moving into areas from which they were previously excluded. But it is far from true that they conform to the rigorous and restrictive requirements for a contested market in contestable market theory.

The results claimed by Baumol *et al.* for contestable market theory have been severely criticised on the grounds that their efficiency conclusions rest heavily on a series of restrictive, and sometimes contradictory, assumptions that are unlikely to exist in practice in most industries (Shepherd, 1984). A key assumption necessary for the results of the theory is that there are no sunk costs associated with involvement by a firm in a market. Every action is costlessly reversible: one implication is that firms can enter a market and instantly enjoy equivalent standing to existing firms. Equally, they may leave the market without incurring closure losses. Firms need no strategies as they can respond costlessly and instantaneously to changing events. If sunk costs are ubiquitous, contestable market theory offers no help (Shapiro, 1989; Gilbert, 1989). This does not mean that potential competition is unimportant for existing firms but that generally it has limited effect rather than the all-important role assigned to it by contestable market theory.

One aspect of retail banking does seem to suggest, however, that contestable market theory might have some use for analysing firm behaviour there. The empirical evidence surveyed in the next chapter suggests that retail financial institutions may be able to offer additional services at similar unit cost to existing ones. The possibility of offering extra services at little or no additional cost suggests that retail banking might offer some good cases of contestable markets in the sense required for Baumol *et al.*'s results. If this were so, contestable market theory would add further justification of contemporary developments in retail banking, even if they lead, as a number of commentators have suggested, to a small number of giant 'financial supermarket' firms (see Fforde, 1983). The threat of new contestants would stop any monopolistic abuse by such firms. But it is questionable whether retail finance actually represents a series of contestable markets in the strict sense. One problem is whether market participants have sufficient information to enable contestability to function as suggested. Characteristics of actual retail financial markets highlighted in the following chapter indicate that information constraints do place bounds on the recognition of contestable market opportunities, whilst market profiles tilt the contest in favour of the established institutions. Moreover, it is unlikely that sunk costs in retail banking are small in most activities. This is especially true where institutions are involved in investment rather than pure intermediation, as getting out of a misjudged position can be exceedingly expensive with system-level consequences as the regulators, legislators and taxpayers in the USA have discovered in the 1980s with the bale-out of insolvent and weak thrifts.

Business strategy

Theories of business strategy recognise the long-term significance of firms' actions and the responses that firms make to one or more competitors. Game theory is frequently used and this necessitates postulating a specific context in which the game is played, its rules and the constraints each player faces. One well-known result is that the outcome of the game depends crucially on the assumptions made, none of which may seem realistic for real world markets. Scepticism has resulted (see Fisher, 1989). But whilst the theory of business strategy does not offer a general theory of the behaviour of firms in markets it does offer a useful antidote to theories which deny the applicability of individual firm actions on market outcomes (Shapiro, 1989). In such business strategy theory firms are also responding to each other's behaviour, which in the financial services literature would correspond to a Keynesian-style view of expectations formation — although without necessarily resulting in an unstable outcome as implied in the chronic instability thesis. (Whether instability results would depend on the parameters of the game.)

Whilst providing no easy answer a theory of business strategy does suggest some general characteristics that are worth considering when examining institutional behaviour in financial markets. Five features in particular seem of relevance to the study of the changing context of the retail financial services industry:

1. *The framework for competition.* This would specify the market structure and rules by which firms can operate. An example would be the limitation until the 1980s of traditional mortgage lending institutions in the USA and UK to house mortgage lending and retail savings as their prime source of funds. Rules would include the requirements of regulatory authorities with respect to financial ratios and aspects of the institutions' activities (e.g. condoning the building societies' cartel for years in the UK and deposit insurance in the USA).

2. *The incentives of key agents.* It cannot be assumed that all financial

institutions are profit-maximising. Some are mutual, 'non-profit' organisations; others are publicy-owned with non-profit-maximising objectives. Similarly, managers may have different incentives from the owners of stock, mutual or public institutions. Situations may arise when managers can take advantage of opportunities to satisfy their own objectives rather than those of the owners, and they may consequently set distinct objectives for the enterprise. The ability to exercise such opportunism is one of the issues between principals and agents examined in contemporary industrial economics which again has not featured in consideration of the behaviour of financial institutions. A classic instance in the traditional mangerialist literature, of course, is when senior managers want to increase a firm's size in order to improve management remuneration and status rather than to maximise profits.

3. *Interdependence.* The actions of any enterprise have to be based on judgements of the impact on the behaviour of major competitors. Misjudgement of the responses can lead to unfavourable outcomes (it will, for example, be argued in Chapter 7 that the building societies in mid-1980s Britain misjudged the response of other institutions to their rate setting behaviour).

4. *Limited information.* Agents in a market may not know important pieces of information, and so have to adopt strategies in relation to such information constraints. An obvious example is the response of competitors to particular innovations by one firm.

5. *Tactical/strategic differences.* One theme that has been stressed in the business strategy literature is the need to distinguish between a firm's strategic and tactical decisions. Strategic decisions involve long-lasting commitments (and hence are ruled out by assumption in contestable market theory), whereas tactical decisions are short-term reponses to the current situation (Shapiro, 1989). Strategic decisions affect a firm's market position as its commitment in the medium term to certain actions, such as moving into a new market, will then affect its short-term tactical reponses. Obviously strategies cannot be rigidly held maxims as they may prove wrong or be superseded by the passage of events. Some tactical responses themselves may be so disastrous as to affect strategy — such as a misjudged reaction to movements in interest rates.

3.5 Conclusion

The merging of retail banking and mortgage finance cannot be understood without adequate theories of financial markets and the behaviour of consumers, institutions and investors. In reality, none of the three general approaches to the development of financial systems approximates to the reality of mortgage finance. Efficient market theory arguments about the role of competition, the continual hunt for arbitrage profit opportunites and the existence of market constraints on individual and institutional behaviour have echoes in certain aspects of mortgage market behaviour. Yet, there is strong evidence of firms being able to exert oligopolistic power and their assessment of risk in a number of respects does not conform to the rationality assumptions necessary for efficient markets. The chronic instability theory's highlighting of the potential for a herd-like formation of market views is borne out by even a cursory examination of retail banking and mortgage markets. The wide debate about the financial supermarket without detailed evaluation of what scope economies really exist has strong 'flavour-of-the-month' echoes. Real estate investment similarly is often fashion led, which is perhaps not surprising as it is one of the most risky and speculative sectors of the economy. Lastly, institutional behaviour cannot be ignored. Firms do form management strategies and operate on them, as suggested by the institutionalists. In some countries, notably Britain with its building societies, those strategies are in part public knowledge and are widely debated. Strategies do have a major influence on the transformation of retail banking and mortgage finance, although often not in the ways intended.

The methodology used in the rest of this book will draw on features emphasised in a number of the theories considered in this chapter in the sense that competition, the formation of expectations and institutional power are fundamental to the analysis. The guiding framework, however, will be a belief that firms' strategies, interaction and the constraints imposed on them will together provide important insights into the processes currently at work in retail financial services and explain why different outcomes have arisen in each country. The contemporary integration of the mortgage market into general retail banking at the same time offers evidence of the validity of the three competing theses of efficiency, chronic instability and strong institutional power. None looks a likely candidate to provide a sufficient explanation. The predictions of efficient market theorists look to be on shaky ground because expectations are not formed in the way that the theory wishes and institutions, to some degree through their strategies, do influence the environments in which they operate. The interplay between expectations formation and institutional reaction, however, does not necessarily imply that markets are chronically unstable — that is an empirical question whose answer varies depending on the structure of the financial market under consideration. Criticism of all-powerful views of institutions were made earlier.

What is missing from the discussion in this chapter is an explanation of the ways in which financial institutions actually compete. Ultimately, of course, the issue is an empirical one concerning the structure of markets and the actions of players within them. Yet, for retail banking a number of general empirical and theoretical issues can be used to provide a general background for such case studies and to help explain the contexts and constraints within which real world markets operate. The next chapter looks at such issues.

4

Competition in retail banking and the mortgage market

Financial deregulation is generally applauded for the extra competition it brings. But how does competition operate in retail finance? Given the similarity and increasing integration of different consumer banking operations, this question has to be asked in terms of retail banking in general rather than of mortgage finance alone, even though the latter is of principal concern here.

Associated with the issue of competition is the nature and size of retail finance institutions. Three aspects are of concern: the costs of providing services in relation to size; the range of services provided, and the position of enterprises in the markets in which they operate.

Most countries' banking sectors have a small number of institutions in control of the majority of assets, although concentration in banking is often not as great as in some other industries. It is only in countries with highly regulated and divided banking systems, like the USA, that financial institutions of widely differing sizes coexist. Everywhere a gradual increase in firm size is apparent. In Britain, a handful of building societies and banks dominate mortgage finance and retail banking. In West Germany, the three financial pillars of private, state and co-operative banks are each dominated by a limited number of institutions, and mergers within each sector continued throughout the 1980s. In Denmark, only three institutions exist in mainstream mortgage finance, and only government legislation limits their expansion through merger and diversification. Table 4.1 shows the degree of competition in banking for several countries. Large enterprises play major roles in banking and mortgage finance everywhere. Government regulation in the past has tended to hold back integration of financial services sectors, but the constraints on integration weakened during the 1980s giving greater impetus to centralising forces in banking. An important element in understanding the nature of competition in mortgage and related financial services, therefore, is to explain why these large enterprises exist.

Table 4.1 International concentration in banking

USA (1985)	The largest five control 12.8% of total assets — out of 13,759 commercial banks. Including assets of the thrifts reduces the percentage to 7.5%; whilst the top 10 institutions control 11.8% and the largest 100 have 33.5%
UK (1986)	The five largest banks control 45.6% of monetary sector assets. The five largest building societies had 55% of all societies' assets in 1981
W. Germany (1987)	The largest six control 37.9% of the total assets of the 316 commercial banks. With the assets of the other 4,232 banking institutions the percentage falls to 8.8%, but an additional 17% of assets are controlled by postal and regional giros
France (1986)	Three banks control 41.7% of all assets of the 367 banks (62.2% if foreign affiliates are excluded). With mutual and savings banks added the figures fall to 29.5% and 44.0% respectively
Japan (1986)	Thirteen banks control 56.7% of the total assets of the 87 commercial banks

Source: OECD (1988b).

The causes could be producer economies with larger banks providing cheaper consumer services per unit than smaller ones. The next two sections of this chapter consider whether producer economies of scale and scope exist in mortgage and other consumer financial services. Data on these topics are fairly limited; most evidence is from the USA. The evidence that exists, however, does not suggest that the largest institutions have lower unit costs than smaller ones. Large institutions could even experience diseconomies, associated with what is often termed 'X-inefficiency'; where the incentives and inefficiencies of internal bureaucratic structures mitigate against cost reduction. Having outlined the evidence against the existence of large production economies of size, the chapter then considers why they are limited. Here it is argued that, given the nature of financial services, it is difficult to see how economies in their provision to consumers can arise to any great extent beyond a limited firm size.

If retail finance firms do not gain any particular economies from size, why do they grow so big? Despite the apparent non-existence of producer scale economies, evidence of the greater competitive ability of large institutions is apparent from their market success and in their ability in most countries to absorb, subordinate or marginalise smaller institutions. But from where do they derive their strength?

An ability to pool risks may enhance the profitability of a large, diversified institution, but again the advantages of risk-pooling cease to increase at a scale way below the size of today's financial giants, as is discussed later. Financial risks, moreover, are not simply known entities, like the probability of getting a pair of sixes on a throw of dice. Risk evaluation may be irrational, guided for instance by over-optimism. Managers of financial institutions may become influenced by fads and skilful marketing of new investment schemes. Insolvency and general financial instability may be the result, as the US savings and loans institutions demonstrated in the 1980s.

All the available evidence indicates that in financial services, as in other industries, market share is a key determinant of profitability. Firms with known and respected reputations gain consumers, even though they might not offer the cheapest or the most efficient form of intermediation. A variety of corporate strategies are possible within this framework. It is not necessary for a financial institution to gain a dominant market share to win a positive reputation. All that is necessary is the creation of an impression of having a clear and successful market strategy. This will be called here a firm's *market profile* (see pp. 66–71 for more detail). From its profile, consumers can easily comprehend a firm's position in the market and accept, with only limited investigation, its ability to maintain that place, at least in the medium term, against competitors.

Although there is wide literature within industrial economics on the reasons for the importance of market shares and position for industrial companies, the financial services literature itself contains virtually none. As a result reasons are suggested as to why market profile might be important to enterprises involved in retail banking and mortgage finance. The suggestions are based on a prior examination of the limitations on the information available to parties in financial transactions. In addition, it is argued that there is often an asymmetry in the information available to the two parties involved; where one party often knows more than the other but has an incentive not to reveal the information, and there is no costless third party existing to redress the balance. Examples of types of informational asymmetry and their consequences are explored. Overall, information limitations give larger firms a competitive edge.

The benefits of size outlined above are unlikely to lead to market outcomes that correspond to the efficiency criteria discussed in the previous chapter. What might be beneficial to an individual firm in terms of enhancing its market profile could be a cost to users of those services and a global or social inefficiency. Examples of such potential cases are considered. The efficient markets view of competition in 1980s mortgage markets is contradicted if these plausible scenarios exist in mortgage markets.

4.1 Economies of scale

Investigations of economies of scale in financial services are fairly limited outside of the USA. The economies measured are the costs in relation to bank size of providing a unit of a particular service or a multi-product bundle. American studies consider retail banking, rather than specialist mortgage institutions. Their results differ slightly but none reveal substantial economies of scale beyond quite small banking sizes. (Recent US studies include Clark, 1984; Benston *et al.*, 1982, and Gilligan *et al.*, 1984. King, 1983; McCall, 1980 and Litan, 1987 provide surveys of other work.) The cost curve with respect to size is L-shaped. Costs per transaction fall through the lowest size categories but then, after sizes considerably below the scale of most of today's giant institutions, they become constant as size increases, although in some studies there are small rises and falls. This pattern is no different from that found in many other industries — although the scale at which cost curves become horizontal, of course, varies considerably between industries (Scherer, 1980; Shepherd, 1979).

Studies of scale economies in banking are not easy to undertake. In most countries the relevant data are unavailable. West European banks do not have to submit regulatory cost returns and carefully guard the information they have under the guise of commercial confidentiality; although US banks do not seem to have suffered because of the more rigorous disclosure requirements there. Even where data exist, measurement problems arise. There are considerable theoretical and empirical difficulties involved in deriving accurate measures of banking output, because banks simultaneously offer a wide variety of services. The assignment of costs to any specific activity inevitably contains elements of arbitrariness. Such problems may account for much of the differences in the results of the US studies quoted above.

The usefulness of data for regression or other statistical analysis is also limited by the low range of bank sizes in most Western European countries. Only a limited number of observations are feasible for Britain, for example, where the small number of clearing banks make regression analysis unviable. In countries like West Germany the links between banks would raise doubts over whether sufficient independent observations could be mustered.

One criticism of most of the US studies is that their data sources relate only to banks with assets of $1 billion or less (see McCall, 1980). Two recent studies of larger banks show contradictory results (Shaffer, 1984; Lawrence and Shay, 1986), with the latter finding significant economies and the other not. Identification problems associated with the multi-product nature of banking services, however, are likely to be found even more with diversified giant banks which may account for the discrepancies. Given such potential data problems, Lawrence and Shay's results cannot be regarded as the definitive investigation overturning the results of so many previous ones. One Japanese study is also said to indicate scale economies (Kuroda and Kaneko, 1986, quoted in Litan, 1987).

Studies of mortgage institutions are limited. British building societies are sufficient in number, varied in size and are required to publish operating cost data, so investigations of economies of scale amongst them are possible. The size distribution of assets, however, is highly skewed — the five largest societies control almost 60 per cent of all assets — which may lead to biased results.

In studies made in the late 1970s and early 1980s, an L-shaped function was apparent when operating costs were compared with asset size, although there was considerable cost variation at each size level and the two largest societies did have slightly lower costs (Gough, 1982; Barnes, 1984). So it would seem that, for building societies, operating costs depend as much on varying efficiencies within particular size categories as on size. The weight of empirical evidence, in summary, does not point towards production economies for large banks and building societies.

Why should size have such a limited effect on retail banking costs? It could be claimed that data and sampling problems hide the real economies that exist. But theoretically it would seem more likely that the studies are revealing what is actually the case — there are simply not many scale economies in retail banking beyond a fairly small size. The logic is reasonably obvious. Particular tasks involving the storage and transmission of financial data require certain labour inputs and pieces of equipment, but being essentially clerical activities they can be reproduced again and again. Payments mechanisms, such as cheque clearing, might be expensive to set up but exhibit the same principles. In any case, they are frequently shared between financial institutions and so do not lead to an optimal institutional size. The costs of personal face-to-face contact with bank customers cannot be reduced as the number of customers increases as long as the staff in question and the physical space and equipment they occupy and use are fully utilised. As long as staff and equipment are fully employed, processes can be expanded on a stepwise basis at similar unit cost. There may be managerial diseconomies of having to control a greater number of operations, although improvements in information technology are likely to have strengthened managerial controls. Only advertising would seem to offer banking economies through being spread over a larger output, but generally advertising is a small, if growing, part of costs. Yet much advertising itself is not a fixed cost, the unit burden of which falls when spread across a larger output. Instead the scale and cost of advertising vary depending on a financial institution's competitive strategies rather than on size alone.

There are not markedly more efficient technologies in retail financial services requiring expensive pieces of fixed capital that cannot be pooled between institutions. Similarly, specialist advice can be hired when needed. Nor are there highly expensive development costs for new products as there are with automobiles, computers or other types of technologically advanced hardware. Innovations in banking practices in the 1980s do not seem to have much affected the absence of economies of scale. The exact impact of new computer technology on scale economies is unclear, but the introduction of new technology does not suggest any noticeable increase in optimal size; in fact the converse could easily be true. The need for special financial intermediaries as a whole could be said to be under threat in the long term because of the widespread availability of relatively cheap equipment that can handle the complex information associated with financial services. The introduction of computers has made it far easier, for example, for large corporations to conduct their own financial transactions rather than being forced to rely exclusively on independent financial intermediaries. This may be one reason that the financial departments of many multinational corporations increasingly resemble the firm's own internal bank.

New technology benefits accrue in three related areas of banking business: databases and communications with them; the execution of transactions, and in service delivery to customers. Computerisation considerably reduces the cost of a transaction, and information about a transaction can now be quickly transmitted virtually anywhere at little expense. Considerable information can be stored or accessed on low-priced machines. Software costs for specialised data handling systems are high, but they reflect as much the costs of innovation as long-run operating costs. In so far as financial services require the assembly and dissemination of information, as long as agencies can plug into the relevant informations systems they can be quite small in size. Such advantages of computerisation must in part explain the meteoric growth of mortgage banking in the USA from the mid-1970s (US mortgage banking is similar to mortgage broking in the UK except that mortgage bankers originate and service mortgages as well as sell them for third parties — the function of British mortgage brokers).

One problem of computerisation is installing the hardware. The costs of automatic telling machine (ATM) networks, 'smart' cards and point-of-sale debiting systems are enormous. Being able to finance their installation is an advantage of size, but here the advantage is that of being able to exclude others from use of the systems rather than stemming from an inherent feature of them. Facilities may be shared, which has occurred particularly with ATMs; or a charge may be made for their use, as with share dealing systems on stock exchanges; or, lastly, they may be provided as a public good by the state, as with the experiments in France where there are schemes to provide all the retail outlets in some towns with facilities for computerised debiting and 'smart' cards. The technology itself, in other words, does not require large enterprises to make efficient use of it. But it may bolster the market position of such firms when installation costs are high and others can be excluded from their use.

4.2 Economies of scope

Scope economies concern the advantages of operating across a range of different products; they exist when the unit cost of producing two products jointly is less than producing them independently. They have been used as a major argument for diversified, rather than specialised, financial intermediaries. Once facilities are available for one type of service, it is argued, they can be used for others at virtually no extra cost. With the advent of computerisation in particular, it is easy for retail financial institutions to offer a variety of products to their customers. The major shift occurring in retail banking is the increase in the range of services offered by each type of financial institution, and the existence of scope economies would explain the trend.

There has been little empirical work on scope economies for producers in retail banking. Gilligan *et al.* (1984) found some evidence of their existence, although the economies were not great. Litan (1987) cites two other studies which show mixed results, and there appears to be no information at all on the joint delivery of banking and non-banking services. So the actual extent of scope economies in retail banking is still empirically unknown.

Banks and specialist mortgage institutions claim scope economies exist when arguing for deregulation or when talking of the benefits of the financial supermarket. The movement towards the financial supermarket has, in fact, been cited in the literature as the best evidence of the existence of scope economies (see Litan, 1987). But, rather than being based on empirical demonstration, the arguments used are theoretical, or discursive — along the lines of 'we can sell holidays and theatre tickets over our counters just as easily as take savings deposits', to paraphrase British building society managers in the mid-1980s prior to deregulation. Yet despite the hopes about scope economies, to date financial supermarkets have not been particularly successful or profitable.

One reason for the inconclusive evidence on scope economies and the difficulty of postulating them precisely may be that they hardly exist beyond the provision of the limited range of joint services currently offered by most retail banks and savings institutions. The point is similar to that made above about the limited existence of scale economies. It is likely to be true that handling, storage and delivery tasks can be repeated again and again at virtually constant cost over a wide range of information, including that about different financial and non-financial products. But it is difficult to see why costs should fall rather than remain constant per unit when two types of transaction are combined in retail financial services beyond fairly small levels of turnover. An ability to sell theatre tickets and collect savings deposits over the same counter at similar cost is not the same as saying that provision of the two jointly is cheaper than separately.

The issue is compounded by the existence of excess capacity. It is well-known that in many countries' financial services there is unnecessary duplication of branches and other consumer interface points. The excess capacity arises from the nature of competition between financial institutions for customers. Given excess capacity, it is understandable that individual institutions might believe they would derive cost savings through providing a wider range of services. Turnover may increase as a result and excess capacity be reduced: yet that is not technically inherent in the nature of financial service provision, and even the hoped-for reduction in excess capacity depends on the outcome of the new competitive situation. Evidence from the countries surveyed in the following chapters does not indicate less excess capacity in countries with multi-product financial institutions. One of the most criticised features of West German financial services, for example, is the high number of bank branches.

One consequence of excess capacity is that it can influence conclusions reached in empirical investigations of economies of scope and scale. When excess capacity exists at all size levels, what is probably being measured is the degree of excess capacity between institutions as much as optimal costs at particular sizes. This interpretation is, for instance, consistent with the wide variation in administrative costs found for British building societies.

Another factor adding confusion to discussions of scope economies is that a banking product is affected by the way it is produced. Attempts to achieve economies of scope may therefore influence the nature of what is being provided. Retail banking involves a set of consumer services, and the nature of a service is that it is consumed as it is produced. Altering the range of services offered may alter the content of individual services. An example of this effect that many people will have experienced is the impact on queues of multi-product delivery. If you go into a bank or post office, for example, and assess the length of the queue, or the queues at each counter, then with a fairly homogeneous service it is possible to calculate quickly and accurately how long the wait will be. With multi-products, where some transactions take seconds and others minutes, uncertainties about waiting time and queue length grow considerably. In Britain, the most variable times seem currently to be at post offices, and the least at automatic telling machines (ATMs); with clearing banks ranking close to post offices, and building societies a little better. Some consumers may find video advertising for those in the queue an informational benefit or at least a diversion from crashing boredom, whereas others find it a gross intrusion. The general point is that with many services, attempts at deriving scope economies alter the service. If a financial service, such as mortgage lending, is delivered in different ways and in distinct combinations with other financial services, its consumption may as a result be different. One implication for competition in financial service provision is that there is always the possibility of product (or multi-product) differentiation, even if the difference is sometimes spurious.

What have been discussed so far are scale and scope economies for producers of financial services. It is also argued that consumers derive them as well. The argument is simple. Consumers save on the transaction costs of time and money associated with acquiring their financial services from individual specialists. The extent of the savings is unclear. They could be low or vary depending on the type of financial transaction. In general retailing, for example, it is widely accepted that for low cost, regular items consumers weigh time savings highly. The benefit falls with less frequent or more expensive items or those with a strong fashion element, where comparison or careful consideration is part of the process of purchase. So supermarkets dominate in groceries, but not in fashion, expensive jewellery or hi-fi equipment, for example. The same could be true for financial services. Withdrawing regular sums of money, buying foreign exchange for travel or putting funds into a savings account may be akin to buying the groceries, whilst buying life insurance or a mortgage may require greater contemplation and consideration of the options. The lack of success of financial supermarkets to date may arise from the simple fact that people do prefer to compare before undertaking large purchases. Why trust one set of advice and calculations when more can be obtained at little extra cost?

One feature of importance to consumers is the cost of acquiring information and the significance of making a mistake. The extra information achieved by searching out cheaper groceries is low relative to the cost of acquiring it. Local supermarkets can be investigated over the course of a few weeks at virtually no extra time and cost, and the favourite one or two selected. The loss of the occasional bargain at the supermarket infrequently visited is hardly worth the effort of finding out. When making a large purchase, like a car or an expensive piece of clothing, the costs of acquiring extra information may easily be balanced by the savings achieved or the purchase of a more suitable product. Even so, for consumers of specialist items, the costs of getting extra information rises as more is known. Full information might, therefore, still be impossible or highly expensive to acquire — although specialist information systems (magazines, etc.) exist to reduce the cost. Yet consumers are not the only parties in financial services faced with informational costs as a subsequent section argues.

4.3   Diversification and risk

Risk is an important determinant of financial institutions' activities. In a variety of ways they may try to minimise it, pool it or pass it on to others. Rates of return tend to vary with risk, with more risky investments yielding higher returns to compensate investors for the greater likelihood of financial loss. So it is not necessarily the case that institutions always want to minimise risk. Risks (in the common usage of the term) and rates of return, however, are neither known with certainty nor are they perfectly correlated. Investors have to make assessments of them both — one of the great disputes in financial theory is the basis on which such assessments are made, as Chapter 3 notes. Efficient market theorists suggest that they are made rationally using the best information available. Others argue that, given the large degree of uncertainty present, irrational factors also come into play. Systematic biases may be generated as a result, such as over-optimism or reliance on fads and fashions.

Optimal portfolio choice can be modelled assuming rationality. The results demonstrate that with known risks and returns a diversified investment portfolio is generally preferable to investment in a single asset. With diversified investments, investors can trade risk against return more efficiently. This result can be applied to retail financial services and empirical estimates made of the average riskiness of an activity (measured, say, by the standard deviation of profitability) as compared with the average rate of return. On the basis of those estimates, optimal portfolios of activities in which specific types of financial institution should be active can be drawn up. Litan (1987) undertakes such an exercise for the USA using data from 1965 to 1982, concluding that 'the average banking organization could have significantly reduced risk if it had been able to diversify into other non-bank activities [such as insurance underwriting and real estate development]' (p. 91).

It may be the case that more diversified institutions can lower risk, improve profitability or achieve some intermediate combination of the two. But whether this is true is an empirical question of the mixes of rates of return and risk in specific activities. Litan's results depend crucially on his inclusion of commodity broking, real estate development and insurance agents in his sample of other possible activities. Without them, sufficient complements did not exist to justify much diversification. Those three activities may also be regarded as too risky for financial institutions to devote large investments to them, particularly in light of the problems of the US savings and loans in the late 1980s.

It is also questionable whether the results of portfolio theory can simply be transferred to particular lines of business activity. In general portfolio theory there is a wide range of assets from which investors can choose, their prices are usually determined competitively, and purchase of particular assets by any individual is unlikely to affect their price. The activities contemplated by financial services firms often do not correspond to those criteria. Markets may be imperfectly competitive and the assets in them over-valued.

A good British example of over-valuation is the movement of banks, building societies and insurance companies into estate agency in the 1980s. Firms acting as agents for buyers and sellers of housing generally have a poor image of providing an over-priced and inadequate service, yet many financial institutions in the mid-1980s decided that they were going to be a prime vehicle through which mortgages and other financial services were to be sold. For some this strategy seemed to work. The financial services group Hambros reported that in 1987 half of its estate agency customers used at least one of the financial services it had offered them. But others were not so fortunate. Estate agencies were taken over by financial institutions at grossly inflated prices. One firm with assets of £0.5 million, for example, is quoted as finding a buyer for £10 million; whilst the largest building society, the Halifax, wrote off £98 million in the 'goodwill' of the estate agents acquired in 1987 (Gates, 1988). By 1989 there were large-scale closures by financial institutions of their new property service outlets, which perhaps illustrates the riskiness of the business. The earlier high purchase prices had been justified in terms of defensive competitive strategies, but in no sense is the acquisition of estate agents by financial institutions a simple exercise in efficient diversified portfolio management. The experience of Merrill Lynch in the USA is an unfortunate portent for UK financial institutions. In 1980, Merrill Lynch was hoping by 1984 to derive 50 per cent of its revenue through its real estate base, but it had achieved only 10 per cent by 1983 and the activity was later put up for sale.

The general point is that risks are neither clearly known nor necessarily estimated rationally, in which case diversified financial institutions might indulge in unacceptably high risk investments, as the US savings and loans did in the 1980s. The limiting of the activities of financial institutions was, after all, introduced originally to counter such excesses.

Within retail financial services, competitive forces may also fail to create a close correlation between profitability and the degree of risk. The precise forms of market competition may be a more important influence on the profitability of particular activities. Diversifying into new product markets, for instance, frequently leads to competitive retaliation in a way that does not occur with the assets of traditional portfolio theory.

The risks of different financial service activities may also be correlated over time. Unsecured consumer lending and mortgage finance, for example, are both likely to exhibit higher defaults in the aftermath of a consumer boom. Risk patterns also change, as occurred with mortgage finance in a number of countries in the late 1970s when, with rising interest rates, high mortgage debt to income ratios and/or falling house prices, mortgage lending ceased to be a low risk activity.

In summary, it cannot be assumed that portfolio theory offers a justification for diversification by financial institutions. Whether diversification is desirable depends on precise empirical circumstances and institutional responses to them.

Whatever the case for diversification, it has little bearing on the optimal size of financial institutions. A diversified institution could, in principle, be of virtually any size above a fairly small minimum threshold. Larger financial institutions in practice tend to be rather diversified, but this does not imply a causality in the reverse direction.

4.4 The effect of information constraints and asymmetries on mortgage and related markets

Lack of information is a central feature of financial markets and transactions. Limited knowledge creates the risks and uncertainties that abound in finance. The distinction here between risk and uncertainty is the formal one. Risks are, in principle, calculable and hence frameworks can evolve to take account of known risk profiles. Uncertainty is incalculable and prudent actions are required to stop such unknowns creating financial havoc.

No-one has full information about the present or the future. The current actions of individuals, institutions and markets are structured by that fact. For many actors, undue risk is to be avoided — households which seem unlikely to repay a mortgage loan will find institutions unwilling to lend to them, for instance. For others, the unknown is a source of profit. Legislative and institutional responses to risk and uncertainty to a great extent created the 'traditional' framework of mortgage finance; whilst long-term shifts in them have contributed to the breakdown of that structure over the past couple of decades. The unknowns to which that legislation was responding were the viability and integrity of mortgage institutions. A number of the contemporary innovations in mortgage finance instruments are an alternative market-based response to such imponderables.

A lack of knowledge is not simply a generalised feature of modern life. In a number of key situations, one party to a transaction also has greater information and will perhaps want to hold it back from the other. A borrower worried about meeting an institution's lending criteria will try to create a favourable impression of his or her current income and debt. Finance institutions have an incentive to suggest that their services and financial instruments are superior to others even when it is not unequivocally true. Parties to financial transactions try to avoid such opportunism in a variety of ways. When they borrow, households are generally required to produce independent evidence of their incomes. Insurance schemes protect depositors. Financial journalists compare competing terms offered to consumers. But the effects of limited information and its often asymmetrical incidence can never be entirely overcome.

A lack of knowledge about such factors as inflation, future interest rates, potential competitors, and the state of the economy are endemic to financial markets. There are, however, five specific types of informational constraint of concern to an evaluation of the competitive structure of retail finance and mortgage markets. They are: (1) limited information on the creditworthiness of retail borrowers; (2) similar limited information on wholesale borrowers; (3) constraints on the ability of consumers to evaluate other financial instruments; (4) limits on the knowledge of the financial institutions themselves about their own cost of funds, and (5) unknowns associated with investment opportunities.

These features will now be considered in turn. To avoid repetition, qualifications will not generally be put on the bounds to the unknowns. The point of the exercise is to demonstrate that informational limitations create a space for specific forms of competitive behaviour and potentials for financial instability.

The creditworthiness of borrowers

Lenders do not know for certain whether borrowers will repay their debt on the terms laid down in the initial contract. Some might hold back repayments for periods of months or default altogether. The advance may as a result be lost in full or part and/or administrative costs may be imposed on the institution rendering the loan unprofitable. The consequences of defaults for a financial institution are substantial. If defaults are large the institution may be unable to pay its depositors leading to bankruptcy. There will also probably be a prior run on its assets if it is a retail deposit institution. In the absence of effective deposit insurance, savings depositors may be concerned about the risk of failure and require higher compensatory interest payments from institutions with higher loan default records. Lastly, even if defaults are a minuscule part of total loans, consumer lending institutions may still wish to avoid them because of the effect well-publicised repossessions can have on their market image (which often rely heavily on attributes such as responsiveness and caring for the customer). Mortgage defaults, in particular, have a wider social and political significance which may rebound on the type of financial institution in question. With a politically charged issue like housing, defaults are taken as an indicator of housing distress, and blame may be apportioned to the offending institutions.

Even though it is an ever-present threat, the risk of borrowers defaulting is a fundamental rationale for the existence of financial intermediaries between ultimate borrowers and lenders. Such intermediaries pool individual default risks so that defaults become a small proportion of a pool of outstanding debt. But the overall level of defaults has to be kept low if the beneficial effects of risk-pooling are to be achieved, and institutions only have limited means through which they can assess borrower risk.

Credit institutions generally screen potential borrowers to minimise the risk of default. Assessment of income and necessary outgoings are usually required of prospective borrowers, and maximum income-related criteria are imposed. With regard to mortgages, for instance, maximum mortgage to income ratios are set. They take the form of imposing limits on repayments as a percentage of monthly disposable income or of setting a maximum ratio of the mortgage advanced to annual household income. In multi-person households, a different weighting is frequently given to each person's income. The permanence of employment may be an additional factor taken into account. Default risk is further minimised via criteria associated with the property on which the mortgage is lent. Independent assessment of its value and structural condition is usually required to avoid the risk that the purchaser has over-valued it. Mortgage lenders also generally have clearly defined repossession rights, with first call on the property at time of its forced sale, or a hierarchy when there is more than one mortgage on the property.

Not all countries have the same screening procedures for mortgage lending. In Denmark no assessment of income is made, though elsewhere income is usually a key creditworthiness device. Some countries have relatively low stipulated mortgage to house price ratios for first mortgages. Sixty per cent is common in most west European countries, as noted in Chapter 2. In Britain, no legally enforced maximum criteria exist and borrowings in excess of 100 per cent have been reported on occasions. Repossession procedures also vary, along with the legal rights of mortgage borrower and lender. In West Germany, full repayment of mortgage debt and outstanding interest is required even when the market price of the property mortgaged falls below the current value of the debt. Penalty interest rates can also be imposed on defaulters. These stipulations caused considerable hardship in the early 1980s in regions like the Ruhr which were hit by high unemployment and falling house prices after an earlier period of rising house prices and large mortgage borrowings (Potter and Drevermann, 1988). In the USA, the courts tend to view the risk of house price falls as a joint responsibility of lender and borrower, and so do not allow repossession to exceed the current value of the dwelling. In the light of the large number of mortgage defaults in the USA in the early 1980s, with homeowners quitting their mortgaged dwelling and giving the key to the mortgage institution, a number of commentators have suggested that acquiring a mortgage is equivalent to taking an investment option on future house prices. If house prices rise, homeowners exercise the option by paying off the mortgage debt; but if prices fall below the value of the outstanding mortgage they may not take out the option and instead walk away from the deal (Foster and van Order, 1984).

Screening devices are not fixed entities. The ability to use them depends on the prevailing legislative framework (which may make them mandatory), the state of mortgage competition and the recent history of the housing market. Highly competitive markets may force lenders to drop screening procedures because of the threat of losing business to more lax competitors. Long periods of rising house prices may create a state of euphoria, downgrading the risks that lead to screening; price falls generate the reverse. A good case is the Netherlands, where it is said that investigations of borrowers' creditworthiness increased markedly with the onset of the years of house price falls in the late 1970s.

Criteria used to evaluate borrowers' ability and willingness to pay are generally based on custom, practice and crude rules of thumb rather than actuarial investigation. Sexual and racial prejudice has sometimes been an unfortunate implicit feature of the rules of thumb adopted. Considerable evidence has been amassed over the years about discriminatory practices in the mortgage field. 'Redlining', whereby neighbourhoods of a city are deemed to be too high a credit risk to lend in, was identified initially in US cities in the early 1970s and later in other countries. The perceived institutional risk had an uncomfortably high correlation with the existence of black communities and other ethnic minorities, although the actual prevalence of redlining is a controversial issue (Canner, 1982). Extra competition is said to be reducing discrimination but the claim has yet to be validated. Some US commentators suggest that discrimination has worsened with deregulation in the 1980s (e.g. Meyerson, 1986).

Extra competition may lead paradoxically to higher interest rates for most consumers. Limits on competition can generate lower interest rates if the constraints enable credit to be rationed in ways which more easily exclude higher risk borrowers. The average profitability of lending thereby rises and all borrowers can be charged a lower rate of interest relative to the mortgage lender's current cost of borrowing. Another way of looking at the issue is to say that part of the interest rate paid by borrowers is an insurance premium for risk of default. The mortgage institution does not know who will default and anyway has little means of discriminating between actual borrowers. If credit is rationed, as many argue it was in a number of 1970s' style mortgage markets where competition was either limited by regulation or cartel arrangements, the stronger customer screening devices made possible by the excess demand in effect lowered the necessary default risk insurance premium in interest rates. The new competition of the 1980s by increasing default risks has forced up mortgage interest rates for all borrowers. This result may partly explain why mortgage interest rates in the US did not fall after deregulation as its protagonists had forecast.

Market segmentation offers another possibility of customer screening but, in practice, it is difficult to generate effective lower risk market segments. Some financial institutions specialise in higher income borrowers, but higher incomes may easily have more risky prospects. In Britain, lower interest rates are offered on larger mortgage loans. In risk terms this may seem perverse, as the larger the loan the greater the risk of default, other things being equal. The discount could be justified in terms of a more socially acceptable screening device for giving discounts to those on higher incomes, but again it is unclear that higher income borrowers are necessarily less risky. A more likely explanation for the lower interest rate is that differential risk is not taken into account at all, but that the low interest rate is a competitive response aimed at an attractive market segment where competition is particularly intense — a classic instance, in other words, of mortgage lending being based on ignorance of risks.

For financial services in general it has been argued by Stiglitz and Weiss (1981) that the interest rate itself may act as a screening device. Relatively high rates of interest, they suggest, affect the risk profile of borrowers. People who are prepared to pay higher interest rates may, on average, be worse risks because they perceive the probability that they will repay the loan as low. They also suggest that higher interest rates may affect the behaviour of individual borrowers. Higher borrowing costs reduce the number of profitable sources of investment, pushing borrowers into higher risk investments, which offer good returns only when successful. Such mechanisms may explain the behaviour of the financial institutions themselves. The activities of many US thrifts in the 1980s, for instance, correspond to its predictions.

What can be concluded from this discussion of lack of information about borrowers is that screening devices are widespread, but that their effectiveness is inevitably limited. In addition, the use of screening varies with market conditions and the nature of competition amongst finance institutions. Higher interest rates may themselves increase the risk of default. For mortgage lending, defaults have generally been limited in the post-war era although in a number of countries they have increased markedly in the 1980s. The low level of defaults is easy to explain given rising real incomes and house prices, and the beneficial effects of inflation on consumer real debt holdings. Government subsidies of mortgage interest also partly shield both borrower and lender from the consequences of over-extended borrowing, as the state is in effect paying part of the interest charges. The 1980s, however, have seen a questioning of a number of these comforting parables as the individual country studies show later in the book.

Limited knowledge of the creditworthiness of wholesale borrowers

Financial institutions fail, so depositors with them need to have some assurance of their viability. Regulatory controls and supervision exist to limit the risk of failure. Most regulatory constraints in mortgage markets have been specifically introduced to ensure the viability of mortgage institutions or to protect the deposits of those that invest in them. To an extent such regulatory controls are a public good minimising depositor risk, but detractors argue that the cost in lost efficiency is too high. Other means of safeguarding investors are possible, they suggest, or investors can acquire sufficient information to be aware of risk and demand a compensatingly higher return from riskier institutions.

In practice, the possibility of discovering details about the financial viability of institutions by investors in them is severely limited. Accounts and even financial returns to regulatory bodies throw only partial light (see Chapter 6). Moreover, the expense of discovering what information is available may be too great for the small investor. The difficulty of knowing how well an investment portfolio of a financial institution is performing is illustrated abundantly in case studies of bank failures and when acquisitions prove disastrous. Even large, sophisticated financial institutions can make serious misjudgements of other financial institutions. Executives of the Midland Bank, one of the largest British clearing banks, declared, for example, at the time of their sale of Crocker Bank, the troubled Californian financial institution, that they had no idea that Crocker's bad debt portfolio was so great when they purchased it in the early 1980s. Similarly, late in 1988 First Fidelity Bancorp of New Jersey announced large and unexpected real estate losses at the recently acquired Philadelphia bank, Fidelcor.

One factor generating limits on knowledge about the detailed financial performance of specific institutions is that those institutions themselves have only limited information about the returns available from specific types of investment that they are currently making. Risk information may be available but it is unlikely to be sufficient to provide an adequate assessment; instead uncertainty abounds. For this reason it is unsurprising how far hunch, fashion and sentiment influence major investment decisions.

Investor reluctance or limited ability to make detailed investigations of the financial viability of specific institutions and the financial instruments they offer can be seen in the structure of the market for mortgage-backed securities. This market is greatest in the USA where it has only managed to achieve such prominence through the existence of federal guarantees of payments on the securities issued, with later expansion encouraged by private insurance on issues not guaranteed under the federal schemes. So the market exists only because the federal government has obviated the need to assess the creditworthiness of issuers. Despite the guarantees, however, investors still face a prepayment risk (see Chapter 6).

Restricted consumer knowledge of the options

Financial services are complex consumer goods because of the variety of terms and conditions associated with them, and the fact that their costs and benefits are often large but accrue over time. The ability of consumers to make rational choices between the different terms offered by competing agencies is limited, especially when a financial package of, say, mortgage finance, life insurance and house insurance is under consideration.

Two factors are important with respect to variations in the prices of financial services — the costs of gathering the available information, and the widespread uncertainties that still exist no matter how much of the available information is known. Together they severely limit consumers' ability to choose rationally between financial packages.

There are costs associated with gathering the information that exists on financial services on offer and on establishing the financial probity of the institution selling them. Newspapers, magazines and specialist advisers may help but all potential options are unlikely to be considered, as the search and evaluation cost time and money. The problem is complicated by the fact that equivalent financial products may have distinct terms attached to them. There may be a choice, say, between a short-term fixed interest mortgage that would have to be renewed after five years or a long-term mortgage attached to a life policy.

It is unlikely that many people are able to compare more than a limited set of options. The problem for the consumer is compounded when financial institutions offer a wide variety of competing products — a cheque account with guarantee card, for instance, which pays only a low rate of interest on deposits and is subject to a series of charges when used in particular ways versus a higher interest deposit account with no cheque facilities and constraints on the withdrawal of funds. There has been a veritable explosion of competing retail financial products in the 1980s. Some offer clear advantages to certain types of consumer and are quickly matched by other institutions, unless they are hopelessly loss-making products. Yet the profusion of products and packages can also be seen as classic examples of oligopolists' spurious product differentiation. It is hard for even the most sophisticated consumer to decide which is which.

Added to the problem of choice for consumers is uncertainty over the future. Choice between a fixed and variable rate mortgage, for example, involves considerable uncertainty and necessitates attempts to forecast the future path of interest rates in ways which few forecasting agencies would dare. Obviously there are times when it is clear that interest rates are going to rise or fall. The introduction of adjustable rate mortgages in the USA in the early 1980s saw new demand switching between them and fixed interest rate mortgages depending on the direction of change of interest rates. But there are plenty of occasions when forecasting the future and an individual's position within it are essentially wild guesses.

The inability of consumers to choose accurately between financial packages gives firms scope to add mark-ups to their prices, rather than always be forced to price at competitive market clearing levels. Not only are profits directly affected, financial products can be cross-subsidised, either as independent entities or within financial packages. So some products can be priced at below cost to gain a market presence or an extra market share. The ability to add mark-ups obviously has limits, but the possibility of doing so gives greater rationale to the contemporary strategies of retail financial enterprises than do empirically weak arguments about economies of scale and scope. Financial institutions in diversified product markets are more likely to be able to offer products with mark-ups and mark-downs than those active in a sector with a homogeneous product. As an example, in the mid-1970s it was difficult for a financial institution to have a range of prices for a standard 25 year, variable interest annuity mortgage when all its competitors were offering the same and the one alternative available was a similarly packaged endowment mortgage. This was effectively the situation in Britain until the 1980s. Yet even then building societies sought to differentiate their products through claims of greater friendliness, easier mortgage availability and better investor security. Even differential prices were tolerated within their cartel to ensure that smaller, aggressive societies did not break ranks. Some smaller societies had an interest rate mark-up justified to their competitors on the basis of higher operating costs and to customers on the not always accurate grounds that they could not get a mortgage from a larger, cheaper society.

Another example of the impact of the interaction between limited consumer information and regulatory frameworks was one effect of the operation of Regulation Q in the USA. Regulation Q put ceilings on the rates offered by deposit institutions. It has been argued, however, that the maximum permissible rates during periods of interest rate variability also became minimum rates as they acted as a signal to consumers of the best deposit rate available which then had to be matched by all institutions (FRBNY, 1987a).

The boundedness of consumer knowledge and the costs to them of acquiring more creates a space on the demand side of the retail financial services market for firms to formulate strategies over the types of product they offer, their price and the ways in which they are marketed. 'The result, at least in the larger and more competitive markets, is a rather bewildering array of available combinations of interest rates, fee structures, balance requirements, and interconnections with other banking services' (FRBNY, 1987b, p. 15). Competition does not seem to lead to product homogenisation with the less attractive packages being withdrawn through lack of custom. Instead, it appears that distinct packages survive side-by-side. A study of retail deposit pricing in the USA in the deregulated environment of 1983–5, for example, showed that banks' and thrifts' pricing strategies were different. 'While competitive factors no doubt are important, the difference in the way bank and thrift rates change over time belies the view that either group of institutions is pricing mechanically off the other's rates' (Mahoney *et al.*, 1987).

The response of competitors, nevertheless, sets bounds to product differentiation strategies, but the nature of the competitive process is such that the limits are not known beforehand. Institutions have to guess competitor responses, and evidence from a number of countries shows that often those guesses are hopelessly wrong. Within the competitive 'game', an efficient market solution is only one of a wide variety of potential outcomes, and an unlikely one at that. Substantial market instability is another, and more likely, market outcome.

Informational constraints on financial institutions as borrowers

Several informational constraints facing financial institutions have already been considered — uncertainties about borrower repayment and difficulties in assessing investment risks are two. Financial institutions also face limited information as borrowers. The interest rate charged and the conditions of repayment are often insufficient guidelines. An obvious case of uncertainty is borrowing in a currency different from that in which the funds are lent, although here a futures contract can often solve the problem.

The classic unknown on which the financing of mortgages through retail financing is based is the uncertainty associated with borrowing short and lending long. Short-term interest rates may rise so that the rates on the contracted long-term loans may fail to cover them — leading to insolvency. The crisis of the US savings and loans in the late 1970s was precipitated by such adverse interest rate movements. Mortgage finance institutions in other countries tend to cover that risk by the matching of the terms and conditions of loans and borrowings (the mortgage bond principal) or by imposing 'on-demand' interest rate conditions on loans (the UK flexible interest rate principle). Both techniques, of course, do not remove the cost of uncertainties but pass them on to others who make, or fail to make, their own market judgements. Some of the uncertainty is passed on to consumers. Under the bond system, consumers may commit themselves to paying high, fixed nominal interest rates for periods of twenty years or more. In the extreme case of Denmark in the early 1980s the commitment was to interest rates of over 20 per cent with high penalty costs of withdrawal. Investors, alternatively, may see the capital value of the mortgage bonds they hold fall as interest rates rise. Conversely, under the flexible rate régime most of the interest rate risk is placed on consumers. Few British households borrowing the record level of new mortgages in summer 1988 could have foreseen the large increases in their mortgage repayments resulting from the rises in interest rates that occurred over the ensuing months.

Another, perhaps surprising, unknown for financial institutions relying on retail deposits for funds is that the cost of servicing retail accounts is often vague. The costs of operating deposit or cheque account systems vary depending on the average size of the balances held in accounts, the number of transactions, the number of enquiries, recourse by account holders to unauthorised overdrafts and other features imposing administrative costs and affecting the effective pool of funds at the institution's disposal. Statistical models can be drawn up to estimate such variables, but such models depend on an underlying regularity in customer behaviour. When new forms of account are introduced there is insufficient prior information on which to base those estimates. Financial institutions in the USA, for example, are said to face this problem (FRBNY, 1987a). In Britain, when Lloyds Bank became the first clearing bank to offer interest on current accounts, it apparently had limited idea of the cost it would incur or the extra funds the move would generate. Lloyds instead justified the innovation in terms of competitive pressures and building a relationship with customers who could then be sold other financial products. Commentators generally regarded the move as a loss leader, suggesting, for example, that 'many people prefer current accounts with an element of cross-subsidy' (*Financial Times*, 26 October 1988). Within months most other large clearing banks and building societies had offered similar accounts, albeit with important differences in pricing and overdraft facilities. Each justified the move as a response to competitive pressures, with (not surprisingly) little idea of the overall impact on profitability.

The difficulties faced by retail savings institutions in estimating the costs of operating particular forms of customer account are compounded by the growth of a wide variety of competing forms of deposit since the late 1970s. Changes in the products offered by competitors make previous assumptions about customers' behaviour with specific types of current and deposit account no longer valid.

An implication of poor knowledge of the real cost of retail funds is that it is impossible to calculate accurate implicit rates of interest for those funds. One particularly important comparison that cannot be made accurately is the cost of wholesale versus retail funds. It is difficult to see, therefore, in many situations how institutions can compete on rates of interest so as to leave only a narrow and universal spread between the cost of borrowed and lent funds. Arbitrage possibilities may still exist, but they will not be known. Similarly, firms might be winning mortgage business financed by retail funds at a loss, but without knowing it. For a diversified enterprise, moreover, the loss might never cause insolvency as other activities in effect cross-subsidise the mortgage business.

Limited investment information

The final informational constraint is limited investment information. Its general existence is obvious, but there is some evidence that many financial institutions do not even use all of the information available to them when undertaking investment decisions. Instead, they take more than reasonable notice of contemporary investment fashion; subsequently justifying its use with excuses like the imperative of 'competitive pressures'. Insufficient consideration of investment gives third parties opportunities for significant profit-taking.

Examples from the USA and Britain illustrate the point. There were strong criticisms in the late 1980s of the purchase of high-risk 'junk' bonds by US S&Ls and of their purchase of particular types of mortgage-backed security. Some commentators have suggested an asymmetry in sophistication between worldly-wise promoters and less sophisticated thrift-institution executives (Kaufman, 1984, quoted in van Horne, 1985). An ex-president of the American Finance Association has suggested that there have been investment excesses, arguing that:

To a degree, a 'herd' instinct appears. In the case of the corporation, a manager does not want to miss out on a perceived good thing if everyone is doing it. Savings-and-loans association, commercial bank and insurance-company executives are attracted to a new repackaging of mortgaged-backed securities, even though they could manufacture essentially the same thing themselves at lower cost. Like ants attracted to a honey pot, this is a bonanza for financial promoters. Each time a ... new type of mortgage-backed security is sold, substantial promoter fees are realized. But do they make money in the old fashioned way by earning it? I think not in many cases. (van Horne, 1985, pp. 626—7)

The activities of the British financial institutions in purchasing estate agents could also be regarded as uninformed; the payment of premium prices at the peak of a housing market boom hardly indicates cautious appraisal.

It could be that institutions' attitudes to house mortgages as a whole is based on limited information. Many seem to be unaware of housing market cycles. Expensive mortgage lending infrastructures are set up during housing market booms that cannot be expected to be profitable in the longer term. The case of the Netherlands in the late 1970s has already been cited (see also Martens, 1988). The US thrift failures in the late 1980s is another example, and the chills blowing over the UK housing market in 1989/90 portend yet another.

4.5 Competitive strategies in mortgage and related markets

The information limitations outlined above and their suggested consequences create one overriding feature of mortgage and related retail banking markets, excess profit opportunities exist and can be exploited by firms with the appropriate strategies. Losses, furthermore, might be unknown or sustainable over long periods of time, enabling particular strategies towards competitors to be adopted. Deviations away from purely competitive situations may only be ones of degree, but they can still be highly significant in terms of market processes and their outcomes. In particular, they are likely to influence firm structures (frequently to the benefit of the larger institutions), the prices of financial products and the costs of providing them. Inefficiencies within institutions will also go uncorrected by market forces, and the overall scale and cost of retail banking and mortgage provision is increased beyond fully competitive bounds. Investigation of the extent of these factors is an empirical issue though certain initial generalisations can be made. The first and most important is that a number of Tobin's efficiency criteria outlined in the previous chapter are simply not met.

Market profile

Firms with known and respected reputations gain and retain consumers even though they might not offer the cheapest or the most efficient form of intermediation. Building up a relationship with consumers is often important to achieve that reputation. Market surveys can be undertaken and niches identified, or a firm may be in a dominant market position and strive to maintain it. Others may react to that firm's situation and its pricing and product strategies. Such positional competition is predicated on enterprises having strategies aimed at achieving a particular *market profile*. A market profile can be defined as the position that an institution has in a market in the eyes of its consumers, suppliers and competitors. It is the perception others have of its market role and expectations they have of its actions. In part, a firm's market profile depends on real factors such as its market share, but also of importance is the image the enterprise has, which may be based on false perceptions (influenced perhaps by general fads and fashions). Firms, of course, can affect their own images through their behaviour and such devices as corporate advertising.

The formation of a market profile is influenced by management strategies, but those strategies are formulated in a competitive context. A firm's ultimate market profile, in other words, is partly outside of its control — because the outcome will be affected by competitive responses to its own actions. Firms may wish, for instance, to expand their market share, but may find that competition from other institutions actually reduces it.

Enterprise attempts to influence and define their market profiles may rely on market segmentation, in which firms identify and specialise in those segments in which they can operate effectively. Tables 4.2 and 4.3 present two examples. The first considers the types of financial consumer existing in the UK as elaborated by a market research survey. The second is a hierarchy suggested in the mid-1980s for S&Ls based on their degree of geographic and product specialisation. Both tables provide informed guesses rather than accurate estimates, yet they do indicate the feasibility of a variety of market profiles in consumer financial services. Strategies to become financial supermarkets is an example of large banking firms trying to alter their market profiles in the face of perceived market changes. Those perceptions and the strategies to which they lead, of course, could be wrong and may create problems later. The difficulties faced by S&Ls in bond and property markets can also be seen in terms of mistaken strategies towards adjusting their market profiles away from mortgage finance and investment.

Market profile is a concept which fills some of the absences over the behaviour of financial institutions noted in financial market theory in Chapter

Table 4.2   Consumer segmentation in UK retail finance

Suggested types of borrower	
Traditionalist	Conservative in approach to money. Savers rather than spenders. Loyal to institutions. Suspicious of change and financial innovations. (26% of population)
Anxious	Derive no pleasure in finances and regard institutions as threatening. Respond well to personal relationships with account managers. (21% of population)
Connoisseur	Informed and sophisticated, though not necessarily in high finance bracket. (19% of population)
Carefree	Money as a means to an end, the route to fun. Tend to have variable relationships with the bank managers. Interested in credit. (19% of population)
Pragmatist	Confident about money matters. Balanced and practical view of money. (14% of population)

Source: based on survey of two thousand adults undertaken for Consumer Finance Segmentation, Campbell-Keegan and Concensus. Reported in the *Financial Times*, 23 April 1987.

3. Expectations and knowledge of potential market opportunities play central roles in most financial theories, but there is no device within the theories through which they are actually put into practice by institutions. Processes of adjustment in efficient market theory are instantaneous so it could be argued that the absence does not matter. But real world processes are not instantaneous, so the possibility arises of the reactions of agents affecting the final outcome. Even in a world of instanteous adjustment, some mechanism must exist through which agents become aware of profit opportunities and react to them, but, as Summers (1986) has pointed out, efficient market theory has no explanation of the processes of identification and reaction. Chronic instability models suffer from the same absence as they implicitly assume that behaviour is common to all agents. Reference is made to some generalisation about expectations formation, such as that of Keynes, which is sufficient to demonstrate the possibility of, say, market instability but not of the behaviours of distinct types of market agent.

Market profile may explain the advantages accruing to size in financial services. Large institutions find it much easier to generate an identifiable market profile and to sustain it. Most people, for example, can name the major financial institutions in their country because of their advertising, the widespread existence of their branches, the attention given them in the media, and the likelihood of direct knowledge of transactions undertaken through them. Such firms have known expertise and will attract customers. They have to demonstrate incompetence to lose business, whereas smaller competitors have

Table 4.3 Potential types of savings and loan association

Local specialists	Serve small local markets as mortgage provider and deposit taker with clear local identity. Small, independent and locally based. Large portion of thrifts (around half)
Consumer banks	Thrifts that have taken advantage of deregulation to provide a wide range of financial services to consumers. Still predominantly in mortgage lending and deposit-taking but have extended into consumer loans, cheque accounts, etc. Buy mortgage-backed securities to diversify their investments and raise some non-traditional loans. Medium-sized, regional concerns. Category covered about one-fifth of S&Ls in the mid-1980s
Full-service financial holding company	Still has consumer orientation but operates on a large scale and with wide scope. Try to attain a national presence, possibly through the acquisition of other S&Ls, consumer finance companies and mortgage bankers. About 5% of mid-1980s S&Ls
Giant S&Ls	Operate in the traditional S&L areas of business but on a large scale, using sophisticated techniques, and measures offered by deregulation. In mid-1980s were ten to twelve giant S&Ls, originating mainly in California
Commercial bank type	Thrifts developing into full service financial institution for any kind of customer in its market area. Finance small businesses via commercial and real estate loans. Active in general consumer lending. Hold portfolios of corporate bonds and equities. Tend to be regional or city based. Vary in size, but usually smaller than the giants. Covers about 5% of S&Ls

Source: based on suggestions raised in an interview with John Tucillo.

to convince consumers of their existence and credibility.

The importance of market profile may explain the significance of market share on banking profits, with a larger market share being associated with greater profitability, as has been found in most US empirical studies. Market share there does not appear to be a simple indication of monopoly — the impact of concentration on banking profits is, from these statistics, far less than for other US industries (Smirlock, 1985; Rhoades, 1982). The reason for the importance of market share is unclear (Rhoades, 1986) but the idea of market profiles would explain the statistical results.

Some negative consequences of competition over market profile

The consequences of the various forms of competition arising from limited information and firms' strategies towards their market profiles are varied and is explored in greater detail in the following chapters. What is noted here are some of the likely global consequences. As competition is generally regarded as beneficial rather than adverse in its forms and consequences, it is worth at this stage drawing out some of the possible negative aspects for retail financial services.

One effect may be an endemic lack of correspondence between the provision and pricing of financial services and their cost. The possibility of cross-subsidising between financial products may encourage institutions to offer unprofitable 'loss leaders' as a way of attracting extra business. The case of generous interest bearing chequing accounts has already been discussed. Price, of course, may not be the only factor used; non-price inducements may be offered as well. Once one major institution offers customers such inducements others may feel forced to match them at least approximately.

The perceived imperative to match competitors' marketing gambits may create a number of inefficiencies and instabilities. If the price of services is not based on cost, demand will be encouraged for the cheaper ones and discouraged for the more expensive. Often the extra services provided appeal only to a limited range of customers; others might be happy to use them as a 'free good' but in the end pay for them via the other services they use.

The leap-frogging of competitors' offers, moreover, may exclude more realistic pricing. An example here is the behaviour of building societies in Britain following the abandonment of the interest rate fixing cartel in the early 1980s. Each society began to offer higher interest accounts, subject to withdrawal restrictions, in order to attract more funds. In the end individual societies gained little extra revenue as their offers were subsequently matched or improved on. The result was higher interest rates on savings deposits with few effective restrictions on deposit holdings. The interest rate paid to building society savers rose relative to other interest rates, and remained so — and were for a number of years substantially above wholesale market rates (see Chapter 7). One outcome was a redistribution away from borrowers towards lenders which may or may not be socially desirable. The new interest rate behaviour by the societies affected the structure of the UK mortgage market as well as the incidence of interest rates. The higher rates enabled other lenders to enter the mortgage market; a consequence that the building societies do not initially appear to have foreseen. All UK households with mortgages have paid the consequences of that strategy in higher interest rates.

The ability of retail finance institutions to improve their market profiles through cross-subsidies may turn out to be illusory. The profits hoped for in, say, selling a wider range of consumer services or real estate may not actually exist. If other competitors are forced to match the interest rates to savers fixed through such a misplaced strategy, the outlook for the whole retail finance sector looks perilous. In Texas, for example, a spectacular property market and banking collapse in the late 1980s seems to have produced this effect. Competition throughout most of the 1980s forced banks and thrifts to pay a 'Texas premium' of about a percentage point more than in other states for retail funds to match the interest rates offered by foolhardy (and sometimes dishonest) thrifts that not surprisingly became insolvent. The high interest rates squeezed Texan banking in general, threatening the viability of the state's financial system, and contributed to the overall US savings and loan crisis in the late 1980s (*Financial Times*, 28 March 1988). During the late 1980s, the interest rate premiums which had to be offered by insolvent thrifts throughout the USA to attract funds generally became known as the Texas premium after the scale of the excesses there.

There is no reason why the least efficient producers should be forced out of business or taken over in market structures of the forms being suggested here. If firms do achieve success through having particular market profiles, the firms with the most successful ones need not be those that are most efficient at delivering the services offered. Lower cost producers may simply fail to achieve an adequate market profile. Large firms in particular may be able to hide or absorb losses in specific lines of their business rather than be forced into liquidation.

Retail finance institution mergers on this hypothesis are more likely to be linked to market profile strategies than to the efficient acquiring the weak. Again evidence is slight but one study in the USA found that takeovers offered no improvement in efficiency. Rhoades's (1986) study found that poorly performing banks typically were not the ones acquired, and that improvements did not subsequently take place in acquired firms' efficiencies.

Common features of oligopolistic activity seem apparent in retail finance markets. There are large-scale duplications of facilities, such as branches, whilst much money is spent on positional corporate advertising. Advertising budgets grew in the 1980s. In real terms, advertising expenditure in retail financial services in Britain doubled between 1980 and 1986, according to MEAL, a UK consultancy (*Financial Times*, 23 April 1987). Building society advertising expenditure alone doubled in just three years up to 1983, following the advent of the new forms of competition.

4.6 Conclusion

Competitive forces have undoubtedly changed in retail banking and mortgage finance during the 1980s. The point of this chapter has been to argue that the nature of that competition cannot be understood within the framework of simple efficient market parameters; instead they have to be seen in the context of the market profiles of firms and transactions where actors have limited information. From this theoretical position it can be seen that the conditions existing in retail finance are unlikely to satisfy the requirements necessary for global market efficiency.

Advantages of greater firm size in retail finance cannot be explained in terms of producer economies associated with scale and scope, because there is little evidence they exist to any great extent beyond fairly small institutions. Risk-spreading associated with diversified activities also has little to offer in explaining the existence of such large enterprises in retail financial services. Large firms conversely may be subject to greater 'X-inefficiencies'. They may, in addition, have a greater ability to cover up mistakes rather than be forced into management overhaul and restructuring when losses occur. Large firms do, however, benefit considerably from their well-known market profiles. Given the limited information available to investors and other customers, large firms win business through the very existence of their major presence in a market, although competition does to varying degrees constrain their actions.

Limited information in mortgage and related financial services markets generates particular forms of competition. Together they create the possibility of significant market instability. A series of informational contraints and competitive responses were highlighted above. Poorly performing institutions cannot necessarily be identified by investors; screening criteria may be insufficient to insure against borrower default; mortgages may be secured on houses with prices that unexpectedly fall; firms may invest or develop market strategies based on wildly optimistic assumptions and a lack of consideration of the options and competitor responses; housing markets may be flooded with institutions anxious to lend, fuelling temporary booms that then turn sour; and retail finance institutions may become trapped in duels for savers' funds bolstered by false hopes of the extra profits from complementary services. The possibilities of instability are substantial. None may happen. The onus of proof, however, lies with those who believe that widespread destabilising behaviour is unlikely in reality: the evidence shows otherwise.

5

The USA
The mortgage market and regulatory controls prior to 1980

In mortgage finance the US scene is one of superlatives. It has the most complex institutional and regulatory structure; mortgage finance was subject to the greatest legislative changes in the 1980s; and there has been the largest post-war crisis among mortgage finance institutions. Around a fifth of savings and loans associations (S&Ls) were insolvent in 1989 and continued to exist only because they were taken under the wing of a federal or state agency. So, ironically, there was a huge *de facto* nationalisation of a major part of the US finance industry during a decade of 'free-enterprise' promoting administrations. The total cost to the federal government of rescuing the industry — closing down the worst cases and finding someone to buy the others — was in mid-1989 put at over $160 billion, an estimate that has risen substantially since the crisis broke.

The causes of the S&L crisis has its roots in the structure of retail banking and mortgage finance prior to 1980; in the reactions of financial institutions to inflation and rising nominal interest rates in the 1970s and early 1980s, and in the competitive behaviour of S&Ls in the years following the deregulatory impetus.

Given the complexity of the situation, analysis of mortgage finance in the USA is divided here into two chapters. This chapter examines the origins of the 1980s' deregulation process. It describes the system of retail banking — including its regulatory controls formulated in the 1930s — and then it evaluates the mortgage market from the 1950s to the 1980s. The US retail finance system as a whole was subject to a series of buffetings in the 1960s and 1970s. A severe 'credit crunch' or 'disintermediation crisis' in the mid-1960s led to adjustment of the system through the extension of interest rate controls to S&Ls. Within the regulatory framework laid out for their operation, S&Ls were subject to periodic shortages of funds and profit squeezes associated with adverse movements in interest rates. These difficulties were compounded throughout the 1970s by rising inflation. The S&Ls were virtually bankrupt in the early 1980s, and they only survived as an independent financial sector through large-scale public sector loans, regulatory 'bailouts' and being allowed to restructure their mortgage businesses and diversify elsewhere.

Chapter 6 concentrates on developments in the 1980s. As a prime purpose of examining the structure of US mortgage finance prior to the 1980s is to facilitate understanding of the two crises in the 1980s, a brief description of the 1980s' crises is necessary at this point. Both arose because of interactions between general economic developments, the legislative framework guiding the behaviour of S&Ls and the actual behaviour of S&L managements — which failed to conform to the desires of the legislators. Three major pieces of legislation in 1980, 1982 and 1989 aimed at major overhauls of the framework of competition inherited from the 1930s to drag the thrifts and banks out of a chronic malaise that lingered on throughout the 1980s and flared up as severe crises at the beginning and end of the decade. The legislation at the beginning and the end of the decade was supposed to encourage an efficient but diversified retail financial services industry. The first measures aimed to create greater competition — but managed to spur the S&L industry into its greatest post-war crisis and failed to improve the position of the banks. The 1989 legislation aimed to overcome the dishonesty and sharp practice brought out by the early 1980s' measures and its destabilising spillover effects. But it might be the case that there are more fundamental problems associated with the structure of US financial services which again could lead to periodic crises no matter how honest all the participants are. Honesty does not lead to perfect foresight and it could be the way that banks and thrifts formulate their views about the future and perceived competition imperatives that are more significant.

The early 1980s' S&L crises came at a time when government regulations of many kinds were being criticised for hampering market efficiencies. Legislative changes in the early 1980s reflected those criticisms and aimed to free retail deposit-taking institutions from many of the controls they had previously faced — most notably through the abandonment of interest rate ceilings. Supporters of the S&L movement were able to persuade Congress to pass deregulation measures that were particularly favourable to those ambitious S&Ls that either wanted to become general banks or to expand rapidly and/or to indulge in high risk investments. In addition, there was a marked weakening of supervisory controls.

Despite strong federal involvement in restructuring of the industry, many S&Ls throughout the 1980s never really recovered from their problems at the begining of the decade, added to which the new deregulated environment generated large-scale fraudulent and reckless behaviour. The S&L crisis of the late 1980s was by far the biggest since the 1930s. It threatened key elements of federal fiscal and monetary policy, as well as the very existence of an independent S&L movement, and it is leading to a substantial restructuring of retail financial services in general and of the regulatory rules under which they operate.

With hindsight, the crisis of the late 1980s can be seen as an inevitable culmination of competitive responses within the new regulatory framework. Policy debate has swung towards reformulation and tightening of regulatory controls in what is still a highly regulated financial services industry. Yet no easy answer is in sight to a problem that could last for years. One thing is clear, however, many of the efficiency benefits claimed for deregulation have not been borne out in practice, and the resolution of the current S&L crisis does not seem likely to encourage them either, as is noted in the concluding section of Chapter 6.

Some terms have to be clarified before detailed analysis can begin. Terminology varies for descriptions of particular types of US financial institution. Savings and loan associations for many years were collectively called thrifts, along with mutual savings banks and credit unions. They are by far the biggest of the three types of thrift. S&Ls specialised overwhelmingly in mortgage finance, and a large part of mutual savings banks assets were mortgages as well; credit unions specialise in consumer loans. After 1982, all three types of institution were collectively called savings associations in official statistical series, although the shorthand term 'thrift' is still commonly used. Here, savings and loan association, S&L, thrift and savings association will be used interchangeably. Reference is to S&Ls rather than the other two smaller types of financial institution, but it should be remembered that S&Ls are only a subset of thrifts as a whole.

American financial terminology differs from that commonly used in Britain. S&Ls differ from banks, because traditionally they have been deposit-taking and mortgage-lending institutions rather than suppliers of a full range of banking facilities, especially cheque accounts and overdraft facilities. Banks with retail functions are generally called commercial banks (the clearing banks in Britain). When the word 'banks' is used in the text it refers to banks with retail deposit and lending functions. Investment banks in the USA deal with the capital markets and have roles similar to traditional UK merchant banks. Current accounts in British terminology are more sensibly called checking accounts in the USA.

5.1 Regulation of retail deposit-taking institutions prior to the 1980s

To the uninitiated the US financial system seems extremely and unnecessarily complicated. Many of its financial instruments and institutional structures only make sense once the regulatory framework is understood. Taxation differences add further complications (although they will not be considered in detail here).

Mortgage finance has since the nineteenth century been dominated by the retail funding of mortgages — in the form of savings deposits placed in savings and loans associations, mutual savings banks, credit unions and commercial banks. Underlying the simple and well-tried principle of using retail funds to finance residential mortgages has been a series of financial crises leading to legislative responses that have successively transformed the conditions under which mortgage lenders operate. Far more so than in western Europe, regulatory change in the US financial system has been induced by severe financial crises. The mid-1930s and the mid-1960s are two major legislative watersheds prior to the early 1980s.

Much of the contemporary structure of US mortgage finance is the outcome of a series of regulatory measures that culminated in the financial reforms introduced just prior to or during the Roosevelt New Deal years of the 1930s. A number of major adjustments were made to the system in the mid-1960s and they will be noted at the relevant points.

The 1930s legislation brought deposit insurance and interest rate ceilings; whilst the US financial system as a whole was further fragmented both geographically — with financial institutions being forbidden from having widespread interstate branching networks — and functionally into separate specialisms. A regulatory structure was created in the 1930s for the savings and loan industry which paralleled that of the already existing Federal Reserve System for banks. The measures enacted between 1932 and 1934 sought to overcome what were seen as major causes of the large number of loan defaults and bank collapses that had swept through the US financial system during the Depression. After spectacular growth during the 1920s, for example, almost three thousand S&Ls folded in the decade after 1929; whilst in 1931 alone, two thousand banks suspended their operations (Ornstein, 1985). The financial collapse was cumulative as interlocking debt triggered off one failure after another and depositor fears mounted over the soundness of the institutions holding their own funds. Excessive competition was felt to have contributed to the failures. There was also concern over the power that large, multi-function financial enterprises could wield over economic activity as a whole. Lastly, malpractice had come to light in the activities of commercial banks in the pre-1929 stock market.

The structure of the 1930s legislation has six features of relevance to contemporary mortgage finance. They are summarised in Table 5.1. The legislative reforms created a unique mortgage finance system with particular linkages to the rest of the financial system. As their consequences are the subject of this chapter, each aspect and its implications needs further elaboration. Much of the structure still remains — so far it has been tinkered with in the face of periodic crises in various parts of the financial system rather than being fundamentally overhauled. The two major changes in the early 1980s were the abolition of interest rate controls and a relaxation of the functional boundaries in retail finance (but not elsewhere). In the late 1980s there was

Table 5.1 The six prime features of mortgage finance regulation prior to the 1980s

1. *Federal regulation*	Federally chartered S&Ls regulated by the Federal Home Loan Bank Board (FHLBB), which also controls the regional federal home loan banks — the central banks of S&Ls
2. *Insurance*	(a) Of *repayments of mortgages* qualifying for the FHA, VA and FmHA programmes. Led to the introduction of the long-term fixed interest mortgage in the 1930s (b) Of *retail deposits*. Retail deposits with S&Ls insured by FSLIC. Currently up to $100,000 maximum. Insurance in principle paid for by a levy on deposits with S&Ls. This mutual insurance principle has been unable to cope with the thrift crisis of the 1980s, so the cost is falling on the federal government. Control of the bankrupt FSLIC was transferred from FHLBB to FDIC, the bank's deposit insurance agency, in 1989
3. *Interest rate controls (Regulation Q)*	Imposed on bank deposits in the 1930s, and extended to S&Ls in 1966. Maximum interest rate set by the Federal Reserve. S&Ls were given a 0.25% interest advantage over banks to encourage funds into mortgage finance. Regulation Q was repealed in 1981, and phased out by 1986
4. *Separation of banking functions*	A prime effect has been to perpetuate a large number of local retail deposit taking institutions. It has made it impossible for either banks or thrifts to achieve a national presence throughout the USA. The retail financial system instead is regionalised
5. *Creation of a secondary mortgage market*	*First phase:* setting up of FNMA in the 1930s to purchase mortgages, funding purchases with FNMA debt sold on capital markets *Second phase:* securitisation of pools of mortgages, with a market in mortgage-backed securities developing in the 1970s. Repayments of mortgages in pools guaranteed — primarily by federally related agencies
6. *Division of regulatory functions*	A number of regulatory agencies with separate objectives oversee the distinct segments of the US financial system, often in conflict. Federal regulation also is not obligatory: institutions can choose to be state chartered instead

some shift of responsibility between government agencies, a reemphasis of S&Ls on mortgages and a general tightening up of thrift supervision and asset requirements. More detailed changes in the 1980s will be considered in Chapter 6 when relevant.

One 1930s' reform was the introduction of stricter *institutional regulation* of S&Ls, undertaken for the first time by federal, rather than state, agencies. Operational rules were laid down and detailed supervisory procedures devised to ensure that participating institutions conformed to them. S&Ls were also given access to lender of last resort facilities through the setting up of regional federal home loan banks. The Federal Home Loan Bank Board (FHLBB) controls the federal home loan banks, and it is also the regulatory body for federally chartered thrifts. It stipulates criteria on capital adequacy, loan portfolios, other allowable asset holdings and permitted sources of finance, and is empowered within limits to alter the criteria set. To bring S&Ls within the remit of the FHLBB substantial tax incentives exist to encourage thrifts to charter federally and to lend mortgages as their prime activity. Thrift deregulation in the early 1980s centred on altering the activities sanctioned by the regulatory agencies.

Federally sponsored *insurance* is the second feature of the post-1930s financial system. Within mortgage finance it has two aspects: insurance of mortgage repayments against default and the insurance of savings deposits against failure of the bank or thrift in which they are deposited.

Federally subsidised insurance against mortgage default has played a major role in encouraging owner-occupation since the late 1930s. Qualifying mortgages are insured by a number of federal agencies — the Federal Housing Administration (FHA), the Veterans' Administration (VA) and the Farmers' Home Administration (FmHA). The FHA enabled the introduction in the 1930s of the present long-term, fixed-interest level payment, self-amortising mortgage. It replaced a variety of short-term 'balloon' mortgages whose loan conditions required that most or all of the principal had to be paid off or refinanced at the repayment date, which was generally only a few years after the loan was made. During the Depression these mortgage instruments had caused widespread personal bankruptcy as they often could not be renewed as their borrowers had planned (Kindleberger, 1987).

Federally insured mortgages played a key role in reviving the owner-occupied housing market in the 1930s and then encouraging its rapid expansion during the 1940s and early 1950s. There is a substantial literature suggesting a strong bias towards owner-occupation and large-scale developers in the formulation and detailed implementation of the National Housing Act, 1934 which set up the Federal Housing Administration, and in other legislation in the 1930s and 1940s (see Weiss, 1987; Checkoway, 1980; Topalov, 1988). Although permissible, FHA insurance programmes funded few rental dwellings. The USA has always had a large proportion of its housing stock in owner-occupation, partly because of the traditional 'family farmer' character of its rural population. In the years following the Second World War, however, suburban homeownership spread among social strata who previously would have generally rented housing in the established urban areas. Large-scale developers were particularly important in the early post-war years. Free-standing private sector new towns built by one developer, such as Levittown, became world famous. But overall, large-scale developers in the USA have not been as successful as many of their critics have claimed. The US housebuilding industry has remained extremely fragmented and subject to bankruptcy in a way that is no longer true in some European countries, like

Britain (Ball, 1988). Yet federal encouragement of homeownership has obviously helped those agencies involved in its provision. Major beneficiaries have been the financial institutions providing mortgages, which for many years predominantly meant the S&Ls.

In the early post-war years over half of all housing units were insured through one federal scheme or another. After that the role of federal mortgage insurance declined proportionately, with FHA-insured units averaging only 14 per cent of all units in the second half of the 1960s (Tucillo with Goodman, 1983). Despite the declining role of mortgage insurance programmes for specific households, the existence of federally insured mortgages has been vital from the 1970s onwards in encouraging securitisation in the secondary mortgage market. Indeed, a variant of federal insurance was implicitly extended to many 'conventional' mortgages — those not federally insured — when agencies, such as Freddie Mac (see below) started guaranteeing pools of conventional mortgages.

The other aspect of insurance, deposit insurance, was introduced for retail deposits with thrifts and commercial banks below a stipulated sum (currently $100,000, although in practice virtually all depositors have been bailed out by federal agencies at times of insolvency). The insurance is funded by a flat rate levy on the deposits of participating institutions. The federal institution administering the scheme for S&Ls is the Federal Savings and Loan Insurance Corporation (FSLIC). Commercial banks have an equivalent agency, the Federal Deposit Insurance Corporation (FDIC). FSLIC bore the brunt of the thrift failures in the late 1980s and was technically insolvent in 1989. Previously its funds had to be substantially bolstered by Congress on a number of occasions. From the 1930s until 1989 it was under the control of the FHLBB but in 1989 it was transferred to the FDIC.

The introduction of deposit insurance considerably reduced the threat of bank runs — when rumours of impending insolvency lead all depositors to try immediately to withdraw their funds, helping to generate the feared insolvency which through interlocking loans may then spread to other banks. In a decentralised financial system, like that of the USA, constant fear of bank runs has meant that deposit insurance has been an important stabilising influence in the US financial system. The thrift crisis of the late 1980s, for example, did not lead to widespread runs on deposits. The danger was present, as can be seen in the speed with which a rescue package was formulated early in 1989 by the Bush administration in its first major legislative move, and also in the repeated public reassurances of the existence of the deposit guarantees made by federal agencies at the time. Even so, large withdrawals of deposits from thrifts still occurred. Twenty-five thrifts in fourteen states had to be taken over by the regulatory authorities in February 1989 which then guaranteed them sufficient liquidity to stop further runs. An attempt by the regulators to stop insolvent thrifts paying depositors high interest 'insolvency premiums' is said to have encouraged that particular spate of withdrawals (*Financial Times*, 20 February 1989).

The next element of the 1930s legislation is the ceiling on interest rates offered to savers under a banking law, which is generally known as Regulation Q. The Banking Act, 1933 delegated to the Federal Reserve the authority to set ceiling interest rates on bank deposits. The aim of the controls was to stop excessive interest rate competition between financial institutions for retail deposits, and its practicability came to depend on how close the interest rate ceilings were to contemporary market interest rates. The ceiling was set at a fixed-interest rate, subject to infrequent adjustment, rather than a mark-up above current market rates, which with hindsight would seem a more viable constraint. Initially Regulation Q was not applied to S&Ls, but a 'disintermediation' crisis in the mid-1960s led to its extension to them in 1966.

The effects of Regulation Q on commercial banks until the late 1950s was limited as market rates were generally below the ceiling set (Gilbert, 1981). One reason for this was that all interest rates were kept low through the operation of monetary policy during the period. The ceilings became temporarily binding during a credit crunch in 1959, and it has been argued that banks were severely credit constrained throughout the period as they were forced to rely only on local deposit markets (Wojnilower, 1980). Banks broke the constraint after 1962 with the advent of certificates of deposit, the interest ceilings on which were gradually relaxed, and through increasing recourse to the Eurocurrency market. By the end of the 1960s deposit rate ceilings were no longer a serious constraint on bank lending activities. The S&Ls, though, could not so easily break out of their retail deposit base, so Regulation Q still had a substantial effect on the flow of funds into them — especially as after 1966 Regulation Q rates were frequently lower than market ones.

The argument used for imposing Regulation Q on thrift deposits was that competition between banks and thrifts was driving up interest rates. Many thrifts also could not pay contemporary market rates for savings, which had risen substantially, because what they could pay for deposits was constrained by the income generated from their portfolios of long-term mortgages, the rates on which had been fixed at earlier lower interest rates. Unanticipated rises in interest rates, in other words, led to a mismatch between the cost of funds to thrifts and the returns they earned from mortgage lending. As such it had many similar characteristics to the thrift crises of the 1980s.

With the extension of Regulation Q to them, thrifts no longer had to match market rates. Not surprisingly the measure did not halt the drift of deposits away from thrifts towards investment mediums outside the remit of Regulation Q. This led to a slight relaxation of the controls in the early 1970s when thrifts were allowed to offer some restrictive, large denomination investment mediums paying higher interest rates (Tucillo with Goodman, 1983; Ornstein, 1985). On their mainstream deposit business, however, thrifts were given an interest rate ceiling advantage over banks of 0.5 per cent (later reduced to 0.25 per cent) in order to channel savings towards them — a slight advantage in view of subsequent high nominal interest rates. The premium was justified by the need to encourage the expansion of housing investment.

The fourth element of the 1930s' US regulatory structure is the *separation of banking functions*. A major objective was to divorce commercial from investment banking (under the auspices of the Glass—Steagall Act, 1933). But other aspects of retail finance were affected as well. The geographical spread of bank branches since the 1930s has been constrained by the need to obtain regulatory permission, which put effective limits on banks having either an interstate or national spread. Other measures have kept financial institutions effectively within one function, such as the tax breaks available to S&Ls that invest primarily in housing mortgages. An important consequence of the continued separation of functions and the constraints imposed on bank holding companies is the large number of independent financial institutions that now exist in contrast with other countries, with almost fourteen thousand commercial banks and three thousand thrifts (see Table 4.1).

The fifth aspect of the 1930s' financial legislation was the setting up of a *secondary mortgage market*. The Federal National Mortgage Association (FNMA, generally known as Fannie Mae) was founded in the 1930s to perform this role. Its prime function up to the 1980s was to buy mortgages from originators. The mortgage purchases were financed by raising loans on the capital markets, which were serviced through the income generated from the purchased mortgages that the FNMA held. Given the regional specialisation of retail deposit mortgage institutions, access to the capital markets has always been essential to channel funds from capital surplus regions into areas where residential investment is expanding rapidly. In the post-war years the major flows have been from the north-eastern states to the West and South. Access to capital markets, through the intermediation of FNMA, has meant that the volume of mortgage funds has never been tied solely to the level of activity in retail savings markets. It was hoped that the creation of this capital market 'safety valve' would smooth out housing cycles, although periodic 'disintermediation' crises have still constrained housing market activity.

In 1968, Fannie Mae was 'privatised'. Its new private status, hwoever, contained a degree of federal sponsorship which ensured that its debt was treated in the capital markets as though it was federally guaranteed. After its reconstitution Fannie Mae expanded rapidly. In 1968 it held $7 billion of mortgages, all of them FHA- or VA-insured; by July 1988 its holdings had risen to $103 billion, 85 per cent of them conventional (i.e. not federally insured). In the late 1970s it was by far the largest holder of mortgages and as such was badly affected by the rise in nominal interest rates. Its considerable holdings of low fixed-interest mortgages generated huge losses as its own borrowings had to be refinanced at much higher interest rates. In 1982, for example it lost $105 million and underwent a painful process of federally assisted restructuring during the 1980s.

Originally, the FNMA also directed federal subsidies to mortgage issuers, but this function was devolved to another institution at the time that its status was transformed in 1968. The new federal agency set up is known as the Government National Mortgage Association (GNMA, generally known as Ginnie Mae). The advent of GNMA created a means through which federal guarantees of mortgage repayments could be used to transform the secondary mortgage market. Investors could purchase paper directly based on pools of mortgages rather than acquire the stock of an institution holding mortgages (the FNMA principle), which requires investors to have faith in the soundness and efficiency of the institution in question. It was through the initial use of Ginnie Mae guarantees that present-day secondary mortgage market instruments emerged. The GNMA is not empowered like the FNMA to purchase mortgages. Instead it guarantees the full payment of the interest and principal of the securities (technically, they are called participation certificates) issued by private sector mortgage intermediaries that are backed by pools of federally insured mortgages. Mortgages are pooled by originators and 'pass through' the GNMA for guarantee, a service for which it charges a fee on the outstanding sum of the securities issued. The GNMA deals only in federally insured mortgages under the FHA, VA and FmHA programmes.

To encourage the development of a secondary mortgage market in conventional mortgages, the Federal Home Loan Mortgage Corporation (FHLMC, commonly known as Freddie Mac) was set up following congressional legislation in 1970. Freddie Mac operates on different principles from Ginnie Mae in that it purchases mortgages and resells them by issuing paper (such as mortgage participation certificates) whose interest and principal comes from the flows derived from the pools or mortgage backing the securities. Freddie Mac guarantees the mortgage repayments and profits from the spread between the cost of its mortgage purchases and the prices of the participation certificates sold. Freddie Mac's shares are held by the savings and loans industry and its board of directors is appointed from the FLHBB. Its profits, which have been good, are passed onto the federal home loan banks and then distributed to individual S&Ls. Freddie Mac's status makes it liable to little taxation — which is another implicit federal subsidy of the secondary mortgage market.

Following the privatisation of Fannie Mae and the introduction of mortgage-backed securities, the secondary market became increasingly significant. By mid-1988, 35 per cent of all owner-occupied mortgages were held in secondary market mortgage pools (see Table 5.2) and around 70 per cent of new originations were funded through it. The secondary mortgage market has taken over much of the traditional role of retail finance because of the inability of savings institutions to cope with inflationary pressures and the heightened

Table 5.2 Market shares of mortgage holdings: the 1950s and 1980s compared

| | Year end, outstanding 1-to-4 family mortgages | | | |
	1950	1956	1985	1988[a]
Life insurance companies	22.7	22.9	0.8	0.7
Mutual savings banks	11.5	14.8	37.8	31.3
Savings and loans	36.0	38.7		
Commercial banks	25.4	18.5	14.5	14.7
Mortgage companies	1.3	1.1	n.a.	n.a.[b]
Federal agencies	3.9	4.0	7.5	6.6
Mortgage pools	—	—	26.1	34.7
Individuals and others	n.a.	n.a.[b]	13.3	13.0
Total ($billion)	37	88	1,467	1,972

[a] Outstanding at end of July.
[b] Not individually itemised in the data.

Sources: data for the 1950s, Tucillo with Goodman (1983); for the 1980s, FRB (1989)

competition for retail funds. The secondary market has also changed the nature of the thrifts themselves. Mortgages can be originated by S&Ls, securitised and sold on the secondary market rather than be held directly. Investment in mortgages can be made subsequently by purchasing mortgage-backed securities. Thrifts, like other mortgage investors, can benefit from the liquidity offered by holding readily saleable instruments — at the cost of a slightly reduced return when compared with holding mortgages direct. By 1986, 13 per cent of all thrift investments were in mortgage backed securities, and thrifts were major purchasers in the secondary mortgage market.

Securitisation, which became so prevalent in international money and capital markets in the late 1980s, owes its organising principles to the US secondary mortgage market. In the 1980s, the FNMA also began to securitise mortgages. More detailed analysis of the secondary mortgage market in the 1980s is given in the following chapter.

The final aspect of the post-1930s US financial system is the *division of regulatory functions*. There is a variety of regulatory bodies, each with different and often conflicting functions. Federally chartered banks, for example, are subject to the supervision of the Federal Reserve Board, the FDIC and the Office of the Comptroller of the Currency, whilst they have to conform to the banking laws of the states in which they operate. Thrifts have distinct, but often functionally parallel regulatory agencies, from commercial banks, although they compete in many areas of business and the functional overlap between them is increasing with time.

Both banks and thrifts can also choose whether they are regulated by federal or state agencies, and individual states have distinct rules sometimes at variance with the requirements of the federal agencies. A number of incentives, such as tax breaks, encourage financial intermediaries down one regulatory route or the other depending on the objectives of the institution.

The welter of regulatory agencies generates considerable confusion, unclear responsibilities when solvency problems arise in the financial system, and serious divisions of interest that make reform difficult. Added to this is the in-fighting and self-interested lobbying of the US political scene which frequently operates outside of the bounds of formal political party distinctions. A number of commentators have questioned the ways in which members of regulatory boards are recruited and their impartiality with respect to the financial institutions that they regulate. A senior Federal Reserve Bank (Fed) official, for example, has been quoted as saying of the thrift regulatory body, the FHLBB: 'The FHLBB was a disaster. It was an industry-controlled organisation and was required to keep its hands off. The industry was totally successful in influencing the Congress and the White House, not only in getting the legislation it wanted, but also in putting its own people onto the FHLBB' (*Financial Times*, 6 April 1988).

One other aspect of the US regulatory system distinguishes it from west European style systems. In the USA, regulation is via legislation and formal instructions from the regulatory bodies. In western Europe, central banks play more direct but discretionary regulatory roles, even over sectors of the financial system not formally within their remit (like the influence of the Bank of England on the British building societies). As a result, financial activities can exist in the USA which would not be permitted by European-style banking regulation. Examples are the setting up in the 1970s of money market mutual funds by independent investment media to take advantage of the interested constraints imposed on commercial banks and thrifts, and the ability of non-financial corporations, like housebuilders and car companies, to set up their own S&Ls. Even non-bank banks exist. They take deposits, insured by the FDIC, but do not make loans — so they can avoid banking regulations through a loophole in the law which specifies that a bank is an institution both taking deposits and making loans. The Supreme Court in 1986 blocked the Federal Reserve Board's attempt to close the loophole (Siedman, 1986).

5.2 The role of S&Ls before the 1980s

From the description of the regulatory structure, it can be seen that mortgage finance in the 1930s legislation was set up as a relatively independent sector with special privileges and tax breaks; a position that was subsequently reinforced by the Regulation Q differential of 1966 and federal encouragement of secondary mortgage markets. But in practice the mortgage market is not independent of the rest of the US financial system nor has it ever been. S&Ls, the traditional prime lenders of mortgages, in particular have never been entirely protected from competition in either the mortgage or the retail savings markets. They have not enjoyed the competitive restraints of an effective cartel in the way, say, that the British building societies did for many years. The US system has not changed from 'no to more competition' but has existed in environments in which competition has taken different forms. The consequences of the changing nature of the competitive environment is best approached by looking at the market share of S&Ls and their deposit and mortgage pricing policies. As S&Ls had no control over the price of their deposits after 1966, the mid-1960s is a convenient dividing line. Regulation Q then becomes of central concern.

Many thrifts are mutual organisations, so it might be thought that their behaviour could not be understood in simple profit-making terms. In one major sense this is true, as much of the industry for many years has made such poor profits that a better return on capital could have been achieved by closing up, liquidating the assets and investing them elsewhere. (The same is true of many US commercial banks.) In terms of their activities, however, thrift behaviour can be explained by examining the profitability of specific actions. In ownership terms S&Ls can be either mutual associations or corporations with stockholders. The split between the two was roughly 70 per cent mutual and 30 per cent stock in the mid-1980s, although stock thrifts tend to be the larger ones so the split as regards assets gave stock thrifts control of 62 per cent of the industry's assets (Brumbaugh and Carron, 1987). The 1980s' reforms encouraged mutual thrifts to convert to stock status, but the distinction in practice between the forms of ownership has little overall influence on S&Ls' behaviour.

Whether S&Ls have been profit-maximising, however, is less clear. Many have gone for growth in a way that contradicts the standard profit-maximising assumption. Yet, as is argued below, the S&Ls have had strong incentives to expand given their inherent economic dilemmas. In addition, for the same reasons they have had inducements to be risk-taking over their investments and optimistic over forecasting the future pattern of interest rates.

The basic dilemma of S&Ls prior to the 1980s is the well-known one of borrowing short and lending long, although such a position is by no means unique but a common feature of many financial institutions. S&Ls, however, lent and held highly illiquid instruments — long-term, fixed-interest mortgages — and funded them with highly liquid passbook deposits. In an era of volatile and rising nominal interest rates after 1966, the S&Ls would have had severe problems even if they could have charged any interest rate on savings deposits. At times of rising interest rates, if S&Ls had matched the interest rates offered elsewhere, their outstanding loan commitments fixed at earlier lower rates would have made their operations unprofitable. If, conversely, they did not match general interest rates then their net inflow of funds would dry up, leaving them with a liquidity crisis as outstanding mortgage debt could not be called in to bridge the funding gap. As S&Ls increasingly faced the interest rate matching dilemma from the mid-1960s to the 1980s, the question is, how did they manage to survive for so long? The answer is Regulation Q and a highly expansionist strategy whenever it was possible.

On the basis of this argument the occurrence of the second thrift crisis of the 1980s is not so surprising. Deregulation in the early 1980s did allow some crooks into the industry and resulted in some spectacular excesses. But it could be said that what thrifts in general were doing was adopting a familiar business strategy — they gambled on getting out of a financial mess by expanding rapidly. The problem of the 1980s was that the deregulators gave the S&Ls even more rope with which to hang themselves. Retail finance in the USA has still not overcome one of its major weaknesses because the late 1980s legislation dampened rather than abolished the incentive towards over-expansion.

The inherent risk for S&Ls of borrowing short and lending long is increased by the ability of US households to cash-in their mortgages at any time at little cost. When interest rates fall, mortgage borrowers have an incentive to trade in their outstanding mortgage for a new one. This means that S&Ls benefit less from holding high interest rate mortgages when general rates are falling than do, for example, the holders of fixed-interest mortgage bonds in West Germany. A further impediment to interest rate matching until the early 1980s' reforms was the frequent ability of households to pass on their own low interest mortgages to the next house purchaser; a right hotly contested in the courts by thrifts in the late 1970s.

5.3 The structure of the mortgage market up to the mid-1960s

Savings and loan associations played a major but not overwhelming role in the mortgage markets of the 1950s and 1960s (Tables 5.2 and 5.3). They were particularly strong in owner-occupied housing (roughly equivalent to 1-to-4 family housing in the data), whereas other financial institutions were more active in rental sectors. The mortgage companies highlighted in Table 5.2 operate as mortgage brokers (more commonly called mortgage bankers). They originate mortgages and sell them to other investors, charging a fee for the origination and continued servicing of the loan. Federally insured mortgages are particularly attractive to mortgage bankers because, as they carry no default risk, they are easier to sell. Mortgage bankers cut down the cost of investing in mortgages for general investors as they are saved the expenses of marketing and servicing mortgages. Although a small part of the market in the 1950s, mortgage bankers in the 1970s and 1980s played a much greater role in originations using the services of Fannie Mae (80 per cent of its purchases were from them in the 1970s) and the secondary mortgage market.

Table 5.3 Percentage of residential mortgage debt outstanding by type of institution, 1950–80

	S&Ls	Mutual savings banks	Commercial banks	Life insurance companies	Federal and related	Other
1950	24	13	19	20	3	21
1955	30	15	15	21	3	15
1960	35	15	13	18	5	14
1965	40	16	13	15	7	16
1970	39	14	13	12	7	16
1975	42	11	14	6	8	18
1980	42	8	16	3	7	25

Source: Ornstein (1985).

Institutional shares in the mortgage market altered after the mid-1950s because two major investors in owner-occupied mortgages, life companies and commercial banks, began to withdraw from the market. The share of life insurance companies direct holdings fell from 23 per cent in 1956 to 12 per cent in 1970 and to less than 1 per cent by 1980 (Table 5.2). Commercial banks adopted a different strategy of expanding lending at the trough of interest rate cycles and cutting back at the peak (Tucillo with Goodman, 1983). With reduced competition, and an inability to follow other institutions into more profitable activities, the share of the thrifts rose to a peak in the mid-1960s. In 1965, thrifts altogether had a 56 per cent share of outstanding mortgage holdings (63 per cent for owner-occupied housing alone). This pattern of increasing mortgage market specialisation up to the mid-1960s is similar to that in western Europe, particularly Britain.

Inflation rose in the mid-1960s and led to severe problems for S&Ls and the mortgage market in general. The nature of the 'disintermediation crisis' and the resultant imposition of Regulation Q on S&L deposits is described in an earlier section. The demand for mortgages also fell rapidly during 1966, associated with the sharpest post-war drop in housing starts (Figure 5.1). S&Ls responded to the drop in mortgage business by putting greater emphasis on non-price competition — using such devices as more branches and free consumer durable offers.

5.4 The years after 1966 and the impact of Regulation Q

The fifteen years from 1966 to 1981 were mixed ones for the S&Ls with their fortunes depending on the pattern of interest rates and the state of the housing market. As both are affected by common economic influences, feast and famine aptly describes their activities over the period.

Funds would not flow into S&Ls for mortgage lending when their Regulation Q controlled deposit interest rates fell below general market rates. With escalating nominal interest rates in the late 1970s the differential between Regulation Q ceilings and market interest rates reached more than 10 per cent (Gilbert, 1981). Thrifts and banks found their deposit bases particularly under threat once the existence of other savings media for relatively small deposits became widely available from the mid-1970s with the growth of money market funds. (Appendix to Chapter 6 gives brief descriptions of the variety of retail savings instruments on offer in the USA in the 1970s and 1980s.)

On the mortgage lending side, the housing market was far more volatile after 1966 (see Figure 5.1). During housing market downturns, the demand for mortgages was greatly reduced. Over time, moreover, homeownership became less affordable for many of the households contemplating a move to the tenure, despite negative real interest rates for a number of years. In 1970, 45 per cent of US families could afford new homes (according to US Department of Housing and Urban Development data); by 1978 the percentage had dropped to 29 per cent (Tucillo with Goodman, 1983). The 'affordability problem' increased defaults among two important sectors of borrowers — new entrants and those with median or lower incomes. The economic crises and the long-term deindustrialisation of certain traditional industrial regions substantially increased unemployment and short-time working, both of which raised defaults further. So the risks involved in mortgage lending grew from the early-1970s onwards.

Regulation Q is the key factor explaining S&L performance in this period. It had contradictory effects on S&Ls. On the one hand, it enabled S&Ls to

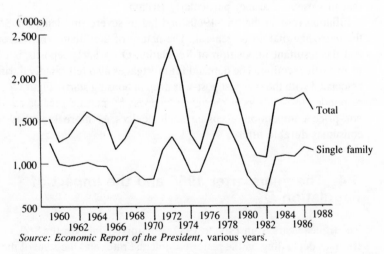

Source: Economic Report of the President, various years.

Figure 5.1 Housing starts in the USA, 1959–87

continue in their traditional business of gathering retail deposits for the mortgage market. This activity was generally profitable because of Regulation Q until 1981—2. On the other hand, interest rate controls caused periods when funds suddenly dried up, forcing S&Ls to curtail mortgage lending and to borrow funds from the Federal Home Loan Banks. Such shortages of funds occurred in 1966, 1969, 1973—4, and 1980—2 (see Figure 5.2).

The periods of low net deposits interestingly came at times characterised by a 'reverse' yield gap between short- and long-term interest rates — when short-term rates rise above long-term ones. Such movements in the yield curve are a central problem for S&Ls as they undermine the profitability of their mortgage business. Their mortgage rates, as is shown below, tended during the 1960s and 1970s to be priced at levels equivalent to general long-term rates, whereas their income was affected by short rates (albeit in a fashion damped by the slow response of the Regulation Q ceilings). Figure 5.3 compared the spread between the current mortgage rate and short- and long-term interest rates (as represented by 3 month Treasury bill and 10 year Treasury bond rates respectively). The difference between the two lines in the graph represents the prevailing spread between short and long rates. It can be seen that up to the 1980s the difference between the mortgage and long-term interest rates was fairly stable, with the mortgage rate between 1 and 2 per cent greater, but that it was highly variable with respect to general short-term rates.

The effect of the yield gap on the S&Ls was mediated by the existence of Regulation Q which resulted in narrowings of the gap being felt quantitatively in sharp declines in net deposit income and mortgage lending, as S&Ls could not match the contemporary increases in short rates. Yet the inability to match other short rates kept S&L spreads healthier than they would otherwise have

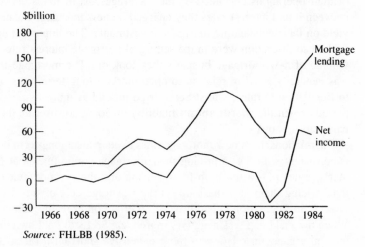

Source: FHLBB (1985).

Figure 5.2 Thrift mortgage lending and net income, 1965—84

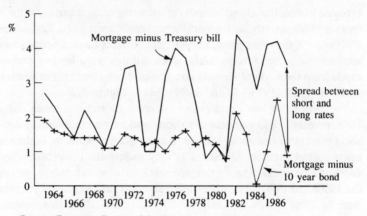

Source: Economic Report of the President, various years.

Figure 5.3 Spreads between new mortgage interest rates and short- and long-term interest rates, 1963—87

been. So it was not just the general *rise* in nominal interest rates from the late 1960s onwards that threatened the viability of S&Ls. The *volatility* of interest rates exacerbated their problems and actually brought crises upon them.

The impact of Regulation Q on S&Ls depended no the actual constraints it imposed on their operations. It only controlled the interest rate on passbook accounts, all other aspects of behaviour were at the discretion of S&L management in the face of changing economic circumstances. The flow of funds into S&Ls may have been fixed by Regulation Q rates, but the profitability of their operations depended on their average cost of funds and the spreads between it and interest rates they charged on new mortgage business and the yield on their outstanding mortgage investments. The important areas where S&Ls had discretion were in the setting of mortgage interest rates and in the volume of new mortgage business they took on. The mortgage interest rate was generally fixed in relation to open market, long-term rates, as opposed to Regulation Q rates, whilst S&Ls tried to lend as much as possible during periods when the short-term profitability of doing so rose, as the following paragraphs show.

The relationship of new mortgage rates to equivalent long-term interest rates is consistent with S&Ls pricing their mortgage commitments at free capital market rates plus a mark-up for servicing and the extra default risk, rather than pricing them at a mark-up on their average cost of funds (which was lower). So Regulation Q had little or no effect on prevailing mortgage rates. When the yield gap was negative, moreover, S&Ls did not switch to pricing their mortgages in relation to more expensive short-term rates. The failure to price at their own marginal cost of funds during these periods could be explained by either of two factors. The first is that Regulation Q protected them from the full impact of exceptionally high short-term rates, but this was not true for their marginal funds which tended to be high denomination short-term money outside of the remit of Regulation Q. The other, more likely explanation is the existence of the secondary mortgage market where rates were priced in relation to capital market rates. The secondary market made it competitively impossible to charge higher rates.

There has been a substantial literature about the impact of Regulation Q on S&L pricing behaviour. All of it emphasises the market determination of mortgage interest rates. Gilbert (1981; 1986; Gilbert and Holland, 1983) argues that S&Ls' marginal cost of funds was not influenced by Regulation Q during the 1970s because of the absence of controls on large deposits. Mayer and Nathan (1983) make a similar point. Kaufman (1987) also notes another unrestrained source used extensively throughout the 1970s (and 1980s) — borrowing from the FHLBs at market rates. Such points, however, do not explain the reverse yield gap periods.

One consequence of S&L mortgage pricing policy was that mortgage borrowers did not gain from the existence of Regulation Q, instead it enhanced S&L profits in certain years at the expense of smaller savers tied to passbook accounts. In this respect it is interesting to note that the Depository Institutions Deregulation Act, 1980, enacted by Congress to ensure the gradual removal of interest rate ceilings, explicitly referred to the need for those with modest savings to enjoy market-level interest rates. Earlier a large literature had emerged on the regressive distributional consequences of the deposit ceilings (see Gilbert, 1981 for an extensive bibliography).

Although they may not have benefited directly from the existence of Regulation Q, many owner-occupiers gained from the overall contemporary structure of housing finance. Homeowners in the 1970s who were prosperous enough to cope with the distortions induced by inflation (such as the 'front-loading' of real mortgage repayments and the higher nominal price of housing — see Chapter 2) enjoyed considerable benefits from federal homeownership subsidies and tax reliefs and from the contemporary organisation of mortgage finance (Gravelle, 1983). Negative real interest rates favoured them and discriminated against small savers. Earlier arguments claiming distributional progressivity for homeownership subsidies and the financial arrangements associated with them rapidly lost credibility in the 1970s.

A central question to ask about Regulation Q is, what would have happened to S&L profitability in its absence? This question can be answered by looking at the spreads S&Ls achieved during the period when they were subject to Regulation Q. The spreads between S&L average cost of funds and the returns on outstanding mortgages and new mortgage business respectively can be compared with those of a hypothetical 'free of Regulation Q' S&L which funded its mortgage investments at contemporary money market interest rates. For simplicity, it can be assumed that the non-Regulation Q S&L could raise money at the best short-term interest rates available (as represented by the 3 month Treasury bill rate); but it only lent new mortgages and held an outstanding pool of them on the same terms as S&Ls on average did in those years. So the returns achieved can be treated as the same.

The three graphs in Figure 5.4 illustrate the effects of the interest rate ceilings. Figure 5.4(a) shows the actual spreads achieved by S&Ls. It can be seen that new mortgage business always had a positive spread, one that was noticeably higher than on existing mortgage holdings. Yet although lower, the spread on existing mortgages was actually negative in only two years (in 1981−2).

Figure 5.4(b) shows the spreads for a hypothetical S&L that financed all of its mortgage business from free market funds. The situation of this S&L is far worse in a number of key respects. The pattern of spreads has similarities with those of actual S&Ls but it is far more volatile. New mortgage business still always has a positive spread from the late 1960s to the early 1980s. The spread during the periods of mortgage boom of 1971−3 and 1975−7 was, in fact, greater than that of Regulation Q S&Ls. The picture on outstanding mortgage business for the 'free market' S&L is again one of greater volatility. The volatility would have led to more frequent years of losses than actual S&L performance — losses would have occurred in 1969 and 1974 as well as in the early 1980s. The losses in the early 1980s, in addition, would have been far worse. The poorest year for the hypothetical S&L was when the spread was −4.1 per cent, whereas for actual S&Ls it was only −1.0 per cent.

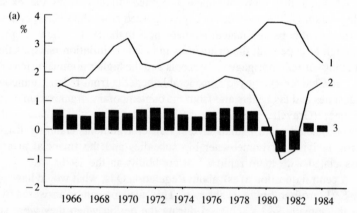

Key
1 New mortgage rate minus average cost of funds
2 Average yield on outstanding mortgages minus average cost of funds
3 Net income as a percentage of average assets

Source: FHLBB (1985).

(b)

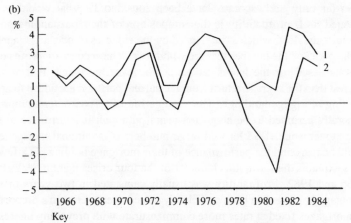

Key

1 Average new mortgage rate minus Treasury bill rate
2 Average yield on outstanding mortgages minus Treasury bill rate.

Source: FHLBB (1985).

(c)

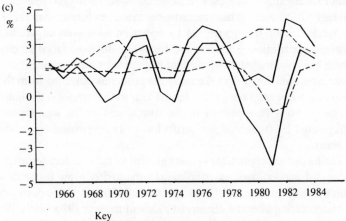

Key
– – Actual thrift spread (as shown in Figure 5.4a).
—— 'Free market' thrift spread (as shown in Figure 5.4b).

Source: FHLBB (1985).

Figure 5.4 The impact of Regulation Q on S&L mortgage spreads,
1965–84
(a) Actual spreads earned on new and outstanding mortgages and S&L
net income as a percentage of assets
(b) 'Free market' spreads between 3 month treasury bill rate and yields
on new and outstanding mortgages
(c) Actual and 'free market' spreads compared

So far only S&L spreads have been considered. What would also have affected S&L profitability is the composition of their outstanding portfolios of mortgage debt, which is influenced by the volumes of new mortgages added to the pool and the number that are withdrawn. The accounting profits of S&Ls are increased (or the losses reduced) whenever mortgages lent at a higher interest than the average return from the current portfolio are added to an S&L's existing mortgage holdings. The average life of a fixed-interest mortgage is generally assumed to be about ten years, although it is sensitive to interest rate movements. If S&Ls sold large numbers of additional mortgages, they could turn around the performance of their mortgage holdings in a few years. This explains the short-run character of the four crises that hit S&Ls between 1966 and 1982. Profitability was usually reinstated in two years or so once mortgage holdings had been sufficiently turned over to contain a preponderance of mortgages fixed at rates more commensurate with prevailing interest rates.

When faced with declining profitability at those times of crisis in the 1960s and 1970s, S&Ls consequently had a strong incentive to issue as many new mortgages as possible as long as the interest rate on them was greater than the average return on their outstanding holdings, because in this way the short-term profitability of their mortgage business was enhanced. Prudency or longer-term expectations of interest rate movements would suggest that such a growth strategy was unwise. When interest rates rose even further than the levels fixed on the additional mortgages, S&Ls ended up with even larger, unprofitable mortgage portfolios. So, since the 1960s, thrifts have faced an environment which has encouraged them to adopt a 'growth or bust' strategy in which new business would hopefully take away the problems inherited from the past. As soon as interest rates once more turned against that strategy, the industry faced another crisis. This pattern of the 1960s and 1970s was repeated in the deregulated 1980s except then thrifts had more investment opportunities open to them.

Thrifts did experience rapid asset growth in the two decades after 1970. As Table 5.4 shows, their asset holdings consistently grew faster in real terms than those of commercial banks. Between 1980 and 1986, during the period of restructuring after the disastrous losses of the late 1970s/early 1980s, thrift assets were growing at twice the rate of GNP. Even this rapid growth, though, did not match the spectacular increase in investment companies — initially taking advantage of the constraints of Regulation Q and later the tax efficiency of their instruments. Such investment funds became the major competitors of thrifts in their quest for extra retail deposits.

The argument that S&Ls have relied on a strategy of trying to grow out of their problems is commensurate with the sharp increases in their mortgage lending after each period of crisis and housing market slump in the 1970s and 1980s (Figure 5.2). Their net increase in deposits did not vary as strongly as mortgage lending, partly because thrifts relied increasingly on sales of

Table 5.4 Asset growth of US financial institutions, 1965—86

	1965—70	1970—75	1975—80	1980—86
Commercial banks	3.3	2.8	3.0	4.3
Thrifts	2.0	5.2	4.0	5.2
Finance companies	2.9	1.8	7.4	7.1
Investment companies	2.2	− 6.0	13.1	20.8
GNP	3.0	2.2	3.4	2.6

Notes
1. Thrifts include S&Ls, mutual savings banks and credit unions.
2. Investment companies constitute mutual funds, money market funds and security brokers.
3. Figures show the annual percentage change at constant dollars. Constant prices derived using GNP implicit deflator.

Source: OECD (1988b).

mortgages on the secondary mortgage market. Originating mortgages and selling them earns income, and the tax advantages of mortgage holdings can be achieved by purchasing secondary market paper.

A final point to note is that S&L depositors did not consistently do badly from the existence of Regulation Q. Regulation Q rates were not changed rapidly, so in periods when short-term rates fell it would produce a ceiling above contemporary market rates. The previous chapter argues that Regulation Q provided a signal to savers about available interest rates from the mid-1960s onwards. It generated expectations in savers which deposit institutions had to match. Thrifts' average cost of funds is not precisely equivalent to passbook rates, but it can be seen in Figure 5.5 that thrift average cost of funds were higher than short-term market rates for a number of years during the 1970s.

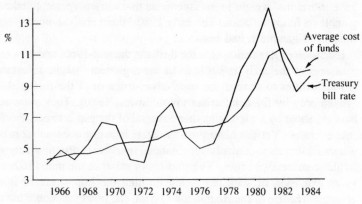

Source: FHLBB (1985).

Figure 5.5 Thrift average cost of funds compared with short-term money market rates, 1965—84

Interest constraints imposed on banks and thrifts, even if they were not deliberately designed to do so, smoothed out the impact of short-term market fluctuations. It was only after 1978 that the imposed ceiling rates fell well behind the market, so it was only then that major opportunities opened up for other investment media, in particular the rapid expansion of money market funds. Lastly, Figure 5.5 shows that following deregulation thrift average cost of funds remained above 3 month Treasury Bill rates, a feature that is discussed further in Chapter 6.

5.5   Conclusion

It would seem in hindsight that the prime consequence of Regulation Q was to sustain S&Ls in their contemporary practices for another fifteen years after the disintermediation crisis of the mid-1960s. Without Regulation Q the industry may have survived the relatively small negative spreads on its outstanding mortgage portfolios in 1969 and 1974. Yet if it had done so, the crisis of the early 1980s would have been vastly worse. Thrifts would have had large incentives in the mid-1970s to take on even more mortgage business than they actually did and they would have 'under-performed' in the early 1980s far in excess of what did happen. Of course, the incentive exists only if thrift managements are irrational in the sense that they did not make sufficient contingency for the high risk of fixed-interest lending at a time of fluctuating but rising inflation. So instead of reining back lending when mortgage rates temporarily rose above borrowing rates they took the short-term view and expanded rapidly. This perspective was encouraged by the existing poor profitability of S&L investment portfolios. The overall position of the industry gave substantial weight to managements that were prepared to take risks and gamble on future inflation. The early 1980s' thrift crisis showed what a poorly misjudged gamble it had been.

Extension of Regulation Q to the thrifts in the mid-1960s and the deregulation measures of the early 1980s both fit the argument that the reluctance of the US authorities to change the legislative structure of the financial system is broken only by financial crises (Wojnilower, 1980). They were also crises brought about by a narrowing then reversal of the gap between short and long interest rates. Yet the history of the S&L industry does not consistently fit the thesis that state control over financial markets is progressively weakened by these successive crises. The first major crisis in the mid-1960s led in fact to an extension of state regulation through the imposition of interest rate ceilings. The use of the Regulation Q controls, however, could have resulted from exceptional political circumstances. The measure already existed in the legislative framework for financial services, and its imposition on S&Ls was claimed to indicate government support for housing at a time of the sharpest post-war collapse in the housing market. Its use also avoided having to formulate and negotiate through the political process more sweeping reforms. Highly contentious issues would have been raised as a wider debate would have had to confront the whole strategy of the government towards a rapidly transforming financial sector. An influential investigation by the Hunt Commission (1971) arguing for general deregulation was widely commented upon but its recommendations did not reach the statute books. Some have argued that the early 1980s' deregulation process was the fruition of the Hunt Commission's recommendations after intensive lobbying by supporters of its ideas for a decade or more. Success was finally achieved in the early 1980s because of the crisis of banking profitability and the growth of 'free market' ideologies (Florida, 1967). Whatever the reason, the S&L crisis of the early 1980s required some form of legislative response.

One characteristic of the Regulation Q years was that the Fed had at its disposal an economic regulator that operated via the money and housing markets. If it was worried about inflationary pressures, it could push short-term rates above Regulation Q levels and refuse to adjust the ceilings commensurately. A mortgage famine would hit the housing market, and housing starts would fall. Usually such falls preceded a general recession (Tucillo with Goodman, 1983). The causes of US recessions cannot be put down simply to monetary policy and the housing market, but a powerful transmission mechanism was nonetheless in place.

The prime advantage of Regulation Q for S&Ls during the 1970s was that it greatly increased the profitability of their mortgage business. It was not, as was supposed by the architects of the deregulation measures in the early 1980s, a fundamental cause of S&L problems with mortgage lending. Arguments which suggest that Regulation Q caused the flow of funds to S&Ls to dry up in the late 1970s fail to address the associated issue of the profitability at the time of using short-term deposits to advance long-term, fixed-interest mortgages, even if interest rates had been unregulated. Other viewpoints claim that Regulation Q held down mortgage interest rates (sometimes put in terms of deregulation raising them), but they do not examine the actual determinants of S&L pricing strategies. All the evidence suggests that mortgage interest rates were hardly affected by the existence of Regulation Q.

By sustaining S&L activity during the 1970s without fundamental reform, the likelihood was increased of an even greater crisis in the future. The framework within which S&Ls operated encouraged their managements to maximise growth and to take (interest rate) risks. Although the constraints on thrift operations changed in the 1980s, these growth and risk factors were maintained — with disastrous consequences.

6

The USA
Deregulation and the savings and loan crises of the 1980s

6.1 The crisis of the early 1980s and its consequences

The difficulties faced by S&Ls in the face of rising interest rates came to a head in the early 1980s — the worst years were 1981−2. Three-quarters of them made losses during the period, with 1,500 disappearing through failure or merger between 1980 and 1986 (Martens, 1988). Kane (1983) estimated that the market net worth of federally insured S&Ls and mutual savings banks at the end of December 1981 was minus $100−175 billion.

Some of the problems in the early 1980s were hidden by the accounting conventions adopted to measure an S&L's net worth. For the regulatory authorities, an S&L is insolvent if the book value of its assets falls below that of its liabilities. This definition is based on historic costs rather than market value, which considerably over-valued the real worth of S&Ls' outstanding mortgage holdings. most companies' accounting principles are also based on historic cost but S&L regulatory rules were particularly generous in recognising income and assets. It was estimated in 1982 that thrifts' overall net worth in that year was 3.69 per cent of assets on regulatory accounting definitions; 2.95 per cent on general US accounting principles; 0.54 per cent on the latter with intangible assets subtracted; and a massive − 12.03 per cent on estimated market value (Brumbaugh and Carron, 1987). Consequently, the true extent of thrift problems in the 1980s is considerably underestimated in the official statistics. Table 6.1 gives data on failed, insolvent and weak thrifts between 1980 and 1986. It can be seen that the problem thrifts tended to remain so, unless they were wound up.

By the mid-1980s there were two sectors of the industry with around one thousand thrifts in trouble and other two thousand or so in far better shape. To add to the already existing problem thrifts, there then came post-deregulation-induced failures — those that faltered through their investment and deposit interest rate strategies after deregulation, particularly in regions where real estate markets collapsed. Altogether the financial difficulties of so many S&Ls brought the whole of the industry into crisis by the late 1980s (See Figure 6.1 showing the pattern of thrift failures from the 1930s onwards.)

Table 6.1 Thrift failures and insolvencies, 1980–6

	Number of FSLIC-insured thrifts			Total
	Failed	Insolvent	Weak	Assets ($ billion)
1980	35	17	280	38.1
1981	81	65	653	159.1
1982	252	201	842	299.8
1983	102	287	883	338.2
1984	41	434	856	463.5
1985	70	466	673	406.4
1986	83	468	515	395.1

Notes:

1. Insolvent as defined under 'Generally Accepted Accounting Principles' (GAAP).
2. Weak defined as a GAAP net worth between 0 and 3 per cent of assets.
3. FHLBB data.

Source: Brumbaugh and Carron (1987).

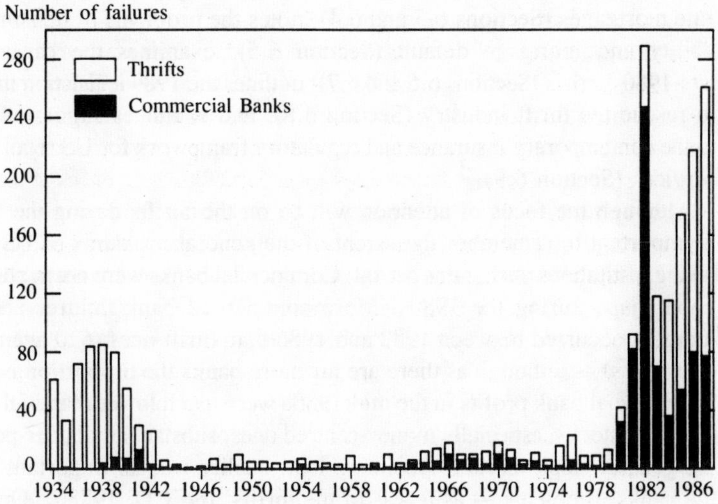

Number of failures

Source: Economic Report of the President, January, 1989.

Figure 6.1 Bank and thrift failures, 1934–87

The two thrift crises of the 1980s are consequently linked. One reason is because the regulators tried from the early 1980s onwards to keep afloat many thrifts that were on the verge of going under. If they had been allowed to sink the extent of the problems in the late 1980s would have been less.

In retrospect the early 1980s' crisis passed quickly. Given the enormity of the problems that had accumulated by 1982, it is remarkable how fast so many thrifts recovered and how rapidly their average spreads became positive again. Falling short-term interest rates were an important reason. Huge sales of the best assets also bolstered income. A large number of new originations in a booming housing market helped — many at variable interest rates — because they changed the maturity of S&Ls' outstanding mortgages. But the turnaround also reflected the rescue operations undertaken by the federal agencies, which included relaxations of accounting rules, a shifting of large pools of mortgages from thrift books into subsidiaries, direct sales of mortgages, swap deals of low rate mortgages for secondary market paper, and other forms of direct or implicit subsidy (see Brumbaugh and Carron, 1987, for a detailed account).

Regulatory relaxation was only part of the response to the first 1980s S&L crisis. The other aspect was abolition of interest rate controls — a move that helped banks as well as thrifts compete with non-regulated deposit-takers — and an extension of the activities that thrifts could undertake. Both measures were part of two finance acts passed within two years of each other, highlighting again how financial reform in the USA tends to be precipitated by crisis.

The rest of this chapter describes the deregulation measures and their consequences (Section 6.2); outlines some dimensions of the late 1980s crisis; considers the increased roles of the secondary mortgage market and adjustable rate mortgages (Sections 6.3 and 6.4); notes the problems of housing affordability and mortgage default (Section 6.5); examines the causes of the late-1980s' crisis (Sections 6.6 and 6.7); outlines the 1989 legislation introduced to rescue the thrift industry (Section 6.8); and evaluates suggested reforms to the contemporary insurance and regulatory framework for US retail financial services (Section 6.9).

Although the focus of attention will be on the thrifts during the 1980s, it is important to remember the extent of the general problems of US deposittaking institutions during this period. Commercial banks were not in particularly good shape during the 1980s. More commercial bank failures and forced mergers occurred between 1982 and 1986 than thrift ones (620 against about 450 S&Ls) — although as there are far more banks the proportion is far less. Commercial bank profits in the mid-1980s were much lower than in the 1970s, and bank stocks, especially money-centred ones, substantially under-performed the general stock market. Declining loan quality was an important cause of the banks' problems — as it was of the thrifts' (OECD, 1988b). Once again the severity of commercial banks' problems was hidden by the accountancy principles used in annual reports. Brumbaugh *et al.* (1989) note that nearly a third of all bank assets late in 1988 were held by especially weak institutions (those with a market value capitalisation less than 6 per cent of the assets they held). 'There but for fortune' may be an appropriate motto for the US commercial banks, and should be remembered when looking at the thrift industry. One consequence was that the threat of widespread collapse of the US financial system was high on the list of concerns of commentators, regulators and legislators during the 1980s — which might explain the remarkably generous treatment by government of the financial services industry in comparison to other 'productive' industries and their problems.

6.2 The 1980s deregulation process and its aftermath

Two acts are the centrepiece of the deregulation process in the early 1980s. The first was the Deposit Institutions Deregulation and Monetary Control Act, 1980 (DIDMC). The second was the Gain—St Germain Act, 1982. The aim of the former in particular was to free regulated deposit-taking institutions, (commercial banks as well as thrifts) from the constraints of interest rate controls which were losing them substantial deposits to money market funds set up by institutions such as insurance companies and brokerage houses. It also enabled S&Ls to invest in consumer loans and commercial paper up to 20 per cent of their assets, and it abolished some lending restrictions. The aim of the second act was to speed up interest rate deregulation and particularly to reduce S&Ls' dependence on the mortgage market. They could now invest in tangible personal property for lease or sale up to 10 per cent of their assets, in a wide range of consumer, commercial and agricultural loans, and had restrictions lifted on loan to valuation ratios and on lending first mortgages only. The effect of the two measures was to free S&Ls from their traditional housing base if they so desired, although taxation considerations still encouraged them to put preponderant weight there. The legal restrictions distinguishing S&Ls and other thrifts from commercial banks were thus weakened. Banks and thrifts now competed effectively with each other in almost all areas of retail banking and commercial lending, and with the burgeoning non-bank retail savings media.

The restraints of Regulation Q were already weakening prior to the 1980 DIDMC Act with the introduction of a number of new accounts with higher interest rates. Money market certificates were introduced for thrifts in 1978, and small saver ones in 1979 (see Appendix to this chapter). The pace of change was transformed by the passage of the act, however, which empowered a Depository Institutions Deregulatory Committee to oversee the gradual but complete removal of all deposit rate ceilings by 1986.

After the passage of the two acts, both the deposit and investment sides of S&L activity were no longer subject to major constraint. They could undertake off-balance-sheet income earning activities, like mortgage origination and servicing, pay the 'market rate' for their funds and invest them in a wide range of assets. Some of their assets would still be derived from the mortgage market (especially adjustable rate mortgages (ARMs) and mortgage-backed securities); others would come from the bond and securities markets (ranging from government stock to 'junk' bonds); plus unsecured consumer lending, and commercial mortgage lending and real estate. S&L exposure to investment risks at a given level of profitability should, in principle, have been reduced as they could now benefit from a more diversified portfolio of investments, in line with portfolio management theory.

During the 1980s, under the impetus of the 1980 and 1982 deregulation acts, thrifts did diversify their asset portfolios substantially. The main changes between 1980 and 1986 are presented in Table 6.2. Thrifts as a whole substantially cut back their investments in residential mortgages; moreover, much of what they still held by the late 1980s were ARMs rather than fixed-interest mortgages. The biggest replacements for direct mortgage holdings are mortgage-backed securities. Non-residential mortgages also grew rapidly, as did real estate activities. Much of the growth in cash and investment securities was for investment purposes in non-liquid assets. Growth overall was high (see Table 5.2).

By the late 1980s, thrifts were an even larger force in the US financial system than they had been a decade before — with total financial assets in 1986 of $1,563 billion (20 per cent of total private intermediated assets), and over a third of total retail deposits. Between 1982 and 1985 thrift deposits rose by an annual average of 15 per cent, although competition and rising short-term interest rates curtailed their expansion subsequently (Brumbaugh and Carron, 1987). By 1986 the thrifts as a whole had more assets than pension funds and insurance companies, and were increasing their share of total personal financial services; whilst the commercial banks, the largest asset holders, had seen their share fall in the 1980s (OECD, 1988b).

Much of the diversification undertaken by thrifts in the 1980s would seem commendable. Yet the large number of subsequent thrift insolvencies has cast a shadow over the asset diversification programmes. Much information about the precise causes of individual thrift failures had not been unravelled at the time of writing, but obvious candidates are fraud and the new spheres into which thrifts diversified. Widespread malpractice has been uncovered with thousands of thrift personnel undergoing criminal investigation in what has been called the biggest white-collar theft in US history. Many of the publicised insolvencies have been said to result from failed real estate projects and wrong-doing associated with them. The collapse of property markets in Texas, for example, has been cited as a prime cause of failure there. In general, much diversification (as can be seen from Table 6.2) was into commercial property either through real estate operations or by lending high interest mortgages on

Table 6.2 Composition of thrift asset portfolios, 1980–6

	1980 (%)	1983 (%)	1986 (%)	Change 1980–6 (%)
Mortgages:	84.1	74.7	69.9	−14.2
Residential	72.4	54.8	44.7	−27.7
Non-residential	7.3	8.8	12.2	4.9
Mortgage-backed securities	4.4	11.1	13.0	8.6
Real estate	0.4	1.0	4.7	4.3
Cash and securities	9.8	13.4	14.5	4.7
Non-mortgage loans	3.0	3.4	6.2	3.2
Other	2.8	7.0	4.7	1.9

Note: FSLIC-insured thrifts.
Source: OECD (1988b).

non-residential property. The information in the table is only that of averages, so some thrifts would have been far more involved in those spheres and others less so. Real estate speculation and lending are highly risky, and S&L managements in the past had had little experience of them.

Unfortunately the 1980s deregulation process failed to understand the nature of the competitive processes it unleashed and the incentives it gave to particular players in the market. The scale of the crisis which broke in 1987 was far greater than that of the one only six years before. In 1981, the thrift industry's accounts showed a record collective loss of $4.6 billion; in 1987, it lost $6.8 billion which turned out to be only the tip of the iceberg. FSLIC was effectively bankrupt. Estimates of the total cost of bailing out the thrifts range from an official estimate of $160 billion to $258 billion by the General Accounting Office to even higher amounts among private analysts, but the true cost may never be known and will be spread over decades. Two quotes from one commentator in 1987 summarise the position well: 'the magnitude of the disaster that has hit this industry is astonishing'; 'somebody is going to lose money, and a lot of it' (Poole, 1987).

The thrift crisis rapidly became entangled with the federal budget deficit and promises made in the 1988 presidential election about not raising taxes. Public funds to aid the thrifts are another large statistic to add to the federal deficit, and all means were tried to keep the crisis off that crucial political balance sheet. This further encouraged regulatory bodies in 1987/8 to try and keep sick thrifts going. Financing schemes to help ailing thrifts were dreamt up, a major requirement of which was that they would not appear in the federal budget even though adopting them could lead to far higher rescue costs. The FLHBB, for example, late in 1988 sold thrifts to private investors with the enticement of large inputs of public money and guarantees against further losses.

One consortium, led by a corporate raider, was reported as buying five Texas thrifts with assets totalling $12.2 billion for $315 million. In the package the FHLBB committed an estimated $5.1 billion and the purchasers' companies gained $900 million in future tax breaks for buying the thrifts. Similarly, the bill negotiated in 1989 between the Bush administration and Congress to rescue the thrifts involved the setting up of a Resolution Trust Corporation (RTC) whose planned $50 billion bond issue does not appear in the federal accounts.

During the worst of the crisis, the weakness of parts of the thrift industry worried depositors, despite the existence of deposit insurance. Considerable fears of bank runs surfaced late in 1988. Deposit outflows forced the FDIC to take over twenty-five thrifts with assets of $12.75 billion late in February 1989 to add to the eleven it had already taken over earlier in the month (*Financial Times*, 29 December 1988; 7, 8, 9 February 1989).

The roots of the late 1980s thrift crisis lay in the deposit-taking as well as the investment side of their activities. There turned out to be in reality no clear 'market rate' for retail deposits. Thrifts and banks could use their new deposit rate freedoms to price savings schemes on the basis of the profits they expected to get from them, rather than on a simple principle such as a viable spread between deposit rates and investment in a range of relatively safe and secure activities. The hoped-for extra profits could either come in the guise of applying theories of scope economies to cross-sell (and cross-subsidise) financial packages or from risky investments in high profit ventures. Over-capacity among deposit-taking institutions dominated the retail savings market of the mid-1980s. Fierce competition for funds driven by the wild optimism of some over their possible uses had a strong influence on deposit rates, in particular regional markets.

The difficulties of thrifts, however, should not be seen simply in the behavioural terms — with new management strategies adopted and over-optimistic expectations generated in the wake of the extra activities sanctioned by the regulators. Much of the behaviour of thrifts in the 1980s has parallels with that in the 1960s and 1970s, when S&Ls also tried to grow out of crises and by doing so implicitly took hopelessly optimistic views of the future pattern of interest rates. In periods following adverse movements in interest rates, thrifts had a strong incentive to grow rapidly through extra mortgage investments to avoid being dragged down by having too large a portion of their investments in low rate mortgage holdings (see Chapter 5). Following the early 1980s' deregulation, interest risk exposure was less marked as thrifts could then invest in more than fixed-interest rate mortgages. Investment-related risk was substituted for a reduction in the risks associated with future interest rates. But even with their wider, but riskier, investment powers interest risk exposure was still there, as most of the areas thrifts could invest in were still longer term than the short-term nature of deposits with them — so their assets and liabilities were by no means 'matched'. This meant that thrifts still faced major risks. Individual thrifts, in particular, because of their perilous positions in the early 1980s may have been encouraged to take on much greater risks in the subsequent years.

An added problem was that most of the traditional activities of S&Ls and many of the new activities into which they diversified experienced intensified competition from the late 1970s onwards. In particular, deposit-taking, other retail banking functions and the mortgage market itself have all become more competitive and, therefore, higher-risk activities. The extra competition could be seen as a boost to operational efficiency, trimming away unecessary costs and leading to optimal product arrays in particular institutions. But any gains in operational efficiency could easily be wiped out by the lower returns and extra riskiness of the markets in question. It is not obvious that the cheapest providers of specific services will necessarily be the ones that get their investment risk strategies right — and are the firms that will survive.

6.3 The secondary mortgage market in the 1980s

The secondary mortgage market became the principal provider of mortgage funds in the 1980s — 72 per cent of originations in 1987 were financed through it. Table 6.3 shows the growth of the market between 1982 and 1987. As can be seen, mortgage-backed securities are overwhelmingly guaranteed by federally related agencies. Derivative securities, which are repackaged income flows from pools of mortgages designed to appeal to specific types of investor, have also been developed over the past decade; the most important of which is the collateralised mortgage obligation (CMO) (see Appendix 2 to this chapter for details). The secondary market has come of age — futures are traded and lenders can negotiate forward commitments with secondary market traders to reduce their exposure to interest rate rises between fixing the mortgage rate

Table 6.3 The secondary mortgage market, 1982–7

	1982	1983	1984	1985	1986	1987
Pass-through securities:						
federally related	54.2	83.5	60.1	108.4	258.9	199.6
private	2.1	2.8	2.1	5.3	n.a.	n.a.
Derivative securities	0.6	5.7	13.4	20.5	58.8	61.5
Total home mortgage originations	96.9	201.9	203.7	246.8	442.3	n.a.
Secondary market as a percentage of total originations	59	46	37	54	72	

Note: all figures are $billions.
Source: Gabriel (1987).

and delivery of a loan. Again, mortgage markets led financial innovation, with GNMA pass-throughs being the first financial instruments traded as futures in 1975 (Wojnilower, 1980). But, as with other developments in mortgage finance, futures and options in mortgage-backed securities have had chequered history. In mid-1989 the Chicago Board of Trade was trying for the fifth time to set up a permanently successful futures contract (*Financial Times*, 7 July 1989).

S&Ls now tend to sell all of their new fixed-interest mortgage originations on the secondary market to avoid the risk of adverse movements in interest rates. In this respect S&Ls have increasingly taken on the mortgage banking function of originating and servicing mortgages rather than holding them. Almost 10 per cent of thrift income in 1986 was derived in this way (Brumbaugh and Carron, 1987).

Mortgage bankers themselves are now major actors in the US mortgage market, originating a third or more of mortgages. Mortgage bankers expanded rapidly with the growth of the secondary market. About a third are subsidiaries of banks, a quarter are owned by thrifts and others — including industrial giants like General Motors and General Electric, whilst around 40 per cent are independent operations (Boleat, 1985). The largest in terms of turnover are as big as the major S&Ls, but there are many small ones. They deal in commercial as well as housing loans.

Housebuilders have also expanded origination functions, sometimes by setting up their own mortgage banking subsidiaries. It is traditional in the USA for housebuilders to provide an 'all-in' package of home, consumer appliances and finance. They can as easily profit from originations and subsequent sales of mortgages as any other institution, and have had tax incentives to do so. Speculative housebuilders (called merchant builders), however, do not build all new single-family homes, so there is still independent space for other mortgage originators. In 1987, for example, 1.1 million single-family units were completed, whilst merchant builders sold 670 thousand units and had roughly the same number of stocks of dwellings for sale as at the end of the previous year, so it can be surmised that they had about a 65–70 per cent share of the new owner-occupied housing market (data from *Federal Reserve Bulletin*, 1988).

S&Ls are obviously not the only providers of mortgages to the secondary market. By giving equal access to all originators of mortgages, the growth of the secondary mortgage market has opened up new competitive pressure in originations for thrifts. As a means of reducing the competitive pressure, thrifts in the late 1980s were lobbying to limit the activities of FNMA and FHLMC so that those agencies would be of less benefit to mortgage bankers (Jaffee, 1987).

The scale of the secondary market and the wide number of institutions with access to it mean that the rate of interest charges on fixed rate mortgages is now determined there, and all issuers have to respond to the competition offered by it. The short-term responsiveness of mortgage interest rates to changes in the yield on 10 year Treasury bonds has substantially increased as a result (Gabriel, 1987).

The US investment banks have also expanded and profited from the growth of the secondary mortgage market. They act as brokers, underwriters, deal in mortgage-backed securities and try to expand investor demand for them. Most of the innovations in mortgage-backed securities have come from investment banks. There are only a handful of investment banks with a major presence in the secondary market, all of them based in New York. It has been suggested that the reason for the small number is the complexity of the market and the need to be known as a skilful operator by institutions wishing to place mortgage-backed securities. There has been criticism of the profits that investment banks have made on some deals with the thrift industry, as is noted in Chapter 4.

Investment banks have tried to protect their role in the secondary market. The underwriting and distributing of mortgage-backed securities has been one of the areas where commercial banks have been unable to increase their investment banking powers. The Securities Industry Association has successfully taken banks to court if they try to underwrite or distribute mortgage-backed securities, even when they come from mortgage pools owned by the banks themselves, on the grounds that such activities violate the Glass—Steagall Act (*Financial Times*, 5 April 1989).

Thrifts are major purchasers of secondary market securities. As Table 6.2 shows, thrift holding of mortgage-backed securities rose from 4 per cent of their assets in 1980 to 13 per cent in 1986. In this way they have considerably improved the liquidity of their mortgage holdings. Holding securitised mortgages, however, does not free thrifts from interest rate risks. If the mortgages in the pools are fixed-rate, the capital value of the bond varies inversely with the direction of change of contemporary rates. Securitising mortgages improves liquidity but it does not make an interest rate matching problem go away. Even the most sophisticated players in the secondary mortgage market have been known to make substantial losses by misjudging the direction of change of interest rates. A Merrill Lynch trader in 1987, for example, took unauthorised positions in the secondary market and lost the firm $250 million (*Financial Times*, 5 May 1987).

Growth of the secondary mortgage market has not been a panacea for mortgage finance. Two problems were particularly apparent in the late 1980s: increased risk of default and a credit crunch.

One problem with securitising assets is that when the originators of the loans no longer hold them they have less incentive to ensure their quality (Duesenberry, 1987). As a result the risk of default on the underlying assets increases, pushing up interest rates or, in extremes, leading to total investor withdrawal from the security. Moody's Investors Services, a major US credit rating agency, expressed concern about the credit quality of securitised assets, including mortgage-backed ones, in 1989. Competition, it felt, increased pressure on underwriters, lawyers, accountants and credit enhancers to lower the quality of their due diligence and review standards (*Financial Times*, 30 March 1989). Whether this aspect of securitisation is significant is a matter of dispute, but it is an indicator of the increased risk potential of key parts of the mortgage market.

A secondary market because it frees mortgage finance from a retail deposit base should in principle avoid a mortgage famine in classic credit crunch periods when short rates rise above long ones. The links are not totally severed, however, if either key sellers of mortgage pools or important buyers are themselves caught in such an interest rate squeeze. In the US secondary market, thrifts are both the major buyers and sellers so problems they face become reflected in secondary market yields and volumes. In early 1989, the crisis-struck thrift industry had few funds with which to buy mortgage-backed securities and was keen to sell mortgages on the secondary market to raise finance, so both the volume fell and the yield rose on such securities. (Something similar happened in the early 1980s crisis.) Rising yields in the secondary market increased the interest rate that had to be charged on fixed interest mortgages. In March 1989 the benchmark Ginnie Mae 10 year security was yielding 134 basis points (i.e. 1.34 per cent) above the equivalent Treasury issue, despite the fact it has implicit federal backing (*Financial Times*, 28 March 1989). The spread between mortgage-backed securities and other long-term rates, in other words, is not fixed, and it tends to increase when the thrifts are in trouble, such as when short rates rise rapidly. Through the indirect influence of the thrifts, the secondary market has not, therefore, entirely removed mortgage finance from its credit-constrained past.

6.4 Adjustable rate mortgages

Until 1981 adjustable rate mortgages (ARMs) were only sanctioned in a limited number of states. The FHLBB then allowed their general use as long as changes in the variable rate were determined by reference to an external interest rate guide outside of the control of the issuing body. Since then ARMs have grown to be a major mortgage instrument. Thrifts generally fund them out of their retail deposits. A number of variants have been offered to consumers although standardisation has gradually evolved. The main form is a variable rate indexed to the 1 year Treasury bill rate, with limits to interest rate adjustments of two percentage points annually and of five to six points over the life of the mortgage; whilst increases in the outstanding principal are precluded (Gabriel, 1987). American ARMs, consequently, are very different from British variable interest mortgages, the rates on which can be changed whenever the issuer wishes to adjust them to whatever rate it chooses.

The interest rate on ARMs, as it is tied to changes in short-term interest rates, tends at the time of origination to be lower than that on fixed-interest mortgages, which are linked to longer-term rates. ARMs in their early days developed poor reputations as some S&Ls deliberately under-priced the initial rates offered on their ARMs. They did this knowing that the interest rate would rise after the first year. This practice caused a number of well-publicised homeowner defaults, but is said to have stopped with greater consumer awareness and tighter insurance criteria.

ARMs are attractive to households that expect interest rates to decline and to those who like lower initial rates either because they plan to move again shortly or because they only qualify for a mortgage on the lower initial monthly payments, which pushes down their mortgage repayment/monthly income ratio. In general, whether households opt for a fixed or variable rate mortgage depends on the fixed interest rate offered relative to the initial rate on adjustable rate mortgages, and on households' expectations of their future circumstances and the path of interest rates.

The effect ARMs have of making more people eligible for owner-occupation has been discounted as a major explanation of the unexpected housing market upturn in 1984 shortly after their introduction (see Figure 5.1). The general fall in nominal interest rates (but not real ones) and demographic factors were major causes of the upturn according to a number of studies (Dhillon *et al.*, 1987; Esaki and Wachtenheim, 1984/5; Goodman, 1985; Stuzer and Roberts, 1985).

The share of ARMs in all mortgage originations varied considerably during the 1980s. They reached a peak of almost 70 per cent in 1984, but then fell away to 25 per cent in mid-1986, only to rise to 58 per cent in 1988. The difference in the share to a great extent reflects the changing spread between the initial rates offered on ARMs and fixed rate mortgages. The greater the difference between the (lower) rate on ARMs and that on fixed interest mortgages the larger the ARMs share tends to be. The flow of mortgages onto the secondary market fell sharply in 1984, when ARMs reached their peak share. It is interesting to speculate that sellers of fixed interest mortgages via the secondary market route would have had to trim their commissions and offer other inducements to sell their products during that period.

The secondary market deals in variable interest rate mortgages, although they are said to be less popular than fixed-interest securities with investors because they present several technical problems and have different risks.

Despite the fact that variable rate mortgages cover much of the interest rate risk that S&Ls and other retail-deposit-funded mortgage lenders face, their introduction has not led to the total supersession of the fixed-interest mortgage, nor is it ever likely to. The existence of the secondary mortgage market means that fixed-interest mortgages are always an option for US homeowners because there will always be investors prepared to offer terms on fixed interest debt. Thus over the last decade another new dimension has entered competition in the US mortgage market: that between the sellers of fixed-interest mortgages funded via the secondary market and the sellers of ARMs funded predominantly from retail deposits.

6.5 Housing affordability and mortgage defaults

At the same time as competition for mortgage business intensified during the 1980s, there were signs that lending house mortgages in general was becoming riskier as well. Table 6.4 shows that delinquency rates on S&L mortgages rose through the 1980s to almost four times the average rate in the second half of the 1970s. By 1985 S&L mortgage delinquency rates were higher than those on consumer instalment loans, an area of consumer lending traditionally regarded as risky.

To an extent, greater housing market risk and increased mortgage competition are correlated, with extra mortgage competition raising the delinquency rate. Competitive pressures push institutions to take on more risky customers. One sign of the move towards more risky mortgage business is rising mortgage to valuation ratios; although part of the greater risk to the lender is generally covered by insurance. Table 6.5 shows the valuation ratios for new and existing housing from 1965 to 1984. It can be seen that the number of mortgages with mortgage/valuation ratios of over 90 per cent rose dramatically in the early 1980s.

Part of the default problem is that the 'affordability' of owner-occupation for the average US household declined in the 1970s and early 1980s. One index computes the cost of a standard quality new home (purchased with an 80 per cent of value mortgage) as a proportion of average household disposable

Table 6.4 Credit delinquency rates compared, 1976–86

	1976–80 average %	1981 %	1982 %	1983 %	1984 %	1985 %	1986 %
S&L mortgages	1.09	1.28	1.90	2.20	2.13	2.80	4.19
Commercial bank consumer instalment loans	n.a.	n.a.	n.a.	2.65	2.59	3.01	3.27

Note: FSLIC-insured thrift mortgage delinquency rate: 1983 0.7
                                                        1985 1.4
                                                        1987 2.8

Source: OECD (1988b); FHLBB Journal, April 1989.

Table 6.5 Mortgage to house price valuation ratios, 1965—84

	1965	1975	1980	1982	1984
Average loan to price ratios					
Newly built homes	73.8	76.2	73.2	76.6	78.6
Previously occupied	72.7	73.5	73.5	71.9	76.8
Percentage with loan to price ratio over 90%					
Newly built homes	n.a.	14	10	21	27
Previously occupied	n.a.	5	9	11	20

Source: FHLBB (1985).

income. From around 25 per cent in the early 1970s the index rocketed to 45 per cent in the early 1980s, but then receded as interest rates came down to stand at around 25 per cent again in mid-1987 (Gabriel, 1987). When interest rates rose in the late 1980s, the affordability index would have worsened again. The decline is less marked if the wealth generating effects of rising house prices are included in the calculation. But, as affordability problems abated in the mid-1980s, it is unlikely that increased mortgage delinquency rates throughout the 1980s can be solely ascribed to its effects.

One feature of the US housing scene that is partly explained by the affordability constraints of the early 1980s is the decline in the rate of owner-occupation. Between 1981 and 1987 the homeownership rate declined by about two percentage points to slightly below 64 per cent. Most of the fall occurred amongst younger age groups, with five percentage point drops recorded for both the under 30 and 30—39 age groups. Another cause of the decline in homeownership is the greater availability of rental accommodation, encouraged by the extra tax-breaks offered from the early 1980s (Gabriel, 1987).

Overall, the US housing market was buoyant for much of the 1980s. Table 2.1 shows that, after a slight downturn in the early 1980s, outstanding house mortgages as a percentage of annual personal sector incomes rose strongly from 50 to 60 per cent between 1984 and 1987. The rapid expansion of mortgage debt created a space for the traditional mortgage institutions to realign their activities without having to go through massive retrenchments. Although the overhang of low interest mortgage investments was a problem for thrifts, they were able to bolster their profits through extra mortgage business as well as through other investments. In some regions housing markets turned sour from the mid-1980s, especially in Texas and southern California. This helped to precipitate some of the subsequent thrift failures. The housing market was heading for a downturn in 1989, one partly precipitated by high interest rates in the mortgage market. In March 1989 the greatest monthly fall in housing permits since the early 1980s housing recession was recorded. On a longer-term basis, all indications are that demographic factors are not going to be so favourable for homeownership in the 1990s; in which case competition in the mortgage market will increasingly be over a stagnant market.

6.6 Deposit insurance and weak regulation as causes of the late-1980s' crisis

As losses in their new areas of busiess, particularly in real estate, have been the cause of so many thrift failures, the question to ask is, why did thrifts diversify into high-risk activities? Two broad answers can be given.

Deposit insurance

The first explanation that has been suggested relates to the structure of the federal deposit insurance schemes. It is widely accepted that they encourage managements to take excessive risk. Many do not question the fundamental principle of insurance. Criticism instead is directed, first, at the comprehensiveness of the current structure of deposit insurance, where some — including President Reagan's last chief economic advisor, Beryl Sprinkel — feel that the insurance should be less than 100 per cent to encourage depositor caution; and, second, at the uniform pricing of the insurance rather than using variable pricing according to the riskiness of the investments made with the deposits gathered. A large literature has developed on the insurance pricing issues.

The traditional principle of the deposit insurance offered by FSLIC to thrifts and FDIC to banks is implicitly that of a mutual, self-financing arrangement by the participating institutions. They pay premiums to the relevant body, which administers the scheme and supervises the participants to make sure that no-one breaks the rules. The object is to cover against the risk of a cumulative run on the deposits of participating institutions, rather than to cover the risks arising from the investments made by individual institutions. In practice, FSLIC on a number of occasions faced such demands on its funds that the contributory insurance has had to be topped up by federal funds. The mutual insurance principle itself, however, can be criticised for making prudent and efficient institutions pay for the excesses of others through higher premiums. During the decades of strong regulatory constraint, the risks associated with individual S&Ls' investment policies anyway were limited by the small range of investments open to the participating institutions. Deregulation in the 1980s changed all that for S&Ls, after which individual S&L investment strategies had a stronger effect on the deposit insurance scheme. The argument of those advocating a repricing of deposit insurance is that presently those greater risks are not taken into account (Kane, 1985).

The insurance schemes mean that when individuals make deposits they have only to know that deposits with the thrift or bank are federally or state insured. Insurance obviates for them the need to know anything about the investment policies of the institution or the quality of its management, which for an individual investor would anyway be difficult and costly. So the insurance has considerable positive benefits for depositors as it closes off for them a major area of information deficiency in the financial system. Even the regulatory agencies with their batteries of powers and experts have found it impossible to estimate accurately whether and when a bank or thrift is going to fail.

The difficulty, according to the anti-flat-rate insurance argument, is that the structure of the insurance system induces 'moral hazard', whereby participants have incentives not to play by the rules of the game because extra risk-taking and imprudent behaviour are unpenalised. In capital markets high-risk borrowers have to pay interest premiums over low-risk ones, and credit rating agencies give assessments of the riskiness of particular institutions. Flat rate, federally organised insurance schemes block such market solutions. The insurance gives risk-loving (or crooked) managers and owners of banks and thrifts a 'one-way' bet. They can, in an unregulated deposit interest rate world, attract funds by offering depositors better than usual interest in order to invest the funds in higher profit, but higher risk, areas. If the investments lose money, or funds are misappropriated, the thrift or bank will fail, but its depositors will be reimbursed by the insurance system. Insolvency will cost the institution's management little — unless they are caught misappropriating funds — as it was not their own capital at risk. They can also pay themselves high salaries and perks whilst the money flows in, until the bad debt rises towards insolvency level and the regulators take over. Shareholders, if they exist, will lose out as their shares may become worthless, but if the risky investments had succeeded they would have been highly valuable as the equity is so highly geared with retail borrowings.

The solution to the moral hazard problem is to match deposit insurance premia to the risks associated with assets in which insured institutions invest (Kane, 1983). The increased insurance costs would also deter depositors if they are passed on by offering lower deposit rates.

Moral hazard has undoubtedly been an important component of the late-1980s' thrift crisis. The low profitability of thrifts would have encouraged managements to take on riskier investments and to try and grow out of their problems as they had previously attempted in the mid-1970s. In addition, dubious practices blossomed in the industry to the extent that the General Accounting Office said that the main cause of thrift losses was crime. The question, however, is whether a reformed insurance system would have avoided these problems.

Criticisms of the 'price' reform of deposit insurance focus on implementation difficulties (FDIC, 1983; Horovitz, 1983; Pyle, 1984; Litan, 1987). First, it is argued that giving banks the appropriate risk incentives is virtually impossible because regulators can only assess the investments that a bank has already made, not the ones it may be contemplating. The problem is made worse by the fact that investigations of banks by the insurers/regulators are expensive and therefore infrequent. The result is that the incentives presented to banks can easily operate in the reverse direction to that desired. Banks that had undertaken high-risk investments but now wished to adopt a lower-risk profile (as regulators would presumably like them to) would face insurance penalties because their current deposit premium would be based on the earlier higher risks. Yet, if they adopt an even riskier strategy they will not suffer extra costs until the results noticeably affect their accounts and are assessed as such.

Second, rough justice and instability could result. Even banks with low-risk investments can still get into difficulty (as low risk does not mean no risk), and under the reform would face higher premiums at a time when they could least afford them.

Third, whilst higher-risk premiums may make the expected return from higher-risk investments less attractive or even negative, that may not deter a risk-loving bank management. The weakness of the deterrent is greatest if the next assessment is expected to be a long way off or if the bank has current investments which are so unprofitable that the extra profits are desperately needed even though their prospect is poor.

Fourth, some risks are difficult to assess. Non-traded assets, such as Third World debt in the early 1980s, are particularly difficult to evaluate. The hardest risk to assess is the impact on the whole financial system of a particular institution failing. After some size, the regulators may feel that the cost of failure to the whole system is too great. Some banks are thus too large to fail. If this fact were generally known, any insurance discipline against risk-taking would be irrevocably weakened. Furthermore, should those large banks be charged higher premiums because of this additional unquantifiable risk? If they were made to pay higher premiums this would handicap their deposit-taking activities against smaller banks. Given these and other practical problems it is not surprising that the FDIC concluded that 'the "ideal system" with premiums tied closely to risk is simply not feasible', although it did support moves towards risk discriminating pricing with an enthusiasm that seems to have grown through the 1980s (FDIC, 1983; Campbell and Horovitz, 1984).

Apart from implementation problems, deposit insurance risk-pricing also rests on the theoretical assumption that a sufficient information exists to make risk evaluation both feasible and comprehensive enough to affect thrift and bank investment strategies. Whilst it may be true that investing in a booming real estate market is riskier than buying treasury bills, a wide range of activities in which a broadly diversified financial institution operates may not present such a clear risk profile. Chapter 4 argues that retail banks face many unknowns, whose nature is more accurately described as uncertain rather than risky in the formal distinction between the two. It may also be unreasonable to assume that future risks will be the same as past ones, but risk evaluation has to rely on past information. The threat of investment losses in general must have increased in retail banking during the 1980s with greater competition, and may increase further with the advancing technological revolution and widespread over-capacity. If uncertainty is prevalent, the risk-pricing of deposit insurance is unlikely to lead to a major reduction in failures.

If the unknowns in banks' investment decisions are great, fads and fashion may rule rather than sober assessment. Real estate speculation has been a major source of current S&L weakness, yet an earlier episode when US financial institutions came badly unstuck in this field had nothing to do with deposit insurance. This occurred in 1973−4 when banks (not thrifts) set up real estate affiliates (REITs) to buy real estate and mortgages on a large scale primarily using certificates of deposit as the source of funds. An increase in short-term interest rates led to the virtual or actual collapse of many of those affiliates (Wojnilower, 1980). That episode can be interpreted as a classic fashion-led investment strategy rather than as a perceived upgrading of risk.

Net worth liquidation

Another suggested regulatory reform is for federal insurance agencies to be far more active in closing institutions when a bank's or thrift's marketable net worth falls below zero, rather than attempting to keep it open for as long as possible. At zero net worth, a bank's assets just equal its liabilities, including the value of the funds deposited with it, which means that any insurance commitment is matched by funds subsequently realised through insolvency proceedings. So, as long as the federal insurance agencies allow only those with positive net worth to operate, their overall risk of loss through paying out insurance claims is low regardless of the riskiness of individual institutions' investment policies. Large insurance losses in reality have occurred only because participating institutions' assets are assessed at book value rather than current market value, so that a thrift or bank is only declared insolvent long after its market value net worth is negative (Horovitz, 1983; Pyle, 1984).

There are problems with this proposal as well. Some of the same objections to risk-related insurance premia also limit the effectiveness of strict implementation of insolvency rules as a discipline on thrifts and banks. Assessment may be too infrequent, for example, to declare an institution insolvent at or near to zero net worth. Predictive models are used by the regulatory agencies but they are not accurate. In addition, it might be impossible to assess the market value of all assets to know when zero net worth is reached.

Given asset valuation problems, regulators may feel safer if they err towards optimistic valuations, because an overly pessimistic stance leading to a declaration of insolvency might result in substantial compensation claims. The too-big-to-fail problem also arises. Would the authorities have been prepared, for example, to face the consequences of closing down most of the thrift industry in the early 1980s when it was saddled with so many low interest mortgages?

Other problems exist with the net market worth insolvency rule. Market value rules reduce the incentive for a thrift or bank to sell bad quality loans at below par because all the remaining loans of that type would then have to be revalued to the new price, possibly dragging the institution into insolvency. The implications for the world's banks of having to do that with their Third World debt in the early 1980s is a good example of such consequences. Regulatory reports, moreover, are currently secret. If they were made available to the public, depositors might be less ready to deposit funds with a bank that is about to be declared insolvent. The chance of widespread bank runs, one of the major fears of US regulators, may also rise if regulators switched to a tell-all policy — especially if a number of institutions are declared to be facing impending insolvency (Litan, 1987).

Global bias and instability

Both the insolvency test and the risk-related insurance schemes arguments focus on individual delinquent institutions, and attempt to devise means through which greater discipline can be imposed on individual banks. The same is true of other reforms aimed at increasing capital adequacy with more stringent net worth requirements, better financial information systems for regulators and a greater preparedness to close down weak institutions. (Some commentators regard such increased stringency as obviating the need for deposit insurance altogether, see Kareken and Wallace, 1978; Brumbaugh and Carron, 1987.) Each of these measures may succeed in reducing the risk of individual failures, although the results may sometimes be the opposite, as the criticisms above showed.

Yet all the reforms fail to confront the possibility of structural biases in US retail finance which lead to persistent problems that may be brought to a head at times of negative yield gaps. The nature of investment and competition in retail banking may contain such biases, so the US retail finance system might contain elements of chronic instability, as characterised in Chapter 4.

The experience of the thrifts in the 1970s and 1980s corresponds to a plausible model of general retail financial institution behaviour along the following lines. When the yield gap between short and long rates is positive, as it usually is, retail deposit-taking institutions are in a 'golden phase' with a wide range of profitable activities into which they can invest their expanding retail deposits. Competition may limit some options but it is unlikely in the short term to threaten well-run institutions. During this phase of the interest rate cycle, there are strong incentives to invest in assets of longer duration than liabilities in order to take advantage of the attractive spread. Expansion during the profitable years may then be brought to a halt by a narrowing or reversal of the yield gap and some thrifts/banks may not be able to adjust quickly enough. Such difficulties are all the more likely to occur as their timing follows the 'golden phase' of expansion and duplication of facilities in retail banking, leading to chronic excess capacity. The excess capacity will be intensified by the reduction in volumes, as well as contracting margins on them, when the yield gap narrows. Some institutions may then fold or withdraw from retail finance, but not all institutions with poorly performing investments will fold. In the next upturn, they will have particularly strong incentives to try to adjust their investment portfolios using retail deposits. In this way optimism in the upswing is reinforced, and 'golden phase' over-expansion begins again.

Not all banks and thrifts have to operate in this way over the yield gap cycle for the effects to lead to general problems of excess capacity and over-optimistic deposit interest rates because the negative effects of a few behaving in that way can easily be transmitted through the financial system. All institutions competing for similar retail funds — be they more prudent thrifts, commercial banks or others — have to match the optimists' deposit interest rates (or the non-price competition over them) or see their share of deposits fall. The higher cost of funds then makes their lower-risk strategies less profitable. The extra capacity also intensifies competition in all lines of retail business. The negative consequences (though not the rewards) of over-optimistic expansion strategies, in other words, are highly infectious. There is no simple market mechanism like the folding of the most risky participants that can then bring the system into long-term equilibrium, instead the situation is a highly unstable one, as the experience of the 1980s has shown. The issue is not one of excessive competition, which is the terminology used to justify the original introduction of Regulation Q. Excessive competition implies a fundamental stability once the excesses have been contained, which is at variance with the incentive structure facing the borrowing and lending activities of retail deposit-taking institutions.

A counterfactual can be cited to the hypothesis of a destabilising structural bias in retail finance in the existence of money market funds. They are retail deposit-taking institutions that are uninsured yet seem to avoid the problems associated with a shifting yield curve — so they may be said to indicate the absence of such structural biases. But they prosper as they are not diversified, and so present a different competitive stance from other retail financial institutions. They offer depositors a limited deposit service (the value of whose deposits depends on the overall value of the fund) and they invest in secure short-term assets to avoid interest matching problems. Such a narrow specialisation and interest-matching is the antithesis of the diversified financial supermarket type of institution.

An implicit assumption of the insurance and net worth regulatory reforms is that financial markets are stable once limited regulatory constraints minimise the impact of moral hazard. This position contrasts with views of financial markets that emphasise their inherent instability. If instability exists, it may be advantageous to devise and regulate a financial structure to avoid the potentially cataclysmic consequences of a major financial crisis at the expense of accepting certain inefficiencies and constraints during years of market calm. Instability is an issue that has plagued the US and other financial systems since their inception through the ever-present threat (even if rare occurrence) of large-scale failures of financial institutions. A variety of factors can undermine the viability of a financial system. They have periodically to face buffetings arising from rapid shifts of opinion or long-term structural problems that suddenly come to a head. Third World bank lending and the interest-matching difficulties of the thrifts in the early 1980s are two examples already cited. They were both problems that should have been foreseen but ended in general crisis. The world stock market collapses of November 1987 arose from rapid shifts of sentiment on a global scale. The problems of financial systems do not necessarily come piecemeal as the arguments over insurance and insolvency control suggest. It is difficult to see what either proposal would have done about bank lending to the Third World (it was not supposed to be risky and was encouraged by governments as a means of recycling petrodollars) or about the concomitant thrift crisis. The net market worth insolvency proposal, if implemented for example, would have led to the unlikely and probably catastrophic event of the majority of the US financial system being declared insolvent in the early 1980s.

There is no easy solution to the reform of retail financial services, but if there are structural biases which may increase the likelihood of instability then they have to be taken seriously. This is particularly the case in the USA where the deregulatory reforms of the early 1980s intensified the tendency for over-expansion in retail services during the subsequent good years.

6.7 Intensified competition and excess capacity as causes of the late-1980s' crisis

Examination of the deposit-taking and investment activities of thrifts in the 1980s highlights how much their low-risk spreads may have narrowed during the decade. More broadly, the market conditions faced by diversified thrifts are similar to those of other retail banking institutions. Margins may, therefore, be under pressure throughout retail banking — suggesting longer-term institutional instability in the US financial services industry.

On the deposit side, after the early 1980s' deregulation, competition for retail deposits intensified considerably. From then on, competitors' interest rates had to be matched. A process of interest rate leap-frogging was often generated, considerably raising the cost of deposits. The notorious 'Texas premium' of around an extra one per cent on deposits is mentioned in Chapter 4. The cost to thrifts of insuring their more expensive retail deposits also rose in the 1980s. By 1989 thrifts were paying substantially more in deposit insurance premiums than commercial banks ($2.08 per $1,000 of deposits compared with $0.83 per $1,000; *Financial Times*, 23 February 1989). The 1989 thrift rescue measures raised the premium even further; under them it could ultimately reach $3.25 per $1,000 of deposits (*Wall Street Journal*, 7 August 1989).

Non-price forms of competition continued. Despite the large fall in the number of thrifts since the early 1970s, branches continued to multiply so that by the late 1980s there were over four times as many as in the early 1970s. Other points of consumer access grew as well, such as free-standing ATMs. Non-price competition in the 1980s led to a sharp escalation in thrifts' operating costs (Hess, 1987). So not only was there pressure on interest spreads, the rise in operating costs squeezed the profitability of what remained, limiting profits and the ability to add to reserves. The profits cushion offered by Regulation Q in the 1970s was sorely missed by the thrifts. One positive aspect for thrifts is that their deposit accounts for some consumers seem to have unique characteristics (although precisely why is unclear). This is an implication of their low interest rate elasticity as reported by Hess.

A feature of deposit competition is that the pricing of deposits may not closely reflect their true cost to the borrowing institution (as Chapter 4 notes). This occurs either because of difficulties in accurate costing or because the deposit-taking institution uses some or all of its rates as loss-leading inducements to potential customers, which others feel forced to match. Overall, then, spreads are squeezed by the optimism of some institutions over the returns they make from investing those expensive deposits and of others over their ability to sell a variety of financial products to their newly attracted depositors.

With respect to thrift investments and other income earning activities, the 1980s was a decade of intensified competition. As was argued above, the mortgage business, despite the shift away from holding fixed-interest mortgages, is still fraught with dangers and mortgage pricing is constrained by additional competition. Thrifts may also be tempted at times to hold fixed-interest mortgages or mortgage-backed securities to take advantage of the contemporary spread between the yield on them and thrifts' own cost of funds. Such a strategy can easily come unstuck if the path of long-term interest rates is wrongly forecast or the spread between long and short rates narrows or reverses.

ARMs (adjustable rate mortgages) offer no respite from tight pricing. Even though their rates are linked to independent short-term interest rate markers, holding ARMs can also still create interest matching problems for thrifts when they fund their lending with retail deposits, despite their rates being linked to independent short-term interest rate markers. There are two reasons for this. First, there are lags inherent in the formulae by which ARM rates can be adjusted to changing short-term rates. The existence of the lags is costly to thrifts when short-term rates turn against them. Second, competition for retail deposits may easily push their effective cost to thrifts above the yield they receive from ARMs, in which case investing in ARMs is obviously not profitable. Arguments that ARMs have entirely removed interest rate risk seem wide of the mark (see Boleat, 1985). The risks may now be more diffuse but they are still important.

Constraints on investment returns obviously limit what thrifts and banks can offer on deposits, so competitive pressures in the deposit-taking and investment sides of a thrift's activities are interdependent. Even diversified thrifts and banks tend to lend longer than they borrow, and they may find that the deposit rates they can offer fall well below those of money market funds (MMFs) at times when short-rates rise above long ones. In April 1989, for example, thrifts were reported to be offering depositors 3 per cent less than MMFs and, not surprisingly, experienced large-scale net withdrawals of deposits (*Economist*, 8 April 1989).

In the light of these problems with the investment spheres in which thrifts traditionally specialise and are knowledgeable, it is perhaps not surprising that the lure of real estate and junk bond speculation often proved irresistible after deregulation. Yet, limiting thrifts' ability to invest in such spheres and forcing them to lend most of their funds as mortgages — as was done in the 1989 legislation — does not take away the difficulties they face in the mortgage market. Nor does restricting thrift diversification actually alter the competition they are likely to confront if they decide to diversify (perhaps through metamorphosis by abandoning their thrift status) into the traditional areas of other financial intermediaries, who are often themselves caught in a profits squeeze.

The fundamental problem for thrifts (and many banks) is that borrowing retail funds and investing them in a diversified range of activities is generally no longer a particularly profitable business in the USA and it is one with appreciably higher risks than prior to 1978.

6.8 The 1989 thrift rescue package

The scale of the thrift crisis in the late 1980s forced the Bush administration and Congress to pass a package of measures in August 1989 which will lead to the greatest transformation of financial services since the 1930s. Their outcome is uncertain but, as the following summary shows, a major restructuring of retail financial services will occur in the 1990s as a result of legislation. Whether the US financial system will as a result be less prone to crisis, however, is still an open question. The principles of the legislation seem to be primarily based on trimming down the thrift industry, raising insurance premia, requiring greater asset strength of what remains and enhanced supervision to avoid fraud. It does not, in other words, adopt measures based on any of the theoretical perspectives outlined earlier. Whether such practical mindedness will do the trick is uncertain.

A brief overview of the legislation shows what it is hoped will happen to the failed thrifts, to those that remain, to the remaining special position of the housing market, and to the opportunities opened for banks.

1. *Closure of seven hundred and fifty or so insolvent S&Ls* via the mechanism of the setting up of the Resolution Trust Corporation (RTC) as a branch of the FDIC. RTC will close down insolvent thrifts, pay off their debts, sell as many of their assets as possible and cover the losses they make in the process by borrowing.

2. *The issuing of a large, open-ended amount of quasi-public debt* to fund the rescue. RTC is funded by sales of bonds, which are 'strippable' so that principal and interest can be traded separately like mortgage-backed securities. Initial sales were of 30 year bonds, though future sales may be of shorter maturities to take account of market variations. The principal of RTC's bonds is guaranteed by zero interest US government bonds; these non-marketable securities are advanced by the US Treasury to RTC so that in theory the government is earmarking funds to pay back the principal of the RTC's bonds at their maturity. This complicated procedure was devised so that the costs of thrift 'bailout' do not appear as government expenditure.

Initially it was optimistically hoped that RTC would need to issue only $50bn of bonds. Within months this was recognised as insufficient. The overall requirement will depend on the costs of closing S&Ls, how many fail, and the success of sales of their assets.

3. *Phasing out high deposit rates.* Many insolvent thrifts had managed to stay in business only by offering high deposit rates. An initial feature of the rescue was to replace those high interest deposits with cheaper ones with the help of FDIC funding. This considerably benefited healthy S&Ls and other deposit-taking institutions like banks which no longer had to match such unprofitable rates. Similarly, the profitability of their lending rates could be improved in the absence of competitors desperate for new business. The closure of so many S&Ls also led to a considerable reduction in the size of the US financial services industry, and therefore considerably improved the market position of the remaining firms. Overall spreads in retail financial services were consequently given a major boost.

4. *Asset sales* RTC aims to sell the assets of the failed thrifts brought under its control in order to pay off those thrifts' liabilities. The cost of this operation will depend crucially on RTC's ability to sell those assets quickly and at reasonable prices. Early in January 1990 it started the sale of $250 billion of

property assets (*Guardian*, 11 January 1990). If the sales are low the costs of the rescue mount substantially. RTC is allowed by Congress to discount the assets by only 5—10 per cent to avoid destabilising the markets in which the sales are made. In 1990, US property markets were weak and many of the thrift assets of doubtful quality. With such an open commitment facing RTC the rescue cost assumed in the legislation could turn out to be very optimistic.

5. *Remaining thrifts will face higher operating costs.* They will pay substantially higher deposit insurance premia ($1.50 per $1,000 of deposits, increasing to $2.30 in 1990 and ultimately $3.50). In addition they will lose their earnings from Federal Home Banks. Furthermore, thrifts will be required to have a much greater tangible capital requirement — 1.5 per cent immediately, rising to 3 per cent of assets by 1994. Along with these measures goes revamped and tougher regulatory supervision. All of these measures are designed to discourage further reckless or fraudulent activity. More own capital will be at risk and the deposit insurance scheme more likely to be self-financing. No attempt was made to charge differential rates according to risk, apart from imposing a greater rate on thrifts than banks. Risk-related deposit insurance was left for further discussion. Some might think that the new measures are rough justice on the model thrifts who did not indulge in the excesses but now have to pay for the sins of those that did. Successful thrifts, however, are likely to do well out of the measures as they are particular beneficiaries of the removal of undesired competition. The rescue package should increase their profitability through the effects it will have on their spreads, bolster as a result their own market value which will be further enhanced by the prospects the legislation opened up for acquisitions of healthy thrifts by banks. Paradoxically, the greater the number of thrifts that are closed or convert to banks the smaller will be the pool of institutions paying into the thrift insurance scheme so that it might still remain underfunded.

6. *S&Ls will be restricted to keeping 70 per cent of their assets in mortgage-related investments.* This measure was introduced on the basis of belief in the greater security of S&Ls' traditional activities, plus providing one of the few sops to the housing lobby. From the history of S&Ls and the earlier analysis of this chapter it is difficult to believe that mortgage lending will actually necessarily be the low-risk activity desired by the legislators. The inability to diversify will also encourage S&Ls to sell out to firms that are not so constrained.

Two other minor gestures towards the encouragement of homeownership — which earlier had been such a powerful force in the creation of the modern thrift industry—were a requirement imposed on Federal Home Loan Banks that they should set aside some of their earnings to subsidise low-income mortgages ($75m in 1990 rising to $150m by 1995) and similarly that RTC must give state and local non-profit housing agencies first refusal on certain low-cost residential properties (*Wall Street Journal*, 7 August 1989).

7. *A gradual ending of the separation between the thrift and banking industries.* Although the legislation still creates insurance, supervisory, capital requirement and asset structure differences between federally chartered thrifts and commercial banks the differences have been considerably eroded to the extent that the distinction between the two might disappear. Federal Home Loan Banks, for instance, will be able to lend to commercial banks that invest in home mortgages. Large thrifts will be encouraged by the costs and restrictions of remaining thrifts to convert to banks; one of the most profitable routes would be through merger with an existing bank. Banks will be able to circumvent interstate banking restrictions easily now by buying a thrift. They may search out bargains from the weak or insolvent thrifts or pay premia for healthy ones. Size is likely to increase in the US retail financial services industry as a result.

The extent to which banks and thrifts will merge is another imponderable of the 1989 measures. Banks may be encouraged to expand rapidly or to take risks with weak thrift acquisitions. As has already been noted, commercial banks are in a weak position overall, and some, like many thrifts, are exposed in the property sphere. Given these imponderables and the new constraints on S&Ls, however, the next major retail finance crisis in the USA, if it occurs, is likely to be associated with the banking rather then the thrift sector.

Conclusion

The scale of the late 1980s' thrift crisis points to there being something disastrously wrong with the provision of mortgage finance in the USA. The thrift industry, the second largest group of financial institutions, is in severe structural crisis. Despite hopes that the problems are simply those of speculative excesses, which can be resolved through bailouts, mergers and greater regulation, it is more likely that on current policies widespread insolvencies will continue in retail banking for many years to come.

A major reason is the nature of the competition for retail funds. The interest rates paid for them are driven up by over-optimistic or reckless investors of those deposits and by institutions that are not particularly concerned with making direct profits from deposit-taking but hope to profit from the cross-selling of a broader range of consumer financial services. Whenever their investment projects or the pattern of interest rates turn against them, the over-optimistic deposit-takers face insolvency. Similar problems may hit institutions who find that cross-selling is not as profitable as they had hoped. Pressures mount on other retail finance institutions because matching the interest rates charged by the optimists squeezes their own margins.

The unstable structure of retail finance cannot be ascribed simply to fraud, excessive competition or excess capacity but to the competitive structure inherent in the contemporary organisation of the US financial system. Regulation Q put a block on that competition, but it was unresponsive to changing macroeconomic events, and biased competitive pressures as it was easily circumvented by some market actors. Virtually all the reforms on the current agenda fail to address the retail deposit interest rate issue. Perhaps their reluctance is understandable in the light of the weaknesses of Regulation Q, a measure that has only just been phased out. Underlying their arguments, however, is the belief that financial markets tend towards a stable equilibrium once insurance pricing systems or a regulatory overseer rules out the possibility of widespread, systematic excesses. That belief in stability is an act of faith as there is no evidence of its existence: rather there is much to the contrary.

In contrast to Britain, the US mortgage finance system offers most consumers relatively cheap credit. New mortgage interest rates are related to long-term capital market rates or less. The US financial system has been successful in this respect in its functional efficiency. But the current US retail financial structure is costly. Competitive forces of the type described above have led to an enormous duplication of facilities. Those facilities have to be paid for by someone, and are hardly likely to constitute an efficient allocation of resources.

General federal subsidies to mortgage finance are substantial through interest tax relief on housing-related debt and the guarantee systems associated with the secondary mortgage market. Many of the costs of the thrift industry's periodic crisis are also borne by the federal government in periodic bailouts, of which the latest at the end of the 1980s was by far the most expensive and open-ended. The federal government then passes them onto taxpayers or (as is currently hoped by the Bush administration) back to financial intermediaries. In crisis years mortgage interest rates are forced up and mortgage finance becomes more difficult to find. The scale of the periodic losses of the thrift industry are a strong counterweight to the 'normal' benefits of low mortgage interest pricing. American households, through the 'backdoor' of federal taxes, are implicitly paying a significant mark-up for the retail financial services they get. More broadly, there could easily be an unquantifiable but significant upward effect on general US interest rates caused by the contemporary behaviour of retail deposit finance institutions, both through the 'crowding out' of alternative uses for those funds and through the impact on general financial instability and the associated risks perceived by investors.

The US government and taxpayers are currently paying much to reduce capacity in the thrift industry. Many of the funds earmarked in the 1989 legislation are being used to phase out insolvent thrifts. This will lead to a significant reduction in the industry's capacity to the benefit of remaining thrifts, banks and other retail deposit-taking institutions. The resultant increased profitability for those that remain will then encourage them and other retail financial institutions to expand their capacity once again.

One way of looking at the problems of the US financial services industry is to suggest that in a number of ways the difficulties are associated with the problem of sunk costs. In contrast to contestable market theory which works only with no sunk costs (see Chapter 3), US financial institutions have demonstrated that once commitments are made they influence future institutional strategy. Loss-making investments have often not led to a smooth withdrawal from lending, but rather have encouraged more investment at higher risk in an attempt to cover losses until the situation improves or becomes desperate. To an extent the problem is a principal/agent one in that the managers rather than the owners of a financial institution have the greatest incentive to expand rather than liquidate. Admitting losses, closing up and handing out the financial pain does not have the same kudos as being the manager that 'had the vision to turn round an unprofitable thrift/bank'. Managers have the sunk costs of their own careers to worry about in a world where imperfect information might lead to unfair judgements of the wisdom of their actions.

What is likely to happen to the current institutional structure of US retail finance? To an extent it will depend on the outcome of the political process and Congressional lobbying. The regulatory bodies are being forced by the thrift crisis to merge. With the passing of FSLIC out of its control, the continued independence of the FHLBB must be under question, especially since it has been so heavily criticised for weak supervision. Without a parallel regulatory structure the thrift industry in effect disappears as a separate entity to be submerged with the general banking system; a move that would be welcomed by the Federal Reserve Board. The Fed itself was increasingly drawn into the late 1980s' thrift crisis, because of the need for it to provide standby facilities to federal home loan banks. The thrifts' official lenders of last resort needed their own saviour. So a major rejigging of the regulatory system is being forced. Congressional maintenance of the remaining barriers to financial mergers has also been severely damaged by the latest thrift crisis, particularly as rescues of weak and insolvent thrifts makes a mockery of the constraints on interstate banking.

The likely outcome of the late 1980s' crisis of retail banking is that larger financial institutions will predominate, as they offer a greater prospect of stability — seen by most commentators, politicians and government officials as being of overriding importance. Concentration has already increased significantly in US retail banking over the last decade (FRB, 1989).

Paradoxically, major financial conglomerates may come to dominate the US financial scene as they do in western Europe, not because they are more efficient intermediaries but because they can use their market muscle and ability to cross-subsidise their activities to hide their investment mistakes and inefficiencies.

Appendix 1: Recent innovations in US savings and cheque accounts

Money market funds

Launched in 1972, money market funds (MMFs) are linked to contemporary market rates of interest and they avoided the contraints of Regulation Q when set up by non-banking institutions, such as brokerage firms and insurance companies. Their initial impact was small, but they expanded rapidly in the late 1970s as inflation and treasury bill rates rose. In 1977, $3 billion was invested in them; by 1982 this had grown to $233 billion. With competition from the new MMDA accounts (see below) assets in MMFs subsequently fell but rose again to $250 billion in 1985.

Money market certificates

Introduced for depository institutions as a weakening of Regulation Q in 1978. A minimum $10,000 denomination certificate with a 26 week maturity and ceiling rates based on the 6 months Treasury bill rate. Denomination minimum later reduced.

Small saver certificates

Another weakening of Regulation Q introduced in 1979, small saver certificates had no minimum denomination but had to have a maturity of 30 months or more. Ceiling rates were based on 2.5 year Treasury bonds, with a maximum rate of 12 per cent at thrifts. (The cap was abolished in 1981 and the minimum maturity progressively reduced to 18 months by 1983.)

Money market deposit accounts

Introduced by the DIDC in 1982 as a counter to money market funds. MMDAs allowed only limited cheque writing — up to six transfers a month, no more than three by draft — but unlimited withdrawals. They were subject neither to interest rate limits nor to minimum maturity but had a minimum balance of $2,500.

Investment retirement accounts

Investment retirement accounts (or IRAs) have been one of the fastest growing savings mediums in the USA since their introduction in 1981. Contributions are tax deductible and earned interest is not taxed. As they are a savings vehicle for retirement, funds tend to remain in IRA accounts for long periods.

NOW accounts + ATS

These are equivalent to interest-earning cheque accounts. The device was necessary to avoid US regulatory controls for most of the 1980s. A negotiable order of withdrawal (or NOW) account is a savings account against which consumers can write 'negotiable drafts'. ATS stands for automatic transfer service. With it, a customer can automatically transfer funds from a NOW savings account into a zero-balance ATS account, whenever a cheque is drawn on the latter.

NOW accounts were originally authorised for Massachusetts thrifts in 1972, and made available nationwide in 1981.

In the late 1980s, NOW accounts came in two forms: regular and super. The distinction originated with a regulatory distinction associated with the transition from the operation of Regulation Q. Regular ones had a 5.25% interest rate ceiling, whilst supers were unconstrained. Super NOWs were, in effect, similar to MMDAs but with unlimited transfers permitted. The distinction between the two types of NOW account was abolished late in 1985, but the terminology remained to distinguish NOW accounts whose rates changed infrequently from those with interest rates changing in line with market rates.

Home equity accounts

Not a cheque or savings but a borrowing account introduced in 1986 following the limitation of interest tax relief to housing only. They enable homeowners to borrow against the equity in their houses at variable rates of interest.

Brokered accounts

Insured savings deposit accounts assembled by broker intermediaries and sold onto deposit-taking institutions. A useful means of avoiding bans on interstate branching.

Appendix 2: Secondary mortgage market instruments

Pass-through securities

Undivided ownership interests in a pool of mortgages, guaranteed either by a federal agency (GNMA) or a federally chartered private body (FNMA or FHLMC). Some pools are privately insured. The guarantee is on the repayment of the mortgage principal and interest, so there is no risk of mortgage default. But the timing of the repayment of the principal is not guaranteed, so there is for investors a risk of the mortgages in a pool being prepaid earlier than expected. There are, in addition, the usual interest rate risks associated with holding bonds whose value is determined by the relationship between the income flows from the bond, the perceived degree of risk in the timing of those flows and the prevailing market interest rate.

Payments of principal and interest on mortgages are passed through to the ultimate owners of the securities. As repayments occur over time the income flow will gradually tail off over the years. The precise profile of repayments of principal and interest is unknown as mortgage holders can prepay their mortgages whenever they wish. As a result investors may find that the income flows from the security have a profile they did not expect. If investors take the view that interest rates will fall, they will expect the value of a bond of known repayment profiles to rise. Yet, with mortgage-backed securities, falling interest rates will also encourage borrowers of the mortgages in the pool to prepay their existing mortgage and take out new ones at a lower interest. With a reduced income flow from the mortgage pool, the security will not be worth as much when interest rates fall as the fixed cash flow bond. Consequently, repayment and interest rate risks are negatively correlated. Expected profiles of prepayments can be derived, although in practice little statistical work seems to have been done on them. Savings and loan associations are said to operate on the basis of 'rules of thumb' for prepayments, sometimes suggesting an average mortgage life of seven years, at other times twelve. One empirical study found, not surprisingly, that prepayment likelihoods are strongly affected by the interest rate fixed on the mortgage relative to current rates (Green and Shoven, 1986).

Derivative mortgage securities

DMSs involve a restructuring of the cash flows from an underlying mortgage pool. Usually they are backed by pass-through securities guaranteed by a federal agency, so they are securities whose income flows are elements of the flows from a prior pool of mortgages. The repackaging of the income flows is designed to cater for different investor preferences for risk and returns. In the light of increase prepayment risks, the pattern of returns from mortgage pools as they mature become more uncertain. Packages can be devised which segment out the more risky parts of the income flows from the less risky ones. Early parts of the stream are less risky in the profile and can be offered at lower returns; whilst investors who are prepared to accept the higher risks of earlier than expected prepayments on later parts of the stream are offered a higher return for their portion of the expected income profile. This example illustrates the principle of segmenting the flows from mortgage pools into derivative mortgage securities, but the flows can be packaged in a wide variety of ways to suit investor tastes for risk and return as can be seen from the description of particular instruments below.

Collateralised mortgage obligations

CMOs are designed to break up the income flows from mortgage pools by issuing securities based on mortgage pools as collateral. Investors are provided with interest payments on an annual or semi-annual basis rather than monthly. A CMO has a sequential structure, which means that bonds of different effective maturities can be derived from the same mortgage pool. If, say, a CMO is divided into four parts, this would mean that the first class of investor would receive the principal from the mortgage pool until they were paid off, whilst the other three classes would receive only interest. Then the next class would be paid off, and so on. Given prepayment risk, longer-term investors are taking the greatest risk. CMOs are issued in the name of the company or trust issuing them, unlike pass-throughs which bear the name of the guarantor. The sometimes obscure names of the issuers has created a little investor uncertainty over the security of CMOs, although if the mortgages in the pool are guaranteed it is irrational.

Freddie Mac, in conjunction with its investment bankers, invented CMOs in the early 1980s. CMOs have advantages for thrifts with poorly performing outstanding mortgages as they are regarded as a debt obligation on the issuing body. Thrifts can securitise low interest mortgages as CMOs, therefore, without having to write a capital loss into their accounts; where the sale of those mortgages as pass-throughs leaves no debt obligation and any capital losses have immediately to be written down. Housebuilders like CMOs for the debt obligation reason as well. When they issue mortgages via CMOs the profits from housebuilding are offset by the CMO debt obligation until the mortgages in the pool are paid off. This considerably delays the time when they have to pay tax on their housebuilding operations.

'Stripped' securities

Here the issuer allocates principal and interest payments from an underlying mortgage pool separately or in any combination to a set of securities. Stripped securities were introduced in 1986.

Senior/subordinate securities

These are securities based on underlying mortgage pools structured into separate
senior and subordinate interests in mortgages. The risk and hence the yield
on subordinate interest exceeds that of the senior interest.

REMIC

REMIC stands for real estate mortgage investment conduit, and was introduced
in the Tax Reform Act, 1986. It is a tax-advantaged vehicle for holding
mortgage assets and issuing mortgage-backed securities. REMIC sponsors have
almost unlimited flexibility in determining the legal and financial form it takes.

7

Great Britain
Pressure on the building societies

By the late 1980s the British were one of the greatest holders of mortgages relative to personal incomes. The mortgage market had expanded phenomenally during the 1980s — outstanding mortgages rose threefold between 1981 and 1987. The 1980s also saw much change in the structure of the mortgage market. The building societies abandoned their long-standing interest rate fixing cartel in 1983, whilst throughout the decade the number of financial institutions offering mortgages grew. Deregulation of sorts occurred in 1986 with legislation that widened the range of activities and investments open to building societies, and the constraints were subsequently relaxed further. Yet this extra competition was associated with a considerable upward shift in mortgage interest rates relative to other interest rates.

The fact that mortgage interest rates have risen relative to other rates, despite intensified competition among institutions lending mortgages, is a paradox that can only be explained in terms of the forms of competition adopted by those institutions. Building societies dominate the mortgage market, although they have lost market share since the early 1980s. So competition has to be seen in relation to them, as well as between individual societies themselves.

One feature of the UK mortgage market that distinguishes it from both the US and West German ones (and most other west European countries) is that it finances homeownership alone. The state of the owner-occupied housing market as a result is of overwhelming importance; it has played a central role in the fortunes of the building societies.

Another unique feature of the UK mortgage market is that extra competition in the 1980s occurred in an environment in which individual institutions had considerable leeway over the pricing of their mortgage products. There is no general tying of mortgage interest rates to shifts in other market rates. Those linkages now exist in the USA — although the spreads do worsen during periods of crisis — and have been the practice for years in most west European countries where the mortgage bond market plays a central role. In contrast in Britain mortgage institutions set the conditions and interest rates on the principle of what the market will bear. In the standard mortgage contract the interest rate can be altered whenever the lender wishes, whilst mortgagees bear penalty costs when they relinquish their mortgage obligations. Fixed-interest mortgages have been offered in the 1980s, as have ones where the variable interest rate is tied to an external marker (such as the 3 month interbank rate), but they have had little impact. The continuance of the standard variable interest mortgage in Britain itself has to be explained in terms of the nature of competition between mortgage institutions.

As can be seen from these preliminary remarks, competition in the UK mortgage market differs from elsewhere because of the unique position of the building societies, the mortgage instruments they use and the behaviour they adopt. Like the USA, however, a major watershed period in the mortgage market is the early 1980s — partly because of legislative changes but predominantly because of limits reached in the contemporary approach of the building societies to retail deposit-taking and mortgage lending. The societies experienced a crisis of strategy, in other words, rather than an actual profits collapse as befell the US thrift industry. The mortgage market in the 1980s has been overwhelmingly influenced by the attempts of the societies to restructure themselves, although the results were often not those envisaged by them. The two major changes adopted by the societies are part of the common themes of retail banking — raise the interest rates offered to depositors and diversify into other areas of retail finance and property markets. During most of the 1980s the societies were lucky enough to have ideal market contexts in which to restructure, but the 1990s do not look so good. Once again, a retail banking infrastructure is being developed which seems far greater than potential demand for its services.

The rest of this chapter elaborates on these introductory comments. First a brief overview is given of the mortgage market since 1970. Sections 7.1 to 7.3 concentrate on the building societies — describing their objectives and behaviour, and the nature of the 1980s liberalisation of their activities. The economic reasons for that liberalisation are then considered in Section 7.4 through an analysis of building society activity up to the 1980s, including the operation of the interest rate fixing cartel. Then a brief overview of the housing market is presented in Section 7.5, following which competition in retail banking and mortgage finance during the 1980s are examined in Section 7.6. The final section draws some conclusions and speculates on likely developments over the next decade.

7.1 The UK mortgage market since the early 1970s

Table 7.1 shows the shares of new mortgage advances by the major financial institutions from 1973 to 1989. The dominance of the building societies is clear. They greatly increased their share to take virtually the whole of the market in the second half of the 1970s — mortgage lending then actually became synonymous with the societies. That position did not survive into the 1980s, however, as first banks entered the market and then other financial institutions — sometimes set up specifically to borrow wholesale funds to lend on as mortgages. The entry costs to the mortgage market for these new competitors, although varied, have often been substantial, and associated primarily with the need to create consumer awareness and to facilitate the easy availability of their mortgage products. Given those costs and the likely future pattern of mortgage interest rates, the new competition is here to stay although market shares will alter from year to year. Building societies' market share declined in 1987 to only 50 per cent, a level not seen since the early 1960s, although

Table 7.1 Institutional shares in the UK mortgage market, 1973–89[a]

	Building societies (%)	Public sector (%)	Insurance companies and pension funds (%)	Banks (%)	Miscellaneous financial institutions (%)
1973	69	14	6	11	0
1974	61	29	8	4	0
1975	74	21	4	2	0
1976	92	4	3	2	0
1977	94	0	3	3	0
1978	94	−1	1	5	0
1979	82	6	4	9	0
1980	78	10	4	8	0
1981	67	7	1	26	0
1982	58	7	0	36	0
1983	75	−2	1	24	2
1984	85	−1	1	12	3
1985	77	−3	1	22	2
1986	74	−2	2	18	9
1987	50	−2	3	35	14
1988	59	neg	neg	27	12
1989[b]	67	neg	neg	26	6

[a] Net advances during period.
[b] First quarter only.

Source: *Housing Finance*, Council of Mortgage Lenders, various dates.

it improved again during 1988–9. By the late 1980s, many societies became determined to increase their share again, as well as branching out into other activities in direct competition with the banks.

Building societies had earlier come to dominate the mortgage market because it was an unprofitable sector for other financial institutions (see p. 141–9) and because of the withdrawal of the state from mortgage lending.

The development of the UK mortgage market during the 1950s and 1960s in terms of the institutions active there shows a similar increase in specialisation to that in the USA. In the 1950s the building societies had about a 50 per cent market share, with another 15–20 per cent accounted for by local authorities and insurance companies. The remaining 20–25 per cent was private loans, often made by landlords selling poor quality accommodation to sitting tenants. Insurance companies slowly pulled out of the market as they found it unprofitable to match the mortgage rates offered by building societies. Banks were only periodically active for similar reasons. One major intervention occurred during the early 1970s housing market boom when a significant share of the upper end of the market was taken for few years by the banks.

The direct involvement of the state in mortgage finance has never been as great as in the USA or West Germany. A social role assigned to local authority mortgage finance was significant for only a decade after the mid-1960s; it was then withdrawn during general public expenditure cuts. Local authority mortgage lending was primarily to lower income households and/or on poorer quality inner city accommodation. The slight upturn during the early 1980s can be attributed to the initial phases of the 1979 Conservative government's council house sales policy.

Looking at changes in the level of activity in the mortgage market as a whole, the volume of outstanding mortgages has grown considerably over the last two decades, but there has been considerable variation in the rate of growth of mortgage business particularly in real terms. As Table 7.2 shows, the value of outstanding mortgages increased at double-digit percentage rates in every year between 1973 and 1988. But the nominal data hide a significant shift in the market between the 1970s and 1980s. In the 1970s much of the growth reflected general price inflation, and there was considerable variation from year to year. It was only in the 1980s that sustained growth occurred. Although even then much of the expansion was concentrated in only three years (1981–2 and 1986), with slower increases in the intervening years, and a sharp fall in 1988–9. Throughout the period, net new advances exhibit substantial volatility, rising in nominal terms by around 50 per cent in some years and stagnating in others, and in real terms the variation is even more marked. Such pronounced shifts in the volume of mortgage business make long-term planning by mortgage institutions a hazardous exercise.

Table 7.2 Growth in the British mortgage market, 1973−88

	Net advances			Outstanding mortgages		
		Percentage annual change			Percentage annual change	
	£ million	Actual	At constant 1985 prices	£ million	Actual	At constant 1985 prices
1973	2,893			18,956		
1974	2,439	−16	−27	21,373	12.8	−2.7
1975	3,730	53	23	25,002	17.0	−5.7
1976	3,928	5	−10	28,856	15.4	−1.0
1977	4,362	11	−4	33,126	14.8	−1.0
1978	5,437	25	15	38,533	16.3	7.5
1979	6,461	19	5	45,001	16.8	2.9
1980	7,333	13	−4	52,424	16.5	−1.3
1981	9,489	29	16	62,060	18.4	5.8
1982	14,141	49	37	77,125	24.3	14.4
1983	14,525	3	−2	91,650	18.8	13.7
1984	17,072	18	12	108,722	18.6	13.0
1985	19,116	12	6	127,838	17.6	10.9
1986	26,581	39	34	154,332	20.7	16.8
1987	28,960	9	5	183,280	18.8	14.0
1988	40,188	39		221,987	21.2	

Note: Constant prices derived by deflating series by the retail price index.

Source: *Housing Finance*, Council of Mortgage Lenders.

7.2 Building society objectives

Building societies are unique legal entities, subject to their own legislative
controls. Their roots are as non-profit-making friendly societies, and as mutual
bodies they are owned and controlled, formally at least, by their members —
all personal depositors and borrowers. They are now regulated by their own
Commission (the Building Societies Commission), and have always been subject
to particular stipulations over capital requirements, borrowing and lending
powers, and the range of activities in which they can participate. As an
independent financial sector the building societies are formally exempt from
Bank of England control (but not its exhortations). So they have not been subject
to many of the constraints imposed upon the monetary sector, especially prior
to the 1980s. Until the mid-1980s, furthermore, the societies enjoyed a number
of tax exemptions, including some on the substantial profits they made from
dealing in government bonds. (They paid no corporation tax on profits made
from gilts nor did they pay capital gains tax on them if held for more than
a year.)

Justification for the special treatment of building societies as financial institutions was based on their mutual status and on their importance since the 1920s in encouraging the growth of owner-occupation. The legislative framework governing the operation of the societies evolved over a hundred years. Additional constraints were gradually imposed on their activities in response to periodic insolvencies of societies and excesses in the movement. Consolidating legislation was occasionally enacted; the last one prior to the 1980s was a 1962 act. Unlike the comparable institutions in the USA, insolvencies among the building societies have always been isolated affairs — the threat of a general run on deposits held by them has never become a reality. This history of financial stability encouraged a relaxed supervisory framework, although the authorities have been swift to close down the occasional rogue (small) society.

Despite the societies' mutual status, their members have in practice had little control over their activities. Widespread criticism was voiced in the 1970s over the self-perpetuating nature of most building society governing bodies. Close personal links were discovered between the directors of some societies and local housing and commercial property interests (CDP, 1976; Barnes, 1984). As mutual institutions, the societies are immune from hostile takeovers but senior managers can gain substantially from friendly mergers with other societies. Since the 1986 legislation societies with the consent of their members can convert from mutual to equity status.

The incentives offered to senior managements help to explain the continual process of merger within the movement. In 1900, there were almost 2,300 societies; by 1988, the number had dropped to 130, despite the huge increase in members and assets during the intervening years. Few new societies were formed — of the ten founded since 1972 only one remained independent in 1987 — so it is a movement whose assets are concentrated in a small number of giant institutions. In 1986, the five largest societies held 57 per cent of the movement's total assets and the twenty largest controlled 90 per cent. Such concentration is not new — even in 1930 the five largest controlled 39 per cent and the twenty largest 65 per cent of total assets respectively. Overall, in the 1980s the movement has an asset base greater than that of the clearing banks. Consequently the largest societies in terms of assets are on a par with their main competitors, the big five clearing banks (Barclays, National Westminster, Midland, Lloyds and TSB). Despite the enormous size of UK retail financial institutions, none of the few available studies contradict the US evidence that economies of scale in retail banking are limited above a relatively small bank size (see Chapter 4).

For many years, from the 1930s to the 1980s, it was virtually impossible for the societies to lose money. The demand for mortgages was good. They operated in an environment constrained by legal restrictions on what they could do, and one where both mortgage and retail deposit interest rates are determined by the movement's own cartel in an environment where competition from others in the retail finance market was muted. Consequently the coercive effects of competition were not marked (Roistacher, 1987).

It might seem odd, given their protected environment, that the societies did not remain fragmented and a sleepy backwater of the British financial system. Instead, the building societies movement has generally been one of the fastest growing sectors of retail finance. Such a role can only be explained in terms of the ideologies of building society management — which are based on an overwhelming concern with growth. The concern to increase the size of their own society led academic commentators to characterise building society managers as classic instances of 'managerialist' behaviour, in which the activities of an institution are driven by senior management's concern with the greater personal financial rewards and prestige associated with larger size (Gough, 1982; Ball, 1983). Yet the need of the societies to increase profits in order to raise their capital bases has meant that concern with growth and profitability have not been mutually exclusive objectives. A major constraint on growth for a mutual body is its capital, which can only be increased through retained surpluses (i.e. profits) rather than via external sources. Capital cannot be raised through issuing equity, although since 1988 the societies have been allowed to issue subordinated debt which is counted as part of their capital.

7.3 Deregulation in the 1980s

The activities in which the societies could participate were considerably extended by the Building Societies Act, 1986. The legislation, following usual practice, was preceded by a lengthy period of consultation after an initial green paper in 1984 (HMSO, 1984). The consultation, again following usual practice, had little effect on the final legislation (Boddy, 1989).

Prior to 1987, when the act came into operation, building societies could only lend, with relatively minor exceptions, first mortgages on residential property. For tax and interest rate reasons they generally only borrowed retail funds, although there were no specific legislative restrictions on their sources of funds. After the act, they could provide many services equivalent to those of general retail banks. A deposit account with a building society could now have characteristics similar to a clearing bank's current account, with the bonus of interest paid on the outstanding balance. A full range of personal banking services could be offered by the societies, such as overdraft, cheque guarantee and credit card facilities. The subsequent introduction by some of the societies of interest-bearing current accounts quickly forced the clearing banks to introduce them as well — ending a tacit agreement between the banks not to offer them.

In terms of their lending powers, the act allowed building societies to invest in unsecured loans, rental housing for sale and other development projects. Lending in such spheres was classified into ascending categories, each with a progressively higher assumed degree of risk. The greater the risk, the smaller the proportion of total funds that could be invested. In the 1986 legislation up to 40 per cent of loans (though less of total assets) could be in non-traditional spheres but the percentage could easily be changed by the regulatory bodies when they wished to (Ball *et al.*, 1984). This framework of control has problems, as it considers the risk of individual types of investment rather than the far more important risk of the overall portfolio of a society's investments. Simple investment percentage rules, however, enable the regulatory authorities to adopt a greater 'hands-off' approach to supervision.

Permissiveness was the underlying characteristic of the new legislation, within a framework that nominally continued to encourage the societies' mutual and housing orientated status. Overall the composition of lending was still required to be concentrated on housing and the regulations made some banking activities difficult to achieve (although this is in practice partially compensated for by lower capital adequacy requirements than banks). The remaining restrictions and pessimism about their likely removal in the near future has led a number of societies to contemplate conversion to public limited company (plc) status. To date only one major building society has actually done so.

Much of the 1986 legislation was structured in such a way that it could be rapidly changed without parliamentary scrutiny. One example was the revision within a year of the limits imposed on wholesale borrowing. In the 1986 act, wholesale borrowing was restricted to 20 per cent of a society's funds — a move aimed at demonstrating the continuing significance of the traditional role of borrowing retail deposits in order to lend them as first mortgages. Contemporary interest rate differentials encouraged the societies to borrow much larger wholesale sums. After some initial lobbying of the societies for an increase to 30 per cent, the limit was raised to 40 per cent in 1987, only nine months later (Boleat and Kaye, 1989).

The remaining constraints on building society expansion and diversification are now the stipulated reserve requirements (i.e. capital adequacy ratios) and limits on the proportion of assets which can be advanced on particular types of higher-risk loan.

Profits have been good during the 1980s but these constraints plus fears about a stagnant mortgage market in the 1990s induced the second largest society, the Abbey National, to convert to limited company (plc) status in 1989 — losing in the process its special building society status. Again the 1986 act gives a new ex-building society plc protection for five years from hostile takeover and allowed, according to a minority of protesting members, the Abbey National's senior management grossly to under-estimate the net worth of the society which had to be paid out to existing members at the time of conversion. In the conversion vote by members the management won overwhelming support for conversion. The Building Societies Commission strongly criticised Abbey National's presentation of the case for plc status to its voting members, but did not stop the changeover from occurring. It is expected that a number of other societies will also abandon their building society status — either independently or through mergers with other financial institutions. A large part of the building society movement could consequently disappear over the next decade.

Despite the 1986 act, deregulation of retail finance has not been as extensive as in the USA, partially because regulatory control was not so restrictive before. Most of the major societies now see themselves as evolving into general financial institutions with a wide range of personal financial services — like a financial supermarket. To date, mergers between different types of retail institution have been limited. The societies are protected from hostile takeover by their mutual status, but they can acquire firms themselves. Large-scale purchases of estate agents by the societies, the banks and life insurance companies took place in the mid-1980s. A trend towards mergers between retail financial institutions and life insurance companies is also discernible, paralleling a similar one in West Germany. Already one society has acquired a life insurance company, whilst a clearing bank, Lloyds, was trying in 1989 to acquire another one, Abbey Life. Abbey Life's members were initially less satisfied with the deal than those of the other (unrelated) Abbey. As part of its privatisation programme, the government sold the National Girobank to the Alliance and Leicester Building Society in 1990. Once again, the legislation regulating the building societies had to be amended to accommodate this sale. It can be seen that regulatory controls are far more flexible in the UK than in the USA.

Legislative flexibility and the whole tenor of the mid-1980s legislation fitted 'the market is always right' philosophy of the Thatcher governments. The point was to facilitate the restructuring of the retail finance sector rather than attempt to control the pattern of development in any appreciable way. Nor was there much focus on providing safeguards against financial excesses. The impact of moral hazard, which has so dominated the US discussion, has not featured in British debate. Official deposit insurance does not exist in Britain, but no-one fears bank runs or failures; either because the deposit institutions are so big in Britain's concentrated retail finance sector that no-one believes that the authorities will allow them to fail, or, with regard to smaller building societies, because the movement as a whole operates a mutual 'depositor bail-out' fund in order to maintain public confidence. If depositors do not fear loss, the incentive structure is similar to that in the USA. Depositors have incentives to search for the highest returns and risk-loving retail finance institutions have incentives to offer them. Uncharted regulatory territory has now been entered.

The success of the control of the smaller societies is rarely tested. One of the most recent cases in 1979 involved the closure of the Grays Building Society. It illustrated both the rapid response of the regulatory authorities and the guarantees given by the rest of the movement, as Grays' operations were quickly absorbed by one of the major societies (Barnes, 1984). But it is interesting to note that under the new regulations the closure of that society would have been unlikely at the stage it occurred.

In a number of respects the UK situation is distinct from that of the USA so a spate of failures of the moral hazard kind in the near future is unlikely. The size of most of the financial institutions is so large that investment losses are likely to be absorbed within depressed profits rather than insolvency. Retail banking is difficult to enter for regulatory and competitive reasons, so new risk-loving institutions cannot set up easily. Off-shore investment funds instead attracted the unscrupulous and have caused a series of insolvencies and investor losses, such as the Barlow Clowes affair in 1988. In addition, the financial community in Britain still has much of the ideology of the gentleman's club in comparison to the USA. Warnings by the governor of the Bank of England periodically issued to the building societies are believed to be heeded. Financial institutions like banks and building societies are trusted not to make too many rash investments. In such an atmosphere strict individual regulatory rules are not regarded as necessary. Such a framework does not stop all such investments, particularly those guided by fashion. Estate agents in the mid-1980s were one such area, as has already been noted (see Chapter 4 for details). Yet no public comment was made by the regulatory authorities on the consequences of that particular investment binge.

The most important cause of the difference between the UK and US situations, however, is the formal and informal cartel arrangements that exist in retail financial services. They are anathema in the USA but have been widespread in the UK throughout the whole of the financial services industry and have influenced the nature of competition in the 'deregulated' 1980s. From 1938 to 1983, the building societies were able to operate through their umbrella organisation, the Building Societies Association, an interest rate fixing cartel. The cartel was far more beneficial to the societies than government interest controls would have been. Unlike the US legislation, for instance, which imposed Regulation Q on the interest rate paid on retail deposits only, the societies benefited from being able to fix both the savings deposit and the mortgage interest rates with profound consequences for the structure of the mortgage market, as is discussed in the following section. The cartel also gave the societies control over the timing of interest changes, which could be vital in confronting potential competitors. The clearing banks also operated a cartel for many years until its abolition in the late 1960s (Wilson Committee, 1980). Certain features of chequing facilities are still openly agreed in formally constituted committees. A much debated one in 1989 was a £50 limit on cheque guarantee cards. The limit was raised only after strong pressure from retailers.

Apart from formal cartel arrangements, informal agreements may be reached or competition may exist in a 'game' framework in which certain bounds are known to the players, transgression of which will lead to immediate retaliation. To an extent, competition in the 1980s can be seen as an exploratory redrawing of those boundaries because, as is shown below, certain key features of other countries' mortgage markets (including the process of interest rate determination) have not come to deregulated Britain.

Cases of bounded competition exist in abundance in British retail financial services. Banks for many years until the 1980s did not wish to compete aggressively with the building societies. The Radcliffe Committee, reporting in 1959, noted that this had been done 'broadly, as a matter of deliberate and concerted policy' (Radcliffe Committee, 1959, para. 132). Banks also limited their opening hours and did not pay interest on current accounts, until the advent of open competition between them and the building societies forced such responses in the 1980s. The withdrawal of life insurance companies from direct mortgage lending in the 1950s and 1960s was replaced by co-operation between them and building societies. Many borrowers of mortgages take out an endowment mortgage which is a tax efficient way of combining mortgage borrowing and life insurance. A policy is taken out with a life insurance company and only the mortgage interest is paid to the building society with the life policy paying off the mortgage principal plus additional profits at the end of the repayment period. Building societies earn substantial but unknown commissions from life companies. Overall, such insurance fees accounted for roughly a third of total building society profits in 1988 (*Financial Times*, 3 April 1989).

The conditions of competition between the societies and the life companies have not to the author's knowledge ever been officially scrutinised. Prior to the Financial Services Act 1986, the societies did not even have to declare a financial interest to mortgage borrowers in the endowment products that they were recommending to them. Since then they either have to give independent financial advice or tie themselves to one life company and declare an interest. But to the chagrin of independent financial advisers, tied agencies do not have to declare the commission they earn on selling life policies whereas the independents do.

7.4 Building society behaviour prior to 1980

The interest fixing cartel was the fulcrum around which building societies structured their activities prior to its abolition. It was a loose but effective arrangement, recommending rates but not overtly enforcing compliance with them. In 1978, for example, a survey found that only 74 per cent of societies actually complied with the recommended mortgage rate, and 56 per cent with the share rate (Gough and Taylor, 1979). Most of the non-compliance, however, was amongst smaller societies which added small premiums to the recommended rate to attract business. The flexibility over the enforcing of the rate aided the longevity of the cartel as it took account of the varying needs of the societies.

The cartel was subject to periodic criticism for the inefficiencies it generated and the shortages of mortgage funds it sometimes created. The absence of price competition weakened the incentives for reducing the cost of services. A government report in the mid-1960s, for example, argued that the cartel led 'to the determination of margins between investment and mortgage rates that are sufficient to allow the least efficient societies to survive and, at the same time, to give generous margins to the more efficient societies' (NBPI, 1966). Other similar criticisms were made with increasing regularity in the late 1970s (e.g. Gough and Taylor, 1979; Wilson Committee, 1980). During most of the 1970s, however, greatest government concern was directed towards the flow of funds into mortgages and the inflationary impact of higher mortgage interest rates. Homeownership and the societies' comparatively low mortgage rates were seen as a 'good thing', so their pricing system was left alone. Pressure to disband the cartel was applied by the market-orientated Thatcher government in the early 1980s, but the cartel essentially collapsed because of growing contradictions in the societies' interest rate strategies.

The interest rates fixed by the societies during the 1970s smoothed out fluctuations in short-term market interest rates and generally kept the mortgage rate below them. The societies could pay low deposit rates because the main competitors for liquid savings, the clearing banks and the government-run National Savings movement, gave even worse ones. The clearing banks seemed happy not to compete fiercely for retail deposits. Their action was partially influenced by government credit control constraints and the tax advantages then given to building society deposits, but also because of a strategic lack of interest in small-scale retail savings.

The benefit of savings deposited with building societies for income tax paying depositors was that the Inland Revenue collected tax due on the interest directly from the societies, estimating an average 'composite' rate of tax for depositors. As many building society savers are elderly or low income households falling below the taxation threshold, the composite rate is to a varying degree less than the taxpayer's contemporary basic rate and thereby boosts the gross-of-tax rate he or she receives on deposits. These composite tax arangements were extended to all retail savings deposits in the mid-1980s. From 1991, however, banks and building societies will also be able to pay before tax (gross) depositor interest.

The societies used extensive non-price competition to attract deposits. Many new branches were set up; opening hours are considerably longer than those of banks, allowing depositors easier access; and a friendly image was carefully cultivated in contrast to the dour image of bank managers. The attractions of building society deposit accounts meant that the societies gradually increased their share of retail deposits, whose overall size was at the same time growing with rising household incomes. In the early 1960s the societies held about a 20 per cent share of liquid savings; by the late 1970s their share, although fluctuating considerably, had more than doubled (Table 7.3). (Hadjimatheou, 1976 and Anderson and Hendry, 1984 provide detailed econometric analysis of building society income during this period.)

Keeping the mortgage interest rate below general short-term money market rates made it difficult for other financial institutions to compete in the mortgage market with the societies. Figure 7.1 compares the mortgage interest rate with the three month interbank rate from 1970 to 1987. Throughout the 1970s, it can be seen that the mortgage market did not provide institutions borrowing on the wholesale money markets with a profitable spread. Monetary control of bank lending, moreover, limited their ability to enter the mortgage market. But, by the 1980s, the 'corset' on bank lending was abolished; whilst mortgage business looked more profitable in part because of increasing competition for other types of banking business. By the mid-1980s, building societies' interest

Table 7.3 Market shares of liquid retail savings, 1973–88

| | Increases in balances Percentage of total | | | | Total retail savings[b] (£m) | Total mortgage advances[c] (£m) | Total mortgage advances[c] divided total savings[d] (£m) |
	National Savings	Monetary sector[a]	Building society	Other			
1973	2	58	37	2	5,842	2,893	0.50
1974	0	61	40	−1	4,892	2,439	0.50
1975	9	2	86	3	4,832	3,730	0.77
1976	8	25	50	8	5,538	3,928	0.71
1977	16	6	71	7	8,304	4,362	0.53
1978	15	31	47	7	10,283	5,437	0.53
1979	−4	44	41	18	14,287	6,461	0.45
1980	9	41	45	5	15,936	7,333	0.46
1981	38	26	45	−10	15,732	9,489	0.60
1982	19	22	58	0	17,783	14,141	0.80
1983	17	21	61	0	16,690	14,525	0.82
1984	16	19	65	0	20,423	17,072	0.84
1985	12	23	65	0	20,478	19,116	0.94
1986	11	36	53	0	22,411	26,581	1.19
1987	9	34	57	0	23,861	28,960	1.21
1988	4	44	53	0	38,254	40,188	1.05

[a] Monetary sector is the banking sector, Trustee Savings Banks (TSB) and some other minor institutions. Prior to 1982, the ordering of data is somewhat different, see *Financial Statistics* for details.

[b] Columns 1–4 are percentage shares of column 5 — where savings are the net change in outstanding balances at the end of the period over the previous year.

[c] Mortgage advances are net advances.

[d] Column 6 divided by column 5.

Sources: *Financial Statistics, Housing Finance.*

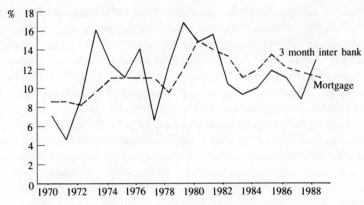

Source: *Financial Statistics*, various dates.

Figure 7.1 Mortgage and three month interbank interest rates, 1970—88

rate setting strategies now made borrowing from the wholesale money market attractive, and not surprisingly many banks and other financial institutions then used the wholesale money market to fund their entry into mortgage lending. So, during the 1970s, the building societies' pricing policies gave them a virtual monopoly of mortgage lending, but as it turned out a precarious one.

If small savers had little alternative to building society deposit accounts prior to the 1980s, larger savers (those in 1975 prices with over £2,000 in deposits) had more options. Deposits of large sums with building societies were found to be highly sensitive to the competitiveness of building society deposit rates in comparison with other short-term rates (HPR, 1977). Whenever the societies were slow to adjust their own rates in line with other short-term rates, they experienced considerable declines in their net inflows of deposits. The times when this effect was greatest occurred during periods of general financial instability, particularly when short rates in general rose above long-term rates in 1973—4 and 1979—80.

Broad annual indications of the effect of the yield gap can be seen in Figure 7.2, which shows the (deflated) increases in net balances in deposits with societies from 1970 to 1986 and the difference in the yield on short and long government stock. Table 7.4 presents this information in a slightly different way by comparing the yield gap with the annual percentage change in real net balances. Periods when net balances fall or grow only slightly are associated with years when the yield gap is small or negative (i.e. short rates are greater than long rates). They occur in 1972—3, 1976, 1978—81 and 1985—6. Their timing differs somewhat from those in the USA, although the first oil-price shock crisis of the early 1970s and the early 1980s' recession are both apparent. Table 7.4 also shows that during these periods the societies had a reduced share

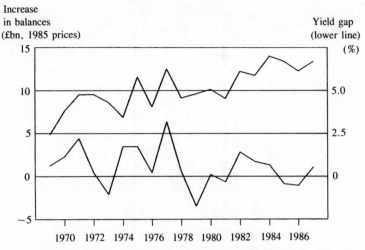

Increase
in balances
(£bn, 1985 prices)

Yield gap
(lower line)

Sources: *BSA Bulletin, Housing Finance* and *Financial Statistics*, various dates.

Figures 7.2 Building society real increases in net balances and the 'yield gap', 1970—87

of increases in short-term savings, losing out to the more competitive rates of the clearing banks and/or National Savings. Lastly, it shows that the effects on mortgage lending of their variations in income were smoothed out by the societies — by adjusting their liquidity ratios and after 1982 by using wholesale funds.

The relationship between short- and long-term interest rates that is so important in determining the timing of the US thrift disintermediation crises consequently has echoes in the British mortgage market. The parallels are far from perfect, however, for a number of reasons. The flow of funds into societies is influenced by a wider range of factors than changes in short-term interest rates. The impact on mortgage lending is also dampened by the societies' ample liquid assets. The societies, furthermore, have not faced the same profit squeezes as the thrifts at these times because they can adjust the interest rates charged on their outstanding mortgages to reflect the new higher rates. Lastly, because of the existence of their cartel, the societies had some leeway in adjusting their interest rates to take account of shifting market spreads.

A consequence up to the 1980s of building societies' reduced income during 'credit crunches' was that periodic mortgage famines were induced. To an extent the societies ran down their liquid assets to offset the effect of the reduction in income. This either limited or delayed the effect of the income shortfall on lending. There was criticism of the societies for not making greater use of their liquid assets in this way (see Wilson Committee, 1980). Building societies are required prior to 1987 to hold 7.5 per cent of their assets in liquid

Table 7.4 Percentage changes in building society income and lending and the yield gap, 1970–87

	1970	1971	1972	1973	1974	1975	1976	1977	1978	1979	1980	1981	1982	1983	1984	1985	1986	1987
Share of liquid savings				37	40	86	60	71	47	41	45	45	58	61	65	65	53	57
Yield gap	2.3	4.4	0.4	-2.1	3.5	3.5	0.4	6.3	0.6	-3.5	0.2	-0.7	2.8	1.8	1.4	-0.9	-1.1	1.1
Percentage change in real deposits	56	25	0	-10	21	67	-30	55	-27	6	5	-10	35	4	19	-4	-9	9
Percentage change in real net lending	28	32	28	-11	-34	46	24	12	20	3	8	-10	22	25	25	1	25	-34

Notes:
1. Yield gap is difference between yield on 20 year government bonds and treasury bills.
2. Change in real deposits is deflated net increases in balances with building societies.
3. Net lending refers to net mortgage advances.

Source: *Financial Statistics, BSA Bulletin.*

form (to avoid running short of transactions funds), but in practice they held considerably more, varying between 16 and 22 per cent from 1974 to 1987. Part of the reason for such high liquidity ratios, at a time when they were supposed to be mortgage lenders only, could have been the attractiveness for the societies of investing in the money and capital markets. The profits earned there were a prime source of the societies' surpluses (i.e. profits). For many years, because they kept their rates below general market rates, the positive spread between their cost of funds and general market rates was substantial, and far greater than on mortgage lending. The need for profits from investing liquid assets was especially important to the societies because of the constraint on their growth implied by their reserve ratios (i.e. capital adequacy).

To summarise, the UK housing market was subjected to 'credit crunches' for two reasons in the 1970s. First, at times of rapid drops in building societies' income and, second, when booming demand for mortgages outstripped supply (the two effects were virtually co-determinous during the 1972–3 and 1978–80 house price booms). With a 'credit crunch' there would be a sudden fall in the number of mortgages advanced. How those credit crunches actually affected the housing market is difficult to distinguish because 'real' factors could also explain the ending of the two 1970s housing market booms. The times when the booms collapsed coincided with or shortly preceded general economic crisis. Lastly, the argument presented above suggests that mortgage credit constraints occurred at specific times rather than as a general feature of the 1970s. This would explain the difference between regression analysis of time series data, which tend to show some credit rationing effect, and cross-sectional interviews (at non-crunch times) with mortgage borrowers who suggested that they were not credit constrained (Ball and Kirwan, 1976; HPR, 1977).

Whatever the impact of mortgage rationing on the housing market, the building societies' interest rate strategy was by the end of the 1970s unsustainable. The increased volatility of general interest rates made it difficult to persuade individual societies to stick to the cartel's recommended rates. The mortgage market was also becoming too big for the societies to fund solely out of retail savings. As Table 7.3 shows, between 1974 and 1981 the mortgage market was absorbing between 45 and 70 per cent of total retail savings, but during the 1980s the volume of outstanding mortgages grew to outstrip total retail savings by 21 per cent in 1987. The traditional building society framework could not cope with the extra demand of the 1980s.

The need to stabilise existing sources of funds and to find new ways of raising income was apparent to the societies in the late 1970s, both individually and collectively through reports published by the BSA — such as the Stow Report (1979). Their options were limited as long as mortgage rates were generally below short-term money market rates. So it was generally recognised that the mortgage rate would have to rise to 'market clearing' levels (see Stow Report,

1979). It is unclear whether the societies recognised the consequences of relative increases in deposit and mortgage rates on their ability to sustain their cartel. Two factors threatened its continued operation. The first was external competition from other potential mortgage lenders. Once mortgage rates rose to be more in line with general money market rates, the entry of other financial institutions into the mortgage market was inevitable. This fact weakened the rationale for the cartel — one of whose prime effects was to exclude such competition. The second factor was increased interest rate competition for funds between the societies triggered off by the introduction of 'high interest' accounts in the late 1970s whilst the cartel was still in operation. In attempts to stabilise their income, individual societies began to offer interest rate premiums on accounts where larger sums were tied up for specific time periods. In 1974 ordinary share accounts constituted over 90 per cent of all accounts; by 1985 they had fallen to only 23 per cent. The interest premiums were not controlled by the cartel arrangements, so soon a lively competition was set up between the societies and it whittled away many of the restrictions on the withdrawal of funds from them — which had been the initial objective of the extra interest.

This outburst of interest rate leap-frogging between the societies proved impossible to contain within the cartel. In order to finance the higher interest savings accounts, the societies gradually raised their mortgage interest rates relative to prevailing general interest rates. Initially they avoided the politically sensitive general rate, adding instead interest rate mark-ups for particular types of borrower — such as for new borrowers during the first year and higher rates on larger loans. These premiums made the mortgages of higher income households increasingly attractive to the clearing banks. They finally re-entered the mortgage market on a large scale in 1981 taking 26 per cent of the market in the first year. The era of mortgage interest rates at below general short-term money market rates had come to an end.

So the history of building society strategy in the 1970s shows that the internal dissolution of the cartel arose because of the responses of the societies to a volatile housing market; to rising but sharply fluctuating short-term interest rates, and to the societies' continual desire to expand. Competition between the societies altered the balancing act between their deposit and mortgage interest rates, and it removed the possibility of keeping the mortgage low enough to be unprofitable to competitors. The cartel had lost its rationale. It no longer protected individual societies from competition over interest rates on deposits, and it could no longer be politically justified on the grounds of keeping down mortgage interest rates and with them general price inflation.

Building societies were also increasingly unhappy in the late 1970s with their sole specialisation in owner-occupied mortgages. The decade had exposed major problems — particularly in the constraints on expansion implied by investing in mortgages only. In real terms the mortgage market had fluctuated sharply for much of the decade rather than grown steadily. Costly branches had sprung

Table 7.5 Building society performance, 1970–87

	1970	1980	1985	1987
Number of societies	481	273	167	130
Number of staff[a]	24,641	49,573	59,432	66,805
Number of branches	2,016	5,684	6,926	6,962
Number of borrowers ('000s)	3,655	5,383	6,657	7,182
Assets (£m at 1985 prices)	55,199	76,086	120,763	148,651
Assets/staff (£m)	2.2	1.5	2.0	2.2
Assets/branches (£m)	27.4	13.4	16.0	19.6
Borrowers/staff	148	109	110	112
Borrowers/branch	1,813	947	961	1,032

[a] Part-time staff are treated as equivalent to a half a full-time employee.

Source: *Housing Finance*.

up, increasing in number by over 2.5 times between 1970 and 1980. The number of staff employed also doubled. Furthermore, by the late 1970s the societies, like other retail finance institutions, had embarked on expensive computerised customer servicing systems, such as automatic telling machines. Performance indicators, such as borrowers and assets per branch and per staff member, showed massive declines (Table 7.5). Between 1970 and 1980, for example, the average number of borrowers per branch virtually halved. To the outsider these indicators show considerable inefficiency in societies' non-price competition. But the excess capacity that resulted could, so the societies hoped, be utilised through the selling of other financial and non-financial services; whilst other housing activities, such as speculative housebuilding and rental housing, offered higher if riskier profits than mortgage lending. Not surprisingly, the movement began to lobby government for legislative reform to increase the permitted range of activities (Boddy, 1989).

7.5 The UK housing market

Throughout most of the post-war years, the overall increase in the housing stock and the growing share in it of owner-occupation has meant that mortgage lending has grown strongly, albeit with periodic downturns. Other housing tenures in Britain make little or no use of owner-occupied forms of mortgage finance, so their decline has not had a counteracting deleterious effect on mortgage institutions. This section considers the nature of owner-occupation in Britain and its implications for mortgage finance.

Some housing supply and demand features obviously affect the operation of the housing market. They include the relative cost of living in particular tenures, changes in government housing policies, demographic factors, living standards, the distribution of income and wealth, building costs and techniques, plus other changes in contemporary structures of housing provision. But, these factors have not influenced the expansion of owner-occupation in a smooth, gradual way; instead they affect the housing market in waves whose scale and duration are strongly influenced by contemporary economic developments.

Table 7.6 shows the changing British tenure structure since 1950. Owner-occupation has increased from 30 per cent in 1950 to almost 65 per cent in 1988. Part of the increase has come from stock transfers from the rental sectors. There were large transfers of privately rented dwellings in the 1950s and 1960s. In the 1980s another major stock transfer took place with over one million council houses sold to sitting tenants.

The overall housing stock has grown rapidly as well. The fastest increase was in the 1970s, when the stock grew by 18 per cent — a greater rate than in the 1960s because less new building was outweighed by more subdivisions of existing houses and fewer demolitions. Additions to the housing stock slowed considerably in the 1980s. The overall stock increased by only 6 per cent between 1980 and 1988, and the rate looks set to be even slower over the next decade — except in the unlikely event of a major revival of new buildings for rental. New building rates halved in the decades after the 1960s. Total completions declined from 85,000–110,000 per quarter in the late 1960s to oscillate around 50,000 during the 1980s — much of the loss of new building occurring in the public rented sector (Figure 7.3). The slowdown in stock increases was mitigated for mortgage lenders by the single-minded encouragement of owner-occupation by 1980s' Conservative governments — in their reforms of housing taxation/subsidy structures and through the policy of large-scale sales of public sector housing.

Table 7.6 Housing tenure in Britain, 1950–88

	1950	1960	per cent 1970	1980	1988[a]
Owner-occupied	29.5	42.0	50.0	56.1	64.1
Public sector rented	18.0	26.6	30.4	31.1	25.5
Private sector rented and other[b]	52.5	31.4	19.6	12.7	9.8
Total stock of dwellings (million)	13.9	16.2	18.7	21.0	22.3
Stock increase over decade		2.3	2.5	3.3	1.3[c]

[a] At June, otherwise year end.

[b] Other includes rented with job or business (around 3% in 1987) and rented from housing associations (around 2% in 1987).

[c] 7.5 years only, equivalent to 1.7 over a decade.

Sources: *Housing and Construction Statistics; General Household Survey.*

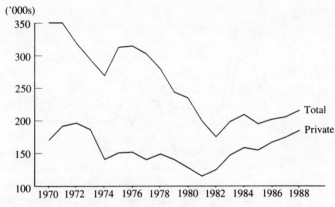

Source: Housing Finance, various dates.

Figure 7.3 Housing completions in Great Britain, 1970–88

The scale of homeownership in Britain means that new house sales now form only a small part of total market transactions. The decline reflects growing sales of existing houses. New housing fell from 25 per cent of all house purchases in 1970 to around only 10 per cent in 1987, even though in absolute terms new housing output was actually the same in the two years (at 170,000 private sector completions). Yet, new housing is obviously still an important source of mortgage demand. Individual building societies sustain their new housing business through marketing arrangements with particular housebuilders. Existing homeowners, nevertheless, have come to predominate with 56 per cent of net advances made to them in 1987. The proportions of mortgage business from existing and new homeowners varies, however, depending on the state of the market. Because of linked chains of sales and other factors, existing homeowners played a more important role during housing market upturns (Ball, 1983).

Underlying supply and demand factors help to explain the mid- to late-1980s' housing boom, which lasted longer than its 1970s' counterparts. The slowdown in net additions to the housing stock occurred in the 1980s at a time when net household formation was on the increase (Whitehead and Kleinman, 1988 and 1989); a pattern again paralleling that in the USA. An added stimulus in Britain was rising incomes. Average real personal disposable income increased by 12 per cent between 1983 and 1987, whereas it had hardly changed in the decade previously.

Another important feature of the owner-occupied housing market is its medium-term volatility. There have been a series of booms during which existing house sales, new completions and house prices rise quickly. They were followed by several years of stagnation with declining output, lower existing house sales, and falling real house prices (see Figures 7.3–7.5). Three boom

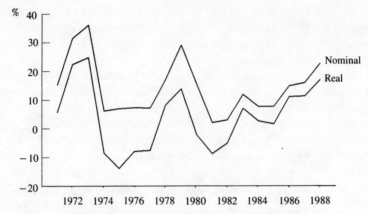

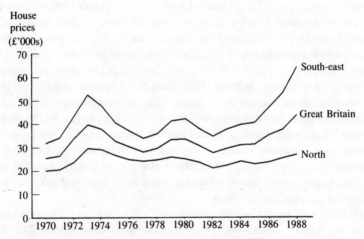

Note: deflated by RPI.
Source: Housing Finance and *Economic Trends*, various dates.

Figure 7.4 Annual house price rises, nominal and real, 1971−88

Note: House prices deflated to 1985 general prices by RPI.
Source: Housing Finance and *Economic Trends*, various dates.

Figure 7.5 Real house prices, 1970−88

periods have occurred since 1970: the first in 1972−3, a second smaller one in 1978−9, and another from 1984 to 1988. Because real house prices fluctuate considerably over time, in the 1984−8 boom they actually only just reached the levels attained in the early 1970s (although in southern England those earlier peaks were surpassed). The last boom was the longest, but unlike earlier ones, it was concentrated in southern England. Between 1985 and the third quarter of 1988, for instance, house prices rose by 111 per cent in East Anglia and

93 per cent in London, but only by 26 and 35 per cent in northern England and Scotland respectively. The latter regions then experienced a later surge and slowing of house prices, giving rise to the notion of a damped ripple effect emanating from the economically strongest region, the South East.

Housing market volatility has a number of implications for mortgage finance institutions in general and building societies in particular. Booms are obviously a good time for mortgage business, with extra advances and useful fee income earned from existing owners when they repay one mortgage and take out another. Conversely, periods of stagnation are relatively unprofitable.

Apart from affecting mortgage demand, the state of the housing market has secondary effects on the volume of funds available for deposit in retail savings accounts. Some of the wealth homeowners realise from house price rises is withdrawn each year. Although some is used for consumption purposes, a significant amount ends up in retail savings deposits, particularly from the proceeds of last time sellers and those trading down market. To an extent, therefore, activity in the housing market helps to generate its own sources of funds via increases in retail deposits with mortgage lending institutions (Ball, 1983; Stow Report, 1979).

Explanations of the medium-term volatility of the housing market vary. Some studies put emphasis on underlying real factors, especially variations in the rate of change of personal disposable income (BSA, 1981). Others add the importance of existing owner-occupier moves and the influence of short-term expectations on demand (Ball, 1983; Hendry, 1984). Considerable emphasis is sometimes put on the supply of credit, suggesting that prior to 1981 — when the banks became major mortgage lenders again — building society credit rationing was the major determinant of market activity. One of the strongest statements of this thesis was published by the Bank of England: 'fluctuations in mortgage supply undoubtedly contributed to the variability in effective housing demand and so played a large part in explaining the two house price "booms" which occurred in 1972—73 and 1978—80 and the subsequent "slumps" during which falls in real prices occurred' (Dicks, 1989, p. 69). Yet the regression results reported in the same paper suggest the claim is exaggerated: 'a small role is found for mortgage rationing' (p. 71). Gough (1982) and Mayes (1979) adopt a similar line.

The problem with discussions of the determinants of housing market behaviour is that variations within it are closely correlated so it is frequently difficult to distinguish cause and effect. Mortgage advances, for example, rise with the level of market activity but that does not mean that increased mortgage credit necessarily caused the extra activity — the reverse could equally be true. The issue of mortgage credit rationing has taken on great importance in the late 1980s because many observers suggest it is the major distinguishing feature between the 1970s' and 1980s' mortgage markets. The previous section argued a different position — that mortgage famines occurred only during the boom years in the 1970s' housing market but that subsequent growth in the demand for mortgages in the 1980s would have meant that relying solely on retail funding would have led to severe rationing then.

Although a sustained housing market boom occurred in the 1980s after the entry of new mortgage lenders, it is unlikely that the boom can be explained purely as a financial phenomenon. Real factors — such as incomes, household and wealth formation and people's expectations about the future trends in house prices — are likely to explain most of it. The restructuring of mortgage finance was a necessary rather than sufficient condition for housing market growth.

Some evidence for this view can be drawn from household income to lending and downpayment ratios from the early 1970s onwards (Figure 7.6). Changes are apparent in both ratios and they differ for first-time and existing owner-occupiers. A decline in the percentage of house price that first-time buyers had to put into their new home might indicate that previously they were constrained in the percentage of the house price they could borrow, but there is no clear major shift in the ratio of average deposit to house price after 1981. With moving homeowners, the picture is somewhat different. Sharp increases in personal funds used to finance house purchase were recorded during the 1973–4 and 1979–80 booms, but this effect was only weakly repeated in the 1980s' one. This might have arisen because existing homeowners were unable to borrow as much as they wanted to during the boom years of the 1970s whereas they could in the 1980s. The decline in mortgage to income ratios after 1974 might also indicate that borrowing constraints were growing in the 1970s, particularly as the decline was reversed in the 1980s. The difference in the ratios for first- and second-time buyers narrowed as well in the 1980s, suggesting again that existing owners might have had easier borrowing conditions in the 1980s. Yet the changes are not that great and the ratios returned to their early 1970 levels again and did not rise to new higher levels. The evidence is clouded further by uncertainty and its effects on consumer borrowing and saving decisions. One plausible explanation of the lower average mortgage to income ratios of the second half of the 1970s is that consumers were concerned about their future economic prospects in the light of falling or static real incomes and the uncertainties associated with stagflation. In consequence they wished to run down their borrowings and increase their savings — the savings ratio also rose during this period.

The causes of the shifts in these ratios, therefore, may be explained by factors other than a pre-existing, permanently binding credit constraint under the societies' cartel. Many variables influencing the demand for mortgages had changed over the period — such as real interest rates, the attractiveness of borrowing house mortgages to fund consumer spending, inflationary expectations and the gains to be made from house price rises, the rate of growth of consumer incomes and, lastly, the size of wealth holdings. There is no

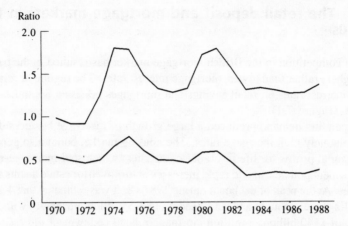

Note: 'Deposit' is average house prices minus mortgages for the relevant group.
Source: Housing Finance, various dates.

Figure 7.6 Deposit to income ratios, first-time buyers and existing owner-occupiers, 1970–88

Table 7.7 Building society mortgage arrears and possessions, 1979–88

	1979	1980	1981	1982	1983	1984	1985	1986	1987	1988
Possessions										
Number	2,530	3,020	4,240	5,950	7,320	10.870	16,770	20,930	22,930	16,150
Percentage	0.05	0.06	0.08	0.11	0.12	0.17	0.25	0.30	0.32	0.22
6–12 months' arrears										
Number	8,420	13,490	18,720	23,790	25,580	41,940	49,620	45,250	48,220	37,440
Percentage	0.16	0.25	0.34	0.42	0.43	0.66	0.74	0.64	0.67	0.50
Over 12 months' arrears										
Number	n.k.	n.k.	n.k.	4,810	6,540	8,260	11,400	11,310	13,000	8,930
Percentage				0.09	0.11	0.13	0.17	0.16	0.18	0.12

Source: Housing Finance.

overwhelming case for a theory of activity determined by credit supply in the UK housing market.

One factor over the past decade that must be of concern to mortgage lenders has been the rise in mortgage defaults. As Table 7.7 shows, arrears and possessions grew in the 1980s and a further increase may be in prospect in the aftermath of the housing market downturn in 1988–9. Altogether, arrears and possessions rose over sevenfold between 1979 and 1987. The rising number of defaults could reflect greater financial strain among owner-occupiers, yet it could also be argued that higher defaults are an inevitable consequence of more relaxed lending policies. The overall level at just over 1 per cent is small, but it may still have a significant impact on lending institutions operating on narrow spreads.

7.6 The retail deposit and mortgage markets in the 1980s

Extra competition in the British mortgage market has resulted in the paradox of higher, rather than lower, mortgage interest rates. The régime of relatively high interest rates on retail savings and mortgages persisted for much of the 1980s (Figure 7.1).

Expanding demand produced a large growth of mortgage business despite the relatively high mortgage rates. The housing market boom also generated substantial profits for life insurance companies, which sold mortgage-related endowment policies, and to rapid increases in turnover for estate agents selling houses. At the peak of the boom during 1987–8, it was estimated that 4 million dwellings were bought and sold, leading to 3.5 million mortgages with a total value of £140 billion; 3 million mortgage-related endowment life assurances worth £4 billion in premiums were sold; and £4 billion of estate agency fees were generated (PA Consultants, quoted in *Financial Times*, April 1989). Given such sums, it is not surprising that so many international financial institutions became aware of the attractions of the British housing market. What is surprising is that even more did not.

For most of the 1980s, the building societies were trapped by the new higher cost of their retail funds into changing mortgage interest rates that were uncompetitive with those of banks and those offered by other financial institutions predominantly relying on wholesale funds. Not surprisingly, the societies massively lost market share. In their worst year, 1987, they only had a 50 per cent share — a figure that would have been thought impossibly low only a few years previously. Yet the societies were not brought into distress by such dramatic falls in their market share because of the buoyancy of mortgage demand. Even in 1987 when their share shrank by almost a quarter from the previous year, the societies still recorded a 9 per cent increase in their outstanding mortgages (Tables 7.1 and 7.2).

The strategy of the new mortgage lenders using wholesale funds helped the societies. They pitched their mortgage rates slightly below those of the building societies rather than pricing them in relation to their own cost of funds. The substantial difference in the spread they enjoyed as a result was taken as profit, making more than worthwhile the investment required to gain a presence in the mortgage market — especially the costs of advertising and of setting up mortgage processing systems.

The societies themselves also took advantage of the wholesale market and profited from the spread derived from its use. After 1981, wholesale funding became increasingly important for them, and they used a variety of methods including the Euromarkets (the major source of wholesale funds) and foreign currency deals (Table 7.8). In 1986, for example, a third of their inflow came

Table 7.8 Building society wholesale funding, 1981–8

Percentage of total net inflow							
1981	1982	1983	1984	1985	1986	1987	1988
1	2	13	14	19	33	18	21

Note: Total funds calculated as increase in retail balance plus wholesale funds.
Source: Calculated from *Housing Finance.*

from wholesale funds — including £1 billion of it from their arch rivals, the banks.

Most wholesale funds — in contrast to the USA — were drawn from the money, rather than the capital, markets. Some capital market funds were utilised via a fledgling secondary mortgage market. Yet, even there, few mortgage-backed securities were issued; instead the instruments used were sales of corporate bonds (similar to traditional FNMA issues in the USA) and sales of outstanding pools of mortgages. The growth of sales of outstanding mortgages can be regarded as a slight development in the UK of the US mortgage banking tradition with institutions originating mortgages in order to sell them on and to profit on the sale and possibly the continued servicing of the debt. A number of medium-sized building societies are now active in this sphere (Boleat and Kaye, 1989). The number of transactions, though, has been insufficient to create a general market with clear, uniform prices.

It is surprising that a mortgage bond market similar to that in other parts of the European Community has not emerged in Britain. Most of the new mortgage lenders have offered mortgages with similar terms to traditional building society ones. Some fixed-interest rate mortgages have been offered, but generally their rate is fixed for only a few years. Mortgages with terms matched to medium- and long-term bonds have not emerged as a major force. Some western European institutions have been reported in the press to be prepared to offer them, but at interest rates similar to prevailing variable ones.

The lack of growth of a mortgage bond system is all the more surprising given persistent government use of short-term interest rates as one of its prime macroeonomic instruments. This has meant that spread between short-term money market rates and long rates has been far narrower than in, say the USA, and frequently the spread has been negative (in 1979–80, 1985–6, and 1988–9). Perhaps mortgage borrowers adhered to the traditional variable rate mortgage because they mistakenly believed government claims that inflation would continue to fall. More likely as an explanation is a lack of consumer awareness, and their suspicion of fixed-interest rate mortgages — paralleling the reverse suspicion of variable rate mortgages in the USA prior to the early 1980s. Mortgage institutions have also not pushed such products.

Given lower interest rates in other parts of the Common Market, especially in West Germany, it is remarkable that more European (or even Japanese) institutions did not enter Britain's booming mortgage market. Exchange rate risks are unlikely to account for their absence, whilst many foreign banks already have a presence in the City. One reason could be the difficulty of establishing a market profile (as discussed in Chapter 4), although others did succeed (like the National Home Loans Corporation after an extensive advertising drive). The advent of financial harmonisation in the European Community over the next few years, plus all the publicity given to 1992 and the 'single European market', may encourage more European financial institutions to contemplate British mortgage lending over the next decade. This would particularly be the case if the exchange rate risk is reduced by Britain joining the European Monetary System (EMS).

The housing boom finally tailed off late in 1988, particularly in southern England. Previously unheard-of price falls were reported in London and mortgage demand plummeted. One of the contributing factors to the fall in mortgage demand was higher mortgage interest rates, which in real terms reached unprecedented levels. The yield gap again turned negative, but a fall in building society deposits did not immediately occur. Record savings flowed into the societies in the months after the stock market crash of October 1987; in addition, one of the main competitors for retail savings, National Savings, had offered poor returns for a number of years, so that there was a large outflow from it. As their own income was not affected — at least not initially — by the interest rate movements, the societies in the face of weakening demand did not raise their mortgage rates by the full increase in short-term rates. So for the first time since the early 1980s the mortgage rate fell below the level that made the wholesale money market a viable source of mortgage funds. This enabled the societies to re-establish their market share. Their success at keeping the mortgage rate down, however, was only a short-lived consequence of the speed of the rise in general short rates and the overall buoyancy of the economy at the time.

Whatever happens to mortgage rates in the future, the experience of the 1980s indicates that greater competition has not resulted in the spread enjoyed by mortgage financial intermediaries being forced down to a small, allocatively efficient level. The wide spreads achieved for most of the 1980s were not caused by a lack of funds to lend on as mortgages. Access was open to the general financial markets which for many years had significantly lower rates. Nor, given the speed with which new competitors took market share, can it be explained in terms of the costs faced by new market entrants. Instead, the obvious reason for the large spread was that everyone else followed the lead on interest rates given by the major building societies. The latter priced their mortgages on the basis of the high retail rates of interest they offered, and on the need to make large profits in order to increase their reserves and to finance the diversification programmes. Competition did not force mortgage and savings rates down.

To illustrate the consequences of this price leadership for mortgage holders, it is worth estimating the savings in mortgage interest payments during the 1980s if all lending had been done by super, but not implausibly, efficient wholesale mortgage finance institutions. They are assumed to have borrowed short-term funds at the three month interbank rate and charged a mortgage rate with a 0.5 spread above it. This spread is not implausible, especially as borrowers are usually charged fees associated with advancing a mortgage. It, for example, is the maximum allowed to Danish mortgage credit institutions (who operate as intermediaries between mortgage borrowers and capital markets). Between 1982 and 1987, years when the mortgage rate rose substantially above the three month interbank rate, the 'efficient' intermediaries would have charged £1,791 million less on Britain's outstanding mortgages. With mortgage interest tax relief, up to a quarter of that extra interest was paid by the Exchequer. The recipients of that extra interest were those holding building society retail deposits (through higher interest rates), the societies through higher gross margins, and other mortgage lenders. Such substantial sums helped mortgage lenders to invest and restructure their activities, to cover the costs of their inefficiencies and excess capacity, to embark on diversification into new markets, and after all that to be left with substantial accounting profits. If Britain does not face a crisis similar to that of the US thrifts in the late 1980s/early 1990s, these oligopolistic profits are a major reason rather than any greater inherent efficiency in the financial system.

A series of new savings and mortgage products did emerge during the 1980s. Accounts equivalent to US money market funds were set up by some institutions, and once the societies' mortgage rates fell below short-term interest rates some societies began offering London Inter-Bank Offer Rate (LIBOR) mortgage rates — the short term interest rate at which banks can borrow. The existence of these developments may suggest that the 1980s were transitional years towards more general wholesale market based pricing. But the domination of the large concerns over the mortgage market, their market profiles, and their beliefs in the advantages of the financial supermarket indicate otherwise.

7.7 A riskier future for building societies?

Building societies are diversifying to reduce their concentration on the retail deposit and mortgage markets. In line with portfolio theory, this should reduce their risk exposure in individual markets, each of which — as in the USA — is becoming increasingly competitive. But the societies have lost their traditional, low-risk control of the mortgage market. The medium-term scenario for them, therefore, is of greater risk all round. At the end of the 1980s' mortgage boom, the societies were lucky enough to find that the contemporary structure of interest rates forced their competitors rather than them to accept substantially reduced margins. Even so, the societies' costs are rising. Investment in cheque account facilities by some of the major societies was expensive and the terms offered quickly matched by the clearing banks. Diversification into estate agency was also copied by the clearing banks and some insurance companies. This inflated the prices paid for estate agents and brought into doubt the profitability of those investments. This illustrates that, however the societies diversify, other financial institutions are already there or correspondingly expanding into the sector, thus raising the costs of diversification and reducing the rewards.

Apart from limiting the societies' profits, expansion by different types of financial intermediary in a competitive race to maintain strong personal sector market profiles results in substantial over-investment in retail banking facilities. A crude estimate of the effect on capacity can be surmised. The building societies and other retail financial institutions are of roughly similar size. Virtually all building societies wish to diversify into general retail banking, amongst other areas, and all retail finance institutions want a mortgage presence. The fashionable 'supermarket' view of the profits to be made from cross-selling financial products, as much as the margins in any particular line, is the driving force. But if all financial institutions are moving into each other's traditional patches, the overall consequence could easily be a doubling of the capacity of the retail financial services sector. Such massive over-investment has little justification. Information technology should be reducing rather than increasing the need for the services of financial intermediaries, so should greater recourse to the capital markets and securitisation. Does the British economy and its population actually need twice as many financial services? The over-expansion is being recognised in some quarters. A financial consultants' report in 1989, for example, talked of 'an increasing problem of a mass of financial company capacity looking for adequate returns' (PA Consulting Group, quoted in *Financial Times*, 1 April 1989).

Although much of the extra capacity is clearly unnecessary, no individual institution feels able to abstain. Individually, they take the risk that others and not they will eventually be hit by the consequences of that excess capacity. European Community financial deregulation in the 1990s could further exacerbate the competitive race. Parallels can be drawn with over-investment by financial institutions in the City during the process of financial deregulation associated with the 'Big Bang' of 1986. Most of the institutions that set up market-making facilities in securities and bonds at considerable cost lost millions of pounds and were forced to withdraw within a few years. Now it would seem that it is retail banking's turn for the rush of investment.

As in the USA, the competition for retail customers — who, it is hoped, can be sold a variety of financial products — is likely to keep the cost of retail funds up. With building societies still the dominant lenders in the mortgage market, mortgage interest rates are generally likely to stay relatively high because the societies are locked into retail deposit competition and wholesale-funded lenders have no incentive to push the mortgage rate much below that offered by the societies. Building societies will probably continue to find that their mortgage market share fluctuates with the yield curve and movements in general short-term interest rates. When interest rates move rapidly against the societies, their market share will fall sharply and vice versa. This means that the societies are unlikely to get the stable mortgage demand they hoped for in the early 1980s.

As excess capacity will prevail over the next decade, profitability in retail banking is likely to be low. Given that most of Britain's retail financial institutions are too big to be allowed to fail, large-scale mergers, forced or otherwise, will be the probable outcome of insufficient profitability over the next decade. But the process could be a stormy one for individual institutions and the regulatory authorities. Merchant banks in 1989 were already lining up insurance companies and foreign banks as potential bidders for building societies (Morgan Grenfell, 1989). Their entry will exacerbate the over-capacity. In the end only a handful of general financial conglomerates may dominate UK retail finance, as Fforde (1983) predicted. Alternatively, the sector may fragment as specialists take advantage of new information technology — but the importance of a strong market profile will probably hold back such fragmentation.

In 1989 the building societies recognised that the continued existence of a large-scale, independent building society movement was unlikely. Some societies were turning into banks, whilst the mortgage market was no longer solely a building society affair. The annual meeting of the Building Societies Association agreed to set up a broader Council of Mortgage Lenders to include other lenders. Its stated aims were information gathering and dissemination and political lobbying rather than a renewed cartel. The new body was seen as a transitional organisation whose activities would be reviewed (*Savings and Loan News*, July 1989). If the building society movement does disappear as an independent entity, subsumed within broader financial groupings, then obviously their influence on mortgage interest rate setting will disappear. But, as it will probably be replaced by the influence of a few giant retail finance institutions, in which case price setting in the mortgage market will still be determined by a competitive game amongst the few rather than be fixed to general money and capital market cost of funds. Unless, of course, a British government decides to change the rules of the game.

8

German universal banking and the mortgage market

with Maartje Martens

There were no major deregulation measures in the West German banking system during the 1980s. Interest rate controls had been abandoned much earlier, in the 1960s, and so no state impediments to institutional competition existed on that front. West Germany also never followed the practice of having a legislatively enforced functional separation of banking activities. *Universal banks* instead have dominated German banking for many years, although some specialist institutions still remain. They undertake most banking activities from retail finance through to investment banking, either within one bank or through the grouping of several specialist banks into one closely linked structure.

The ownership of West German banks is also unique. There are three independent pillars of the banking system: commercial banks, public sector banks and a co-operative banking structure. Within each the universal banking principle operates, although the emphasis on specific banking functions does vary between them. As most of the West German banking system is publicly or co-operatively owned, it might seem that non-market principles have an important influence on many banks. But in practice the profit motive always plays a central role, and has most influence on bank responses to changing market situations. What the distinct ownership forms do mean, however, is that mergers and linked relations between banking institutions occur only to a limited extent between the three pillars; although within them mergers, acquisitions, joint ventures and other forms of co-operation have been extensive over the past twenty years. This effectively restricts the degree of bank centralisation without the need for complicated controls like those of the US banking acts.

Regulation of West Germany's banking system, however, is strict in terms of reserve requirements, and it extends to the sanctioning of the types of financial product that may be sold. Many of the innovative financial products of the 1980s in countries like the USA and the UK as a result do not exist, including anything like the high yielding money market funds which have had such a devastating effect on traditional retail deposit-taking in the USA. Even credit cards are rarely used and automatic telling machines are far less prevalent than in countries of equivalent size and wealth. The lack of innovation cannot be put down simply to government regulation, as the banks and insurance companies themselves seem content for most things to remain as they are. The big commercial banks, for example, have put up a long fight against the widespread introduction of credit cards. 'Conservative' is a compliment in the German banking world, and competition though fierce in some areas has definite bounds.

One characteristic common to the major institutions whatever their ownership is that they are all interested in expanding their retail banking activities. The financial supermarket is known as *Allfinanz* in Germany. In a number of respects it is far more developed than in the two other countries under study. The strategy is not only being adopted by banks but also by a major Bausparkasse (building and loan association) and by insurance companies. The latter two either try to compete directly with the banks or they are pursuing mutually advantageous link-ups in the retail sphere.

Part of the reason for the greater development of Allfinanz is the prior existence of the universal banking tradition but it also reflects the particular nature of competition between West German banks. Allfinanz is about product competition but not necessarily about price competition. Bank deposits, for example, play a much greater role in the West German financial system than in either Britain or the USA. Yet one noticeable feature of German retail banking during the 1980s was that the rate of interest on retail deposits was not forced up towards general money market rates as they were in both Britain and the USA. In this respect German bank customers get a poor deal. The ability of West German banks to attract such large volumes of relatively cheap deposits helps to explain the heavy reliance on bank lending by firms and individuals.

Economic conditions in West Germany during the 1980s differed from those of the two previous countries surveyed. The economy picked up only sluggishly after the early 1980s' recession, although growth did improve in the late 1980s. Unemployment remained stubbornly high. Huge balance of payments surpluses were recorded, and both inflation and interest rates were low compared with other leading west European economies. Partly because of the general macroeconomic climate, housing activity was low. Rental housebuilding plummeted and the owner-occupied market was depressed. For many years prices in the secondhand housing market fell. No mid-1980s housing market boom occurred similar to those in Britain and the USA. Although, like those two countries, mortgage defaults became an issue of concern for the first time since the Second World War. Consequently the mortgage market of the 1980s was not a particularly attractive one for lenders.

The owner-occupied housing market, however, is seen as central in the strategy of Allfinanz. A variety of factors encourage potential German homeowners to save for long periods to help fund the final purchase of a new home. Mortgage borrowing, futhermore, generally does not take the form of a single mortgage instrument, but a package of first and second mortgages — plus possibly other borrowings and insurance policies. So both during the savings years, and when mortgage packages are assembled or parts of them refinanced, financial institutions are able to exploit the possibility of selling other products as well.

From these brief introductory comments it can be seen that, once again, a unique institutional and competitive structure exists in West German retail banking and mortgage markets. Because of the diversified sources of borrowing available to the universal banks, mortgage credit rationing has not been a major issue in West Germany, but other features do suggest that competition does not lead to a simple or unequivocally universally beneficial outcome.

The following sections elaborate on these issues. Section 8.1 gives a broad overview of the West German financial system and the role played by the major institutions within it. Section 8.2 presents a similar picture for the mortgage market after which West Germany's rapidly changing housing market is evaluated in Section 8.3. Then greater analysis of the development, interlinkages and functioning of each type of institution is given in Section 8.4, concentrating on their activities in mortgage finance. Section 8.5 draws together competitive processes in retail banking and mortgage finance, followed by some concluding comments.

8.1 An overview of the West German financial system

Many people in western Europe and North America are familiar with Germany's giant private sector universal banks, such as the Deutsche, Dresdner and Commerz Banks. Not only do they have branches throughout the country but they also have close links with industry, with seats on the boards of most major companies. In the Bundesbank statistics those banks are even referred to as the 'big banks'. On the basis of such information, the mistaken impression is often derived that such banks have an overwhelmingly dominant position in the Federal Republic's financial system. This, however, is not the case. In the personal, small business and agricultural sectors in particular they have traditionally played only a minor role. Collectively, public sector savings banks and co-operative banks, plus their co-ordinating and clearing organisations, are far more important in domestic banking than the big banks.

The respective roles of the different types of bank can be seen by looking at their relative size as measured by their balance sheet activities (Table 8.1). Not all the categories of bank are independent of each other — all the mortgage banks, for example, are at least partly owned by other institutions. The picture is also complicated by the existence of many off-sheet activities, such as foreign exchange dealing, underwriting and so on, but an idea of each type of bank's

Table 8.1 West German banks and their 1988 market shares

	Percentage of total business[a]		
Universal type banks[b]			
Commercial banks	24		
Big banks		9	
Regional and other		11	
Branches of foreign banks		2	
Private banks		2	
Foreign banks[c]	4		
Public sector banks	38		
Regional giro institutions[d]		16	
Savings banks		22	
Co-operative sector banks	17		
Regional inst. of credit co-ops[e]		5	
Credit co-operatives		12	
Specialist banks			
Mortgage banks	14		
Private		9	
Public		5	
Banks with special functions	7		
Postal giro and savings banks	2		
Total	100[g]		(DM 3,984 billion)
Bausparkassen	100		(DM 157 billion)
Private		68	
Public		32	
Insurance companies[f]	100[g]		(DM 607 billion)
Life		61	
Pension		12	
Health		5	
Indemnity, etc.		13	
Reinsurance		7	

[a] Domestic and external liabilities/assets as reported in balance sheet totals, plus several off-sheet liabilities.
[b] Strictly only the broad categories of commercial, public and co-operative are universal banks (see text).
[c] Not included in total.
[d] Including Deutsche Girozentrale.
[e] Including Deutsche Genossenschaftsbank.
[f] Assets.
[g] Totals subject to rounding errors.

Source: *Monthly Report of the Deutsche Bundesbank.*

relative importance can be ascertained, especially in their deposit-taking and lending activities. Table 8.1 shows that the big banks account for only 9 per cent of total banking turnover. Regional commercial banks have a greater share, and the co-operative sector and its central organisations are almost twice as large. Foreign banks play a small role in contrast to Britain. The largest group of institutions are the public savings banks and their central organisations with 45 per cent of banking turnover. Altogether private sector commercial and specialist banks have only 40 per cent of total banking turnover.

Apart from the banking sector, Table 8.1 also shows the size and composition of the insurance sector and the Bausparkassen. The function of the insurance companies is obvious. Bausparkassen, however, are uniquely German. They are building and loans associations involved in long-term savings schemes for owner-occupied housing. After a contracted period of savings Bausparkassen give a low interest second mortgage (see later for details). Both public and private Bausparkassen exist, and they may be owned by other institutions, such as a bank or insurance company.

Although universal banking is common throughout the German financial system, differences of emphasis can be seen within each sector. Table 8.2 provides information on the deposit-taking and borrowing of banks from the non-bank sectors of the economy. It can be seen that the commercial banks tend to specialise in sight (current account) and time deposits and have only a small presence in savings deposits and bonds (savings bonds are non-marketable financial instruments). Savings banks and credit co-operatives are more evenly spread across all forms of deposit-taking. Most sight and time deposits are held with them, but they also play a dominant role in the much larger market for savings deposits. Half of all savings deposits and 60 per cent of all savings bonds are accounted for by the savings banks alone. In terms of banks' reliance on the capital market, most long-term bank borrowing is undertaken by mortgage banks through the bond market. Banks with special functions and the public regional giro institutions borrow most of the rest of the capital market funds used.

The German financial system is far more orientated towards bank deposit-taking and lending than the UK and US ones, where non-bank financial instruments are more important. Table 8.3 shows the financial assets and liabilities of the non-financial sectors of the German economy. Around half of assets are held as bank deposits — a much higher proportion than in the USA, where, for instance, only a quarter of personal sector financial assets in 1986 were held as bank deposits and currency (OECD, 1988b). One particularly noticeable feature is the very low holdings of shares — only 7 per cent of total financial assets (although the low amount partly reflects their undervaluation in the accounts of the banks and insurance companies that hold many of them). Turning to liabilities, not surprisingly their composition reflects the pattern of asset holdings. Almost 60 per cent of liabilities were bank loans in 1985, whereas capital market liabilities in the form of bonds and shares

Table 8.2 Banks' deposits and borrowing from non-banks, January 1989

	Sight deposits	Time deposits and borrowed funds		Savings deposits	Bank savings bonds	Other[a]	Total sources	
		<4 yrs	≥4 yrs					
	(%)	(%)	(%)	(%)	(%)	(%)	(DM bn)	(%)
Big banks	18	18	4	8	7	2	192	10
Regional banks	13	17	9	6	8	5	183	9
Regional giro	4	8	17	1	1	46	137	7
Savings banks	33	27	1	50	59	3	654	33
Credit co-ops[b]	22	25	4	28	25	2	404	21
Mortgage banks	0	1	44	0	0	15	200	10
Other banks	9	6	20	6	1	29	190	10
	100[c]	100[c]	100[c]	100[c]	100[c]	100[c]		100[c]
Total (DM bn)	276	278	423	731	193	59	1960	
Source type as percentage of all sources	14	14	22	37	10	3		100

[a] Loans on a trust basis.
[b] Includes central institutions of credit co-operatives.
[c] Totals subject to rounding errors.

Source: *Monthly Report of the Deutsche Bundesbank.*

Table 8.3 Composition of non-financial sector's financial assets and liabilities, 1970 and 1985

	1970	1985
Assets		
Bank deposits		
Sight	15.1	12.5
Time	17.1	17.7
Savings	24.2	18.9
Bausparkassen	4.6	3.7
Insurance companies	10.1	13.8
Bonds	7.7	12.8
Shares	6.9	4.3
Other, including abroad	14.2	16.7
Liabilities		
Bank loans		
Short-term	15.1	11.6
Long-term	45.9	47.2
Bausparkassen	4.0	4.4
Insurance companies	5.7	5.5
Bonds	4.9	8.1
Shares	7.1	4.1
Other, including abroad	16.7	19.3

Notes:
1. Non-financial businesses debt/equity ratios (mid-1980s at replacement cost): West Germany 1.3, Japan 1.3, UK 0.6, USA 0.6.
2. Data subject to rounding errors.

Source: OECD (1986).

were correspondingly low. The pattern of assets and liabilities has remained remarkably stable since the early 1970s — again in contrast to Britain and the USA — with only a small decline in bank deposits and loans.

Part of the reason for the structure of the financial system is the relatively small equity base of the business sector in West Germany, which relies instead on bank borrowing. The high gearing of German firms is well-known (see Table 8.3). Matching the high level of bank borrowing in both the business and personal sectors is the correspondingly important role of bank deposits. The financial system is organised in a way that puts emphasis on channelling funds into banks, which then lend them on directly. The move towards securitisation in the international financial system has not yet had much effect on the German domestic scene. The securities market itself is primarily a bond one. Sales of shares in 1988, for example, were only one-fifth of the value of the bonds sold. Industrial bonds, furthermore, are only a tiny proportion of the bond market; only 0.2 per cent of outstanding bonds in 1988 were industrial bonds (DB, 1989).

The role of bank deposits is encouraged by the tax incentives given to savings in general, which again contrasts with countries like Britain and the USA where most subsidies are given to financial instruments that encourage capital market activity such as life insurance policies and pensions. Many of the German subsidies are linked to contractual savings schemes, which stimulates the role of medium- to long-term deposits with banks. Another aspect of the German financial system is the near permanent surplus on the trade balance. This means that capital is exported — much of it through the banking system — rather than the converse of a deficit encouraging the development of money and capital markets to cope with the inflow of capital as is required in countries with chronic trade deficits. The money market itself is primarily an interbank market (OECD, 1986).

With almost 4,500 banks the number falls in between the small number in Britain, less than 700 banks and building societies, and the 17,000-plus US banks and thrifts. Yet, per head the number is similar to that in the USA. The number of West German banks had declined considerably over the past thirty years from over 13,000 in 1957 (Table 8.4). All banking types were affected, with the exception of regional and foreign commercial banks. A slight increase in the number of private mortgage banks was more than offset by a decline in public ones. In the public and co-operative spheres there was much rationalisation from the late 1950s onwards. The number of co-operative banks in particular declined by over two-thirds.

Both the savings banks and the credit co-operatives have central organisations, the Deutsche Girozentrale and the Deutsche Gennossenschaftsbank respectively. They and a middle tier of regional institutions even out liquidity between member banks, and act as clearing centres and universal banks. The importance of the roles of the middle and upper tiers has grown in recent years.

Table 8.4 Number of banks and their branches by category of bank, 1957 and 1987

	Banks		Branches	
	1957	1987	1957	1987
Commercial	364	311	1,917	6,291
Big banks	8	6	787	3,120
Regional and other	96	157	1,020	2,814
Branches of foreign banks	15	58	6	31
Private bankers	245	89	104	326
Regional giro institutions	14	12	191	231
Savings banks	871	586	8,192	17,307
Regional insts of credit co-ops	19	6	89	42
Credit co-operatives	11,795	3,476	2,305	15,910
Mortgage banks	44	38	19	32
Private	25	27	8	26
Public	19	11	11	6
Banks with special functions	16	16	34	84
Bausparkassen	n.a.	20	n.a.	21
Private		17		21
Public		3		0

Source: *Monthly Report of the Deutsche Bundesbank.*

Although the overall number of banks is large, there are few specialist housing ones in contrast to their importance in both Britain and the USA. Housing is particularly important for the mortgage banks and the sole sphere of the Bausparkassen. But neither of these types of institution have an extensive branch network — the public Bausparkassen have no branches at all (Table 8.4). Both instead sell their products through other financial institutions, and in the case of the Bausparkassen through large networks of door-to-door sales personnel.

The branching system in German banking is extensive as the data in Table 8.4 show, and it has grown considerably in recent decades. The branching networks of the savings banks and credit co-operatives are particularly large. That of the credit co-operatives grew sevenfold from the late 1950s. To put the scale of the branch system in context, comparison can be made between the German savings banks, the British building societies and the US thrifts. In contrast to the savings banks' 18,000 bank offices, the building societies have 7,000 and the thrifts around 22,000. Yet in West Germany there are two other types of retail financial institution with extensive bank office networks, the commercial banks and the credit co-operatives (Table 8.4); whereas Britain and the US have only commercial banks in addition. Obviously, population size and density, the level of incomes and transactions all affect the comparison. But West Germany's banking office network is on a par with that of the USA, a country with four times the number of people and a much larger land area, and it is vastly bigger than Britain's. Such a network is obviously expensive to run and reflects the nature of competition between retail financial institutions, which is based on service rather than on price.

With this overview of the financial system in mind the next two sections examine the mortgage and housing markets.

8.2 The West German mortgage market

The mortgage market is used by social housing institutions and private landlords as well as for owner-occupation. Some mortgage instruments, moreover, are restricted in their use. As housing in West Germany is expensive — especially in the owner-occupied sector — this means that packages of mortgage borrowings are common. Mortgage bonds, for instance, can only finance first mortgages up to 60 per cent of the value of a property, whereas Bausparkassen loans are for second mortgages only. (First and second refer to creditor priority in recovering loans if the borrower defaults.)

The 1970s were a period of considerable increase in residential mortgage finance. The depressed years of the 1980s were the converse but, as with Britain and the USA, the changes of the 1970s are a central component of explaining the contemporary mortgage finance situation. This is all the more true of Germany because of the absence of new institutions and mortgage instruments in the 1980s. There was no mortgage finance revolution in the 1980s: that had occurred in the 1970s. The 1980s rather was a period of retrenchment and consolidation.

Before the 1970s, fixed-interest loans were the norm. Housing costs were relatively low, as were inflation and interest rates. For owner-occupiers, such loans would frequently be topped up by Bausparkassen borrowings. Rising housing costs, inflation and nominal interest rates changed all that during the 1970s. By 1983 outstanding mortgage loans amounted to 48 per cent of all domestic lending to firms and persons, up from 41 per cent in 1970. The major area of growth was in second mortgages — they rose from 29 to 46 per cent of outstanding mortgage credit during those thirteen years (DB, 1984).

Table 8.5 shows the institutional shares of the mortgage market in 1970 and 1983. The dominant position of the mortgage and savings banks in the lending of first mortgages is clear, although their combined share did fall from 93 per cent in 1970 to 84 per cent in 1983 as a result of increases for the other universal banks, the commercial banks and the credit co-operatives. Both the latter aggressively expanded into a market that had been previously of little importance to them, using second rather than first mortgages as the vehicle. The traditional structure of the mortgage market, however, was weakened rather than transformed, as in 1983 the three traditional lenders — savings banks, mortgage banks and Bausparkassen — still had almost 80 per cent of overall (first and second mortgage) business. Changes in shares by type of lending

Table 8.5 Mortgage lending to domestic firms and private individuals, 1970 and 1983

| | Percentage of outstanding debt, year-end | | | |
| | First mortgages | | Second mortgages | |
	1970	1983	1970	1983
Commercial banks	4.0	6.8	7.7	15.2
Savings banks	43.9	41.3	12.9	20.3
Credit co-ops	3.2	5.8	10.7	16.4
Mortgage banks	48.8	43.2	2.6	3.6
Bausparkassen	—	—	62.7	42.5
Others	0.1	2.8	3.4	1.7
Total (DM billion)	135.7	379.7	55.3	321.7

Source: Adapted from tables provided by Dr Wagner, Deutsche Bank, Frankfurt am Main.

agency hides, however, the considerable shifts in ownership and in joint ventures that took place, as is discussed in Section 8.4.

To some extent there was a traditional division of labour in first mortgage lending between the mortgage and savings banks, with the former concentrating on lending to corporate developers — including the social housing institutions — and the latter to individuals. The increased role of individual investors in the rental as well as the owner-occupied sectors resulted in mortgage banks losing the greatest market share during the 1970s and 1980s, with their share falling from 35 per cent of overall lending in 1970 to 25 per cent in 1983. The savings banks' share declined only slightly, by around 3 per cent.

The area where there was the most change after 1970 was in second mortgages. In 1970 the Bausparkassen had almost two-thirds of this market, but during the following decade they significantly lost share to all three types of universal bank — although until the mid-1980s their aggregate business continued to rise.

The increasing role of second mortgages in the 1970s reflected the growing importance of owner-occupation, changes in social housing subsidies and the decline in social rented housebuilding. The social housing institutions began to take out second mortgages for their new dwellings from the mid-1960s onwards, after state subsidies no longer covered all the costs above the permissible value of a first mortgage.

Up to the mid-1970s mortgage credit was lent mainly for new building. But inner city gentrification and the extension of housing subsidies to existing housing in 1977 resulted in a considerable boost for mortgages on the existing housing stock. Large-scale sales of previously socially rented housing in the 1980s further encouraged the trend.

The new emphasis on owner-occupation and the concomitant growth of second mortgages were prime causes of new competition in the mortgage market. The mortgage banks had to adjust and find ways of encouraging individual housebuyers as well as corporations to use their financial products. The Bausparkassen and savings banks were traditional lenders to owner-occupiers, but they had to respond to the commercial banks and credit co-operatives' attempts to increase their shares of new mortgage business. The enhanced competition was not only fierce in mortgage lending, it was also intense in attracting funds from personal savers.

Several specific circumstances favoured the universal banks in expanding their role in mortgage finance from the early 1970s onwards. First, the mortgage market was growing rapidly which made it relatively easy for new institutions to enter. Second, rising personal wealth encouraged the universal banks, particularly the biggest three commercial banks, to intensify their activities in the personal sector. Lastly, rising and unstable nominal interest rates, characteristic of the 1970s and early 1980s, had less effect on the mortgage lending activities of the universal banks than on the mortgage banks and Bausparkassen with their less flexible financial instruments. Before examining the functioning and changing roles of each specific lending institution, though, the role of homeownership in West Germany needs to be elaborated in greater detail.

8.3 The West German housing market

Owner-occupation in West Germany is a much lower proportion of the total housing stock than in either Britain or the USA. For many years after 1950 the homeownership percentage even declined and only rose again after the mid-1970s. Only around 40 per cent of the stock is owner-occupied, more is rented from private landlords and about 15 per cent is socially rented. In urban areas the proportion of owner-occupied dwellings is even less. Part of the reason for the traditionally low level of owner-occupation is the nature of housing subsidies which are more even-handed between tenures than in Britain and the USA, and to an extent have even favoured rental housing. (The even-handed nature of the subsidies makes it notoriously difficult to get breakdowns of key data by tenure — as the statistics frequently refer to housing under differing types of promoter (individual or corporate) and house type rather than specifically to tenures.)

Owner-occupation in West Germany plays a somewhat distinct social role. Households traditionally move into the tenure at quite a late stage in their lives — if at all. The average age of new entrants is generally 35+ years. In 1982, only 17 per cent of owner-occupier head of households were aged under 40. To buy a house substantial savings are often accumulated, and households envisage settling down in their final dream home in a suburban or rural location.

In contrast to much of the rest of the housing stock, owner-occupied dwellings tend to be large and expensive single-family units. The broad up-market characterisation was offset by several factors. In some industrial regions, traditional nineteenth and early twentieth century working class housing was occasionally built for owner-occupation, whilst social housing subsidies have from the 1950s onwards increased owner-occupation amongst middle to lower income groups. The traditional role was also changed slightly following the rundown of social housebuilding and sales of some dwellings to existing sitting tenants, and by some inner city sales of privately rented housing. Despite these caveats, owner-occupation tends still to be an expensive form of housing provision, so much of the expansion of owner-occupation since the mid-1970s has been amongst the highest 40 per cent of income earners (Potter and Drevermann, 1988).

The expense of homeownership is highlighted by a survey of recent buyers from the early 1980s that found that mortgage repayments were on average 40 per cent of net income, despite the fact that 30 per cent of the house price was financed by own savings (Weissbarth and Hundt, 1983). A comparison of the construction cost of a new single family house with average manual earnings also shows that the homeownership costs rose substantially during the 1970s. In the mid-1960s, the multiple was five times average manual earnings; by 1976 it had risen to seven times; and eight times by 1982 (Köster and Mezler, 1979). Transactions costs are also high. Estate agents charge 4−6 per cent for arranging a sale, whilst legal costs and taxes have to be added. One estimate put transactions costs at 13 per cent of the already high purchase price (quoted in Potter and Drevermann, 1988). As Table 8.5 shows, new construction costs continued to rise throughout the 1980s. An indication of the high price of housing in West Germany can be seen from a survey in the mid-1980s which found that a person on average earnings in most western European countries would need between eight to ten thousand hours of work to be able to buy an average owner-occupied home; but in Germany they would require around twenty thousand hours of work to do so (Nationwide Building Society, 1987).

One consequence of the position of owner-occupation in West Germany's housing system is that the secondhand housing market is relatively unformed. People tend to buy houses late in life and then remain in that dwelling rather than move again, so trading up or down the market and linked chains of purchases and sales are uncommon. Given a preference for new dwellings amongst first-time buyers, low mobility means that the market for secondhand dwellings is limited. The secondhand market tends to be segmented from that of new housing and also localised. Clear uniform prices do not always exist and long periods may lapse before sellers and purchasers are matched. Indicative of the underdeveloped nature of the secondhand market is that there are no accurate national price data for either new or existing owner-occupied housing. The only indicators available are crude unweighted averages drawn up from information provided by estate agents.

The secondhand housing market was severely depressed for much of the 1980s. Prices did rise rapidly in the late 1970s, a,development encouraged by the extension of housing subsidies to existing housing in 1977. But in the 1980s there was considerable reaction to those inflated prices. Neither real incomes nor the number of households grew significantly, whilst sales of previously rented dwellings increased the supply of secondhand dwellings coming onto the market. The result was five or six years of falling house prices from 1981 onwards — dropping by an estimated third on average but much more in some urban areas, with prices marked down most for flats and cheaper properties in general.

Falling house prices created problems for households that defaulted on their mortgage loans during the 1980s. The law and the policy of mortgage finance institutions does not allow defaulters to walk out of their mortgage obligations as is possible in the USA. When house prices fall a forced sale does not necessarily cover the outstanding debt; whilst any unpaid mortgage repayments are capitalised into the outstanding mortgage sum on which a high penal interest rate may be charged when the borrower defaults. Again it is difficult to get an accurate picture over time of arrears and defaults but they seem to have risen substantially during the 1980s, even if they still remain a very small proportion of total outstanding mortgages. Defaults and foreclosures probably doubled between 1980 and 1985. The complex financial packages taken out by homeowners — with a mix of loans of varied repayment dates and interest rates — adds to the likelihood of default because households are not necessarily aware of the precise commitments they have made, nor of the fact that a key low interest loan may after a few years have to be refinanced at a much higher interest rate (Brambling *et al.*, 1983; Potter and Drevermann, 1988).

Housing subsidies for owner-occupation in Germany take specific forms. Unlike those in Britain and the USA, they are not tied specifically to mortgage finance. House purchase is treated as an investment by the German tax authorities, and homeowners claim depreciation allowances on their investment rather than relief from the finance costs of homeownership. The principle subsidy is an accelerated depreciation allowance which can be claimed for the first eight years. Extra tax allowances are given for the number of children housed. Lower income homeowners can apply for social housing subsidies as well which gradually decline over a twelve to fifteen year period. The investment allowances can be claimed only once (twice by married couples). This discourages trading up and gives households an incentive to wait until their maximum income years before house purchase in order to benefit from the greatest tax relief. (Then they will be on their highest marginal tax rate and be able to purchase a more expensive dwelling with correspondingly greater depreciation allowances.) Owner-occupiers can also take advantage of subsidies offered to new rental housebuilding by a fiscal device known as the 'two-family house' whereby part of the structure is rented out during the years that subsidies can be claimed, with the building often turning into sole use subsequently (often called the Bauherren model). A mortgage interest rate tax deduction was introduced as a temporary measure by the West German government in 1982 in an attempt to revive flagging construction demand. Partly because of that temporary tax allowance, housing subsidies rose substantially during the early 1980s — rising by 47 per cent between 1980 and 1984 (OECD, 1988c).

The housing market stagnated throughout the 1980s as Table 8.6 shows. Housing costs rose in all tenures. Rents rose above the rate of inflation, whilst rising construction costs offset the fall in interest rates for house purchasers. Housebuilding tumbled, falling to only just above 60 per cent of its 1980 level by 1987 although there was a slight revival in 1988. Apart from macroeconomic factors, common explanations of the fall off in housebuilding are the young age of the housing stock after years of high building rates and a reduced rate of household formation (OECD, 1988c). The 'capital promised for residual building' column in Table 8.6 refers principally to the money allocated by mortgage finance institutions. It can be seen that the 1980s were not good years for mortgage business. Some of the increase of the early 1980s is an artefact of improved data collection, and from 1983 the level of funding remained fairly constant (or declined slightly in real terms).

One final feature of German homeownership is important for mortgage finance institutions. Much of it is not mass house provision by building firms,

Table 8.6 Selected housing market indicators, 1979—88

	Residential building orders[a]	Capital promised for residential building[b] (DM million)	Price index for residential buildings[a]	Rent index[a]
1979	101.3	6,493	90.4	95.3
1980	100.0	6,906	100.0	100.0
1981	89.6	6,580	105.7	104.4
1982	90.4	7,009	109.2	110.2
1983	109.3	8,637	111.4	116.5
1984	87.9	8,513	114.3	120.9
1985	68.2	8,673	115.1	124.7
1986	64.8	8,693	116.8	127.2
1987	61.0	8,479	119.2	129.5
1988	68.2	8,565	121.7	132.9

[a] 1980 = 100.
[b] Loans promised by savings banks, regional giro institutions, mortgage banks and Bausparkassen for new housing, modernisation, the purchase of existing dwellings, and debt rescheduling. Before 1984, non-new housing loans only partly recorded.

Source: *Monthly Report of the Deutsche Bundesbank.*

but one-off 'self-building'. In US terminology self-building is more accurately described as custom building, whereby the purchaser acquires the land and orders a prefabricated house from a catalogue or arranges for a general builder or separate building trades to erect an individually designed dwelling. A survey in 1980 found that two-thirds of new owner-occupied house approvals were for self-building (quoted in Martens, 1985). That type of market structure favours lenders who already have an established relationship with the mortgage borrower through holding their bank account or having a pre-established savings scheme. To a considerable extent it explains, therefore, the traditional pre-eminence of the savings banks and Bausparkassen in this sphere.

8.4 The West German mortgage-lending institutions

This section describes in greater detail each type of institution active in the mortgage market and examines the changes that have occurred to them over the past two decades. The roles of the three universal banking types — the savings banks, the commercial banks and the credit co-operatives — will be considered first, followed by the specialist institutions — the mortgage banks and the Bausparkassen.

Until the early 1970s the mortgage market tended to be divided into well-defined segments in which each type of institution had a clearly defined position, and one of them was usually dominant. The market segments revolved around a mix of characteristics: first or second mortgages, rural or urban areas, high or low income groups, rented or owner-occupied housing, and individual or corporate lenders. But from the early 1970s these specialisms began to weaken with the extension of the universal banking principle throughout each of the three banking pillars — then all types of universal bank began to compete for a share of each market segment. This process was intensified in the 1980s with the enunciation of the strategy of Allfinanz. The result was that the earlier divisions were shattered, but the effects were a two-way process. The mortgage market was transformed, but at the same time universal banking was affected by the increasing integration of mortgage finance within it.

Savings banks

Savings banks are one of the oldest types of financial institution active in Germany today. They date from the second half of the eighteenth century, and grew to prominence with the rapid urbanisation of the late nineteenth century. Savings deposits are often medium- to long-term contracts entered into by depositors, and they are generally used for medium- to long-term lending. The savings banks' traditional role is to provide credit for housing, small companies and municipalities and regional governments. Small companies have been one of the mainstays of post-war West German economic growth. With their public finance roles, in addition, savings banks have for many years been a key part of Germany's wholesale, as well as retail, banking systems.

Most savings deposits are from lower to middle income households, which also tend to hold current accounts at the same bank. Savings banks as a result are sometimes referred to as the banks of the 'little man'. For most West German men and women, in other words, their regular banking facilities are at the local savings bank.

There are restrictions on the activities that savings banks can undertake. Regional savings bank laws lead to variations in the precise constraints. In general, savings banks are excluded from certain risky ventures, like speculating in shares. They also cannot raise money from the bond market — instead they rely overwhelmingly on retail funds as their source of finance. Deposits are guaranteed by the Savings Bank Association.

Most savings banks are publicly owned and operate solely within the jurisdiction of the local or regional (Kreise) public authority that owns them. Such a geographical ownership pattern obviously limits competition between them. Their ownership structure also means that their business is guaranteed by the public authorities owning them, and gives them tax privileges. Both these features generate a competitive edge over other banks (EAG, 1981). The sizes of the 589 savings banks varies considerably with the largest one based in Hamburg (Hamburger Sparkasse). Branching networks are similarly varied.

Each state in the Federal Republic has a Landesbank which acts as a giro institution for the savings banks active in the state and provides other services. At a national level the Deutsche Girozentrale is the savings banks' central organisation, although each savings bank is an independent entity — sometimes fiercely so. The Landesbanken are usually jointly owned by the state savings bank associations and the state governments. Some of the Landesbanken are amongst the largest institutions in the country. The Westdeutsche (WestLB), Bayerische and Norddeutsche Landesbanken are giant concerns active in international markets as well as in West Germany. The WestLB, for instance, is the country's third largest banking group (after the Deutsche and Dresdner Banks).

Alongside the public sector savings banks there exist other public financial institutions, particularly mortgage banks but also insurance companies and Bausparkassen. Once again most of these other institutions are partially owned by, and operate within the jurisdiction of, specific states. There is considerable co-operation between public sector financial institutions. A local savings bank as a result can offer its customers a package of financial services by drawing on the products and resources of other public financial institutions. Savings banks were, in fact, the first type of bank to offer a wide range of retail financial services via their branch networks.

There have been mergers between savings banks, with the number falling by about a third between 1957 and 1987. Several Landesbanken have disappeared in a similar way. In 1988, for example, two of the largest (WestLB and Helaba — the latter is based in Hessen) entered unsuccessful merger talks that would have created the country's second largest bank — although the talks did lead to the Hessen government selling its share holding of Helaba to the state's association of savings banks giving it full ownership. Two other smaller Landesbanken, however, did succeed in merging in that year. Greater talk of further restructuring existed in the late-1980s than for many years for reasons that are considered in Section 8.5.

In the decades after the foundation of the Federal Republic, savings banks benefited from the weak competition they faced for personal sector savings, which helped them expand to become the largest banking sector. Their growth was aided by rising personal sector incomes and a high propensity to save. State subsidies on contractual savings schemes, although not specifically directed towards them, also encouraged their growth because they were the major savings deposit-taking institutions.

Competition between savings banks is limited, partly because of their geographical spread. But interest rate competition is restricted through the practice of fixing interest rates on deposits in relation to guidelines set by the Association of Savings Banks and Girobanks (OECD, 1986).

Savings banks' investments are directed towards small business and the personal sector. About half their assets are housing loans, which are usually lent to individual homeowners. Loans carry variable interest rates and so are unattractive to corporate investors in rental housing. Retail funded mortgage sources may frequently give cheaper initial interest rates than the fixed rates offered by mortgage banks, but they contain an unacceptable interest rate risk for corporate mortgage borrowers. With rising inflation, moreover, they may also be more expensive over the full period of a loan.

Impetus for change within the savings bank sector has been driven by increased competition in retail financial services from the early 1970s onwards — much of it stemming from the commercial banks and credit co-operatives. In the late 1980s extra pressure from the commercial banks was also being applied in the market for the banking services of small businesses: a sphere where the savings banks have traditionally been predominant. The savings banks in turn are trying to expand in the domains controlled by the commercial banks. The Landesbanken, in particular, are trying to increase their wholesale and international banking activities. The costs of computer systems have been another recent stimulus to restructuring.

Commercial banks

Until the end of the 1960s commercial banks concentrated on lending to trade and industry. Because of this specialisation their share in the banking business declined substantially during the 1950s and 1960s, as industry was needing less external capital and the personal sector was becoming of greater importance (EAG, 1981). The decline in market share was most significant for the three big banks, so they tried to reverse the trend by increasing their involvement in personal sector finance and through aggressive entry into the mortgage market.

Expansion into personal sector financial services required a major attack on the hold that the savings banks had on the personal savings market. This necessitated attempts to increase the limited number of households holding current accounts at the commercial banks. To achieve this branching networks were extended. The big banks were also amongst the strongest supporters of interest rate decontrol which came into effect in 1967. The introduction of VAT in 1968 helped the commercial banks as it took away some of the tax privileges enjoyed by the public and co-operative banking sector (Schnitzer 1972; Francke and Hudson, 1984). By the late 1960s the commercial banks' competitive position in the market for personal savings had much improved. But expansion in the personal sector generated competitive responses with other types of bank increasing their branching networks and services to avoid losing market share. The big banks had the advantage of the prestige associated with having an account with them, but the majority of accounts are still held with the savings banks and credit co-operatives. Commercial banks, in particular, have had limited success in the savings field. They still have only a 14 per cent share of savings deposits and 15 per cent of bank savings bonds (Table 8.3).

Commercial banks' business in the mortgage market, especially that of the big banks, grew significantly in the early 1970s. They then acquired, through a complex set of share interchanges, majority shares in most of the private mortgage banks. Commercial banks from the 1950s onwards had bought mortgage bank shares as investments, but the big banks had failed to acquire majority stakes. This changed when in the early 1970s the three big banks actually exchanged their shares so that they all gained control over at least one mortgage bank. At the same time this share exchange activity received considerable press publicity and came to be known as the mortgage bank carousel. After acquisition by the commercial banks the mortgage banks continued to operate as relatively independent subsidiaries retaining their own identities and offices.

The acquisition of mortgage banks proved highly profitable for the commercial banks up to the late 1970s. In a similar way to the public banking sector they could now offer a full mortgage service to their clients. First mortgages were put together by the mortgage banks which were complemented by second mortgages advanced by the commercial banks. In this way the commercial banks not only profited from the business of their mortgage banks but could at the same time develop a new stake in housing finance through offering second mortgages. As was noted earlier, the commercial banks increased their second mortgage business considerably during the 1970s (see Table 8.5).

Customers for the commercial banks' mortgage products came from the traditional higher income clientele. Commercial banks were active in the 1970s in the development in the mortgage field of what is known as the Bauherren model, as a way of increasing their mortgage business with high income households by maximising the housing-related tax relief and subsidies available for personal investors in the higher tax brackets.

Co-operative banks

Co-operative banking in Europe has a long established tradition. In Britain the Co-operative Bank is a relatively small institution, but in other western European countries co-operative banks play a far greater role. The Credit Agricole is France's largest bank, Rabo Bank in the Netherlands is the third largest; whilst Spain and Italy have significant but fragmented co-operative banking sectors. The largest co-operative banking sector in terms of assets, however, is in West Germany. The 3,500 credit co-operatives and their central institutions undertake 17 per cent of total banking business. With almost 19,500 bank offices they surpass the savings banks by about a thousand offices to have the largest physical presence in the West German banking system — although in total credit, co-operatives have less than half the business of the savings banks (Tables 8.1 and 8.4).

Co-operative banks differ in ownership from the savings banks. Whilst the latter are owned by local and regional governments, the co-operative banks are owned by their depositors — in a similar fashion to the mutual thrifts and building societies in the USA and Britain. They originated as general banks from within two agrarian self-help movements, one of which catered for small artisans whose livelihoods were threatened by industrialisation (Volksbanken) and one which aimed to assist poor farmers (Raiffaisenbanken). The two groups finally merged in 1972.

Like the savings banks, credit co-operatives have a three-tier structure. Individual co-operatives rely on regional institutions for general banking and clearing facilities and there is a central institution — the Deutsche Genossenschaftsbank (DG bank). Traditionally the role of the DG bank was to undertake certain co-ordinating and general banking functions and to place excess liquidity in the co-operative system on the money market. But, in the 1980s, the role of the DG bank has expanded considerably and it is playing a central role in restructuring the co-operative sector.

The number of independent co-operatives has shrunk by more than two-thirds over the past thirty years, yet there are still six times as many as there are savings banks. In contrast to the savings banks, however, the regional institutions of the credit co-operatives have declined considerably in number as well — falling from nineteen in 1957 to only six in 1988. In part the decline results from the merger of the two co-operative movements in 1972. But the reduction may also reflect the absence of local state ownership — as local pride and other political factors may have inhibited mergers amongst the Landesbanken. In the late 1980s the top tier of the co-operative movement, the DG bank, is trying to absorb the remaining middle tier institutions into it to make the country's second largest bank. According to a press interview with DG bank's chief executive, two of the regional banks are in favour of merger and so are going ahead with it whilst two others are totally opposed (*Financial Times*, 28 April 1989). It is interesting to note that in the co-operative sector the top tier institution is making the running in the restructuring of the sector, whereas amongst the savings banks it is the middle tier of Landesbanken that is instigating mergers and international expansion. This illustrates that ownership structures have important influences on competitive responses, and that the ownership differences that matter are not simply the equity/non-equity divide.

The funds of credit co-operatives are drawn mostly from personal bank accounts and savings. They traditionally specialise in lending to agricultural producers and small, rurally-based artisans. Credit co-operatives, however, face similar restrictions to the savings banks. They cannot issue bonds and are thus primarily restricted to attracting retail funds. Until 1974 co-operative banks were confined to lending to their own members, which made them the nearest of German general banks to a pure closed system of deposit-taking and lending within a specific group of households and small enterprises. Like the savings banks, competition between credit co-operatives is limited by their geographical spread and by the practice of offering deposit interest rates fixed by the Association of Industries and Agricultural Co-operatives.

Credit co-operatives have traditionally been the strongest competitors for the savings banks in their deposit-taking and lending activities. A spatial division of the market tended to exist between credit co-operatives and savings banks — with savings banks servicing the towns and credit co-operatives the rural areas. Yet both banking sectors served a similar clientele of middle and lower income households.

Prior to the late 1960s housing loans did not belong to the mainstream business of the credit co-operatives. Then during the 1970s they expanded their mortgage lending in a way similar to the commercial banks. Their central bank, the Deutsche Genossenschaftsbank, acquired the largest private mortgage bank and also gained control of a smaller one. Second mortgage lending was increased at the same time. So, like any other banking sector, they were able to offer clients a full mortgage loan package. The traditional rural base of the credit co-operatives helped them to raise their mortgage business through the financing of one-family housebuilding.

Mortgage banks

The mortgage banks used to be the largest issuers of first mortgages but their overall importance has diminished since the mid-1970s. They differ from the US mortgage banks which operate as brokers — originating loans and then selling them on. West German mortgage banks hold mortgage portfolios and issue bonds in their own name to fund their lending.

The origin of the mortgage bond system goes back to the large landowners of eighteenth century Prussia who, after a war with Austria, were looking for ways of financing the rebuilding of the agricultural sector. Money was raised through bonds issued by associations the landowners formed, with the associations collectively guaranteeing the debt paper. The guarantee and the use of landed property as the ultimate security for the bonds ensured the success of the flotations on the primitive capital markets existing then. The mortgage bond system grew rapidly and spread to other European countries, but never took off in Britain or the USA (Pleyer and Bellinger, 1981; Martens, 1985). With the creation of the Credit Foncier in France in 1852, the mutual mortgage bond system was for the first time transformed into a banking system — with mortgage banks acting as general financial intermediaries between borrowers and lenders, rather than as organisations whose object is to facilitate borrowing for their members.

Mortgage banks specialise in mortgage and municipal bonds. The former are debt papers secured by urban real estate and agricultural land and buildings, and the latter are debt papers guaranteed by public authorities. Municipal bonds form an important and, until the mid-1980s, a growing part of the business of West German mortgage banks.

Mortgage banks have a considerable advantage over other types of bank in the bond market as the reserve/capital adequacy ratios required of them by the monetary authorities are far less than for other types of financial institution. This privilege has given them overwhelming dominance in the bond market. Similar privileges exist for specialist banks lending mortgages for activities like shipping (classified under 'other banks' in Table 8.3). In general, mortgage banks are restricted in the spheres in which they can operate, although two banks have a long-standing privilege to combine commercial banking with mortgage bond business. They are the Bayerische Hypotheken und Wechsel Bank (West Germany's largest property lending bank with an expanding international presence) and the Bayerische Vereinsbank. These two banks are classified as regional commercial banks in the official statistics.

Mortgage banks can only use their mortgage bonds to finance first mortgages, and first mortgages are restricted to 60 per cent of a property's value. These restrictions both encourage the existence of a second mortgage market and effectively restricted mortgage banks' role within it. Because mortgage banks have to use other sources of funds to advance second mortgages, and they do not have access to cheap sources of retail funds, they were effectively excluded from the growing second mortgage market in the 1970s. In 1983 their market share in second mortgages was still less than 4 per cent.

Mortgage banks, conversely, complement the activities of institutions that wish to enter the second mortgage market using their own cheap sources of retail funds. This explains the takeover of all the private mortgage banks in the early 1970s, when a number of institutions — particularly the commercial banks and credit co-operatives — earmarked the second mortgage market as a means of expanding their retail lending. The savings banks as traditional first mortgage lenders had less need of mortgage bank link-ups. They could co-operate with public sector mortgage banks to offer fixed interest first mortgages as part of mortgage packages when desired, but generally have not encouraged the public sector mortgage banks to move into the individual homeowner sector.

Mortgage banks are not permitted to have any interest rate exposure, so mortgage bonds are matched in their interest rate and maturities with the pools of current mortgage offers they are financing. The interest rates are fixed, and the length of the mortgage offered depends on the terms of the bond issued. Mortgage banks offer annuity loans and, like all long-term mortgage loans in West Germany, the amortisation rate of these loans is fixed at 1 per cent. The precise repayment period, therefore, depends on the interest rate at the time the loan is being arranged.

The repayment period usually used to be twenty to thirty years, but this period has reduced substantially in recent years. Most mortgages are now of less than ten years in duration, although longer times are possible. Their short duration, in contrast to British and American practice, may not create the same difficulties it would in the latter two countries. A number of reasons can be suggested for this although in practice they might be of varying relevance. Other mortgage sources exist and larger corporations rather than individuals use these instruments. Furthermore, when individuals contemplate the use of a mortgage bank as part of their mortgage package, the generally higher average age of the time of first-time house purchase by individual homeowners means that they do not necessarily require very long-term loans and may be happy to roll over the debt in new mortgage bank borrowings — especially if they expect nominal interest rates to fall in the medium-term. Individual homeowner purchasers, in addition, may not simply be owner-occupiers but private landlords or a mix of the two. So financial needs are distinct in West Germany's housing market from those in Britain and the USA.

Individual homeowners have been of importance to the mortgage banks only since the 1970s. The home loan markets previously served by the mortgage banks consisted mainly of rental housing, where they lent to the larger public and private housing developers. As mortgage banks usually negotiated with relatively few large borrowers and funded their advances through the capital markets their overheads were low. They needed a branch network neither to attract clients nor to collect funds. Even with the growing importance of individual homeowners, their branching networks have grown only slightly as loans are made through the branches of their parent organisations' retail banks. The interest rate spread on which mortgage banks operate as a result of their low overheads is low — around 0.5 per cent between that on the mortgages they offer and the bonds they issue, compared to savings banks' roughly 3 per cent average spread.

Amongst the mortgage banks, the fortunes of the public (Realkreditanstalt) and the private (Hypotheken bank) ones has varied. Two-thirds of the market share of the mortgage banks in 1970 was taken by the public mortgage banks. This was largely the result of the expansion of social housebuilding during the 1950s and the fact that most public investment at that time was allocated via public institutions. Private mortgage banks became more important during the 1960s with the recovery of the private housebuilding market. As a sector, mortgage banks have lost ground over the past fifteen years, and much of the decline has been concentrated in the public sector.

The reduced market share of the mortgage banks has resulted from a combination of three developments: interest rate volatility, the changing nature of the housing market, and their integration with the universal banks.

Mortgage banking works best in an environment of low inflation and stable interest rates, so economic developments since the early 1970s have not favoured it. Table 8.7 gives details of the shortening repayment term structure of mortgage bonds mentioned earlier. As can be seen, it changed dramatically between 1970 and 1983. In the 1960s most mortgage bonds had repayment terms of twenty-five years or longer, whereas by the beginning of the 1980s short-term repayment periods predominated. Strong fluctuations in interest rates during the 1970s contributed to the reduction, with two cycles and peaks in 1973−4 and 1980−1. The business of mortgage banks is particularly affected by interest rate volatility. In periods of volatile interest rate levels, mortgage banks are caught between the interests of investors and borrowers. When interest rates are rising but expected to fall again in the future, borrowers are unwilling to commit themselves to long-term, high fixed interest rate loans. When rates are falling, but expected to rise again, investors are less likely to invest in bonds for fear of the subsequent capital loss. The matching of the requirements of investors and borrowers can consequently be achieved only by using much shorter-dated bonds. Even when the yield gap turns negative, making mortgage bond fixed-interest terms more attractive than retail financed ones, the expectation of subsequent falls in interest rates makes fixed-interest loans unattractive to borrowers. In general, because of the interest rate fixing practices of retail banks in West Germany, the initial rates offered on variable loans are lower than those on mortgage bank fixed-interest loans. Inflationary expectations may still tip the balance for some individuals in favour of the

Table 8.7 Repayment periods of debt papers issued by private mortgage banks, 1969–83

Period (yr)	1969	1979	1980	1983
1–4	1.4	17.1	31.7	43.0
4–8	5.1	47.3	47.9	43.0
8–10	0.3	6.4	4.0	5.0
10–15	2.4	28.6	16.4	9.0
15+	90.8	0.6	—	—

Source: Verband Deutscher Hypothenbanken e.V (1984) *Geschäftsbericht 1983*, Bonn.

fixed-interest loans, but the interest rate advantage of variable loans helps to explain the declining role of the mortgage banks.

One consequence of the shorter redemption periods of bonds and mortgages has been an increase in the operating costs of the mortgage banks. Overhead costs have risen as both bonds and mortgages need to be renegotiated more often. The result has been a further squeeze on their profit margins.

Associated with periods of greater interest rate volatility have been the onset of housing market slumps, which depressed the overall demand for mortgages, particularly in the areas in which the mortgage banks operate. Investment in 'self-build' housing is said to be less influenced by short-term market fluctuations (Ball *et al.*, 1986), but that is the market segment covered by the savings banks (and to an extent the credit co-operatives) rather than the mortgage banks. The housebuilding slump of the mid-1970s marked the beginning of a long-term decline in large-scale housing developments and the building activities of corporate investors. The run-down of social housebuilding hit the public sector mortgage banks especially badly.

Whilst interest rate movements and the housing market have both over the long-term moved against the mortgage banks, they, in addition, have faced greater competition from other mortgage lenders. The integration of mortgage banks in the universal banking system meant that they lost their ability to compete independently, although integration did enable them to use the branching network of the universal banks to reach individual clients. During the first phase of integration, until the mid-1970s, universal banks used the mortgage banks as a vehicle to enter the then very profitable area of housing finance. But since the late 1970s universal banks have increasingly 'invaded' the traditional lending areas of mortgage banks. They frequently have curtailed the housing loans refinanced by mortgage bonds to below the 60 per cent limit in the packages that are put together. Things have been most difficult for the public sector mortgage banks because savings banks already dominated the issuing of first mortgages to individual housebuyers and so wanted to restrict the expansion of public mortgage banks into this area. But even if mortgage banks had remained independent, it is difficult to see how they could have improved their position any further in the market for individual household mortgages when their universal bank competitors can fund variable rate mortgages from very cheap retail funds. Only at specific times have the yield curve and consumer expectations about inflation and interest rates benefited them.

The results of these interlinked adverse movements for mortgage banks can be seen in the trend of net sales of mortgage bonds from 1971 to 1988 (Figure 8.1). It can be seen that they fluctuated considerably during the 1970s and early 1980s with the state of the economy and the housing market; but, in real terms, there was a long-term downward trend. Since 1983 net sales have plummeted and were increasingly negative from 1986 to 1988 (i.e. redemptions were far greater than sales).

The other area of business for the mortgage banks is public sector bonds. During the late 1970s, local, regional and central governments all substantially increased their borrowings from the bond market (Table 8.8). So, whilst the share of the bond market taken by mortgage bonds declined substantially, that of the public sector as a whole increased. This shift particularly benefited the public sector mortgage banks, as communal bonds were channelled through them. Yet, even this market has been a declining one for the mortgage banks in the mid- to late-1980s, with public expenditure cuts reducing the role of communal bonds and central government adopting a strategy of placing its bonds directly rather than through financial intermediaries. About 40 per cent of outstanding bonds are held by the banking system (the figure was 37 per cent, for example, in 1985). Savings banks are the principal purchasers, followed by the credit co-operatives, the Girozentralen and the commercial banks. With such holders' additional financial intermediation is perhaps unnecessary.

Given the problems mortgage banks have faced in their main lines of business since the late 1970s, it may be the case that they still recognisably exist only because of their special regulatory privileges.

Bausparkassen

The Bausparkassen were founded in the 1920s to encourage collective savings schemes for individual housebuilding. Everyone who saves is eventually entitled to borrow, with the current savings of some members financing the borrowings of others. The Bausparkassen scheme is consequently in principle self-contained — a 'closed' system as it is known in Germany.

The formality of the saving and borrowing process is that individuals take out a savings contract with a Bausparkasse. The contract stipulates an agreed

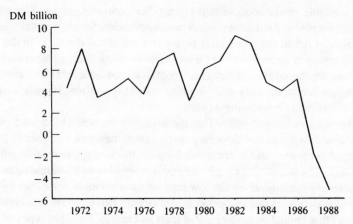

Source: *Monthly Report of the Deutsche Bundesbank*, various dates.

Figure 8.1 Net mortgage bond sales in West Germany, 1970–88

Table 8.8 Issuers' shares of outstanding bonds, 1974–88

	Mortgage bonds (%)	Communal bonds (%)	Public bonds (%)	Other bonds (%)	Total (DM billion)[a]
1974	26	32	20	22	267.9
1976	22	36	23	19	365.2
1978	16	35	26	22	461.5
1980	19	37	24	20	548.6
1982	17	40	23	20	690.3
1984	16	39	27	19	850.0
1986	14	35	32	18	1,017.7
1988	12	32	38	18	1,151.6

[a] Nominal value.

Source: *Monthly Report of the Deutsche Bundesbank*.

amount that will be advanced by the Bausparkasse to the individual at some future date. The person then deposits with the Bausparkasse an agreed flow of savings each year, the amount of which is calculated as a proportion of the agreed future advance (usually the annual savings are around 5 per cent of the advance). A fixed, low rate of interest is paid on those savings and credited to the saver's account. Once a sum equivalent to 40 to 50 per cent of the advance has been deposited, the saver is eligible to receive the advance — the loan amount being the difference between the advance and the savings accumulated. The advance is made, however, only when the Bausparkasse has the available funds accumulated from other contracts, as the Bausparkasse cannot borrow to fund its savings contract advances. Savers generally get their advance seven to ten years after taking out the initial contract. In the closed Bausparkassen system, savings deposits must equal loan advances minus an amount for liquidity and reserves (contracts can be cancelled early). Like mortgage banks, the only other housing market specialists, Bausparkassen are not allowed any borrowing exposure.

The rates of interest offered on the savings contracts of 2.5−4.5 per cent bear little relation to contemporary market rates; neither consequently do those charged on loans, which are a mark-up on the savings rate of usually 2−3 per cent. The low savings imply substantial negative real interest rates during inflationary periods. Even the low interest rates on loans are offset by a high annual amortisation rate of 7 per cent. This means that loans are repaid relatively fast, so that annual outgoings are at least as great as for other types of higher interest borrowing.

Bausparkassen savers benefit from state subsidies — which from 1952 to 1972 were particularly generous and added 25−35 per cent to the sum saved — and the interest paid on savings deposits is partially tax-exempt. State subsidies greatly improve the attractiveness of the Bausparkasse principle. Since 1972, however, the savings bonuses have been reduced considerably and a failure to raise the income-related limits on their availability has excluded progressively more households from eligibility. But the subsidies did help to make Bausparkassen savings contracts a popular savings medium in West Germany, and even at their lower rates they continue to do so. Many households have at least one Bausparkassen account. The number of accounts reached a peak in the early 1980s when 24 million contracts were outstanding. Most savings contracts are arranged through the offices of banks (especially with the public sector ones) or via the Bausparkassen's vast army of door-to-door sales agents and staff (especially with the private ones). The Bausparkassen themselves have few offices (Table 8.9).

Not all Bausparkassen contract savings schemes take the standard form described above. They are now being promoted as a means of repaying endowment mortgages and general bank loans as well, especially for those households still eligible for the state-funded savings premiums.

Bausparkassen building loans finance the second mortgage zone of 60−80 per cent of a property's value. This is because legally Bausparkassen loans have only second charge on a property and they cannot generally lend above 80 per cent of a property's value. Households have to find the remaining 20 per cent of the house price from their own savings or other borrowings. People do not necessarily have to wait for Bausparkassen savings contracts to become available before purchase as they can usually borrow an interim loan from the Bausparkasse or another financial institution until their Bausparkasse loan becomes available, using it as security.

Table 8.9 Bausparkassen activity, 1974–88

	1974	1978	1982	1984	1986	1987	1988
Number of associations	30	30	32	31	29	29	29
Loans under savings contracts (DM billion)	49	70	104	109	106	104	97
New contracts entered into ('000s)	60	94	71	75	82	86	101
Savings accounts deposits (gross, DM billion)	22	27	28	25	23	24	25
Housing bonuses received (DM billion)	3.1	1.9	2.0	0.9	0.9	0.9	0.9

Source: *Monthly Report of the Deutsche Bundesbank.*

Table 8.10 shows the consolidated accounts of the Bausparkassen. Around three-quarters of their income comes from savings contracts. Most lending is associated with contract loans, although interim and bridging loans are an important part of their business.

The attractiveness of Bausparkassen contracts has depended on state subsidies, inflation and interest rates. From the mid-1970s onwards, Bausparkassen schemes became less attractive. State savings subsidies were reduced and other sources of second mortgages grew. The long savings periods at low rates of interest began to look less attractive when other nominal rates were rising. General price inflation and house price inflation in particular made

Table 8.10 Bausparkassen finances, 1988

Liabilities	DM billion	%	Assets	DM billion	%
Savings deposits	115.6	74	Loans under savings contracts	97.8	62
Deposits and borrowing from banks	15.7	10	Interim, bridging and other building loans	33.8	22
Sight and time deps, non-bank borrowing	5.9	4	Lending to banks	19.8	13
Bearer bonds	2.7	2	Securities	2.1	1
Capital incl. reserves	8.2	5			
Balance sheet total	156.6	100		156.6	100

Note: certain minor items excluded thus individual items do not add up to balance sheet total.

Source: *Monthly Report of the Deutsche Bundesbank.*

the long savings period onerous. Bausparkassen contracts taken out in the years prior to house price booms were even less likely to fill up the 60—80 per cent slot when prices continued to rise. Such hedging against house price rises may help to explain why households take out multiple Bausparkassen contracts, although the savings subsidies and tax benefits may also explain them.

When economic circumstances move against Bausparkassen saving, less money is put into savings contracts overall, so people have to wait longer for their offer of a Bausparkassen loan as there are fewer funds in the scheme to go around. During the extra waiting period, inflation continues to erode the real value of the savings and the promised cheap loan. Despite these problems, however, the Bausparkassen managed to expand their turnover for much of the 1970s and early 1980s, although real growth was limited. In the late 1980s, declining inflation and low interest rates on other savings media made the schemes more attractive again.

The existence of the Bausparkassen, their encouragement by governments and their popularity helps to explain the 'package' arrangement of German mortgage finance. The mortgage package also induces Bausparkassen to consolidate links with other financial institutions and it encourages other institutions to set up their own Bausparkassen. The various types of financial institution can compete to offer households the best package to suit their needs — from the resources of the specialist institutions they own or with which they have links — whereas prior to the 1970s households would usually assemble their own packages. Borrowers may be only vaguely aware of the constituents of the loan packages drawn up for them.

The public Bausparkassen are integrated into the savings bank system. They are often departments of the Landesbanken, and so are generally known as Landesbausparkassen. The private ones have varied ownership. In 1983, the largest was owned by the trade unions, the second by the co-operative banks, the third was a private company and the next four were owned mainly by insurance companies. One of the big banks — the Dresdner — had a 50 per cent shareholding of the fourth largest (Boleat, 1985).

Wüstenrot, the only large private Bausparkasse that is independent, has increasingly diversified into other financial activities. To avoid legal restrictions on Bausparkassen owning subsidiaries it set up a holding company structure. Within the holding company is the Bausparkasse, a bank, an insurance company and a real estate company (the latter was set up in conjunction with the Deutsche Bank) (Schäfer *et al.*, 1986). It is expanding its branch network — and through its holding company structure increasingly takes on the guise of a universal bank.

In the late 1980s interest in the Bausparkassen system was growing amongst the financial institutions. All of the big three banks set up their own Bausparkasse in a process reminiscent of the mortgage bank carousel of the early 1970s. The Deutsche Bank set up its own Bausparkasse, forming an alliance with a Swiss insurance company (Zurich Insurance) with one thousand sales staff and agents active in West Germany. Dresdner Bank sold its previous shareholding in a Bausparkasse to set up its own one — and the Commerzbank subsequently bought a major share stake in the Bausparkasse Dresdner had abandoned (*Financial Times*, 3 December 1988).

Interest grew because of the strategy of Allfinanz, especially the growing integration of the retail banking and insurance spheres, and the fact that the salesforces of Bausparkassen visit people at home and could sell them a variety of other financial products as well as contract savings schemes. Door-to-door salesforces are also a cheaper way of expanding customer contact than expensive branch offices in an already saturated branching system.

8.5 Allfinanz, institutional restructuring and price competition

West Germany's complex mortgage finance system of retail savings banks, capital market mortgage banks and Bausparkassen has over the past twenty years metamorphosed into part of an overall retail finance system based on a distinct ownership pattern rather than financial function. Universal banking has been redefined as Allfinanz but the underlying principle is the same — large financial institutions offering a wide range of wholesale and retail financial services under one roof. Allfinanz emphasises the fact that the large institutions are moving away from aiming simply to provide all banking services to a desire to provide all other financial services as well, which includes moves into pensions and insurance.

Ownership structures have determined the precise evolution of the Allfinanz process. The distinction between the commercial, public sector and co-operative banks is important and affects the pattern of institutional change. In addition, the major insurance companies are reacting to invasion of their territory. Once previously independent institutions are drawn into a particular Allfinanz ownership structure they are usually kept identifiably functionally separate. This is done for marketing reasons and so that they can continue to enjoy their regulatory privileges — like the low reserve requirements of the mortgage banks, and the Bausparkassen's reserve, taxation and savings subsidy advantages.

Ownership is not the only factor affecting the realignments. German banks are specifically excluded from some of the strongest provisions of the anti-trust act on mergers and cartels. They have greater leeway than other industries, therefore, not only in acquisitions but also in forming marketing arrangements, including the many they have with insurance companies. Often these arrangements are cemented through cross-shareholdings. When one major institution decides to expand into a new area they have a variety of ownership and co-operation options open to them. Conversely, shifts of strategy by one or more of the major institutions lead to reorderings of the complex network of marketing agreements.

The effects of the distinct types of ownership and the marketing arrangements on the process of financial restructuring can be illustrated with a few examples.

Deutsche Bank, West Germany's largest bank, has been one of the main leaders in the Allfinanz process. It has put considerable emphasis on retail financial services, and on the use of housing finance as a means of selling a variety of financial products. In its expansion it has used its own financial independence and strength to set up major new subsidiaries in areas like life insurance and Bausparkassen. In moving into these areas, it was forced to abandon previous 'cosy' relationships with the insurance companies, including Allianz, Europe's largest insurance company. The Allianz has responded to the double loss of its marketing links with Deutsche and the advent of a new insurance competitor by setting up a joint marketing agreement with Dresdner, the second biggest bank. The agreement covers much of populous central Germany. In addition, Allianz has market pacts in Bavaria with the region's co-operative banks and the commercial bank, Bayerische Hypotheken und Weschel Bank, in which it has a 23 per cent share stake. That Bavarian bank itself has a 25 per cent stake in a Hamburg bank, with which Allianz is also likely to make a marketing agreement giving it new marketing arrangements throughout the country (*Financial Times*, 2 March 1989).

The Allfinanz process is also taking root amongst the public sector banks. The smaller savings banks are said to be losing some of their small- to medium-sized corporate customers to the commercial banks, which are making inroads through marketing their ability to set up international financial deals. Consequently, part of the regrouping is a response to that threat, as size is important in international wholesale banking. But again the retail side is a major impetus. The Hessische Landesbank (Helaba) after its failed merger with the West Deutsche Landesbank, discussed earlier, negotiated with the region's savings banks to form a more closely co-operating network. This followed the decision of the Hessen state government to sell its stake in Helaba and a public sector insurance company to the state's savings banks (*Financial Times*, 25 May 1989). Here, negotiation and co-operation are paramount because of the need to win the agreement of enterprises that cannot be taken over through share purchases. One result has been said to be a general weakening of the position of the public banking sector, but such a public pronouncement could itself be part of the intra-public bank negotiations. A similar process of negotiation, although spurred on by a different set of pressures, is occurring in the co-operative banking sector, as is described in the section on the credit co-operatives above.

The reasons for the changes in the structure of retail financial services, both in the move to Allfinanz and the organisational regroupings, seem over-whelmingly to be driven by marketing rather than production cost considerations. Market profiles are being shifted and expanded in a process of competitive interaction. Scale or scope economies do not seem to be a central issue. There may, in fact, be inefficiencies in the Allfinanz process. The wider the range of complex retail financial services sold by staff the greater is the training and skill they require. There must be doubts as to whether, for example, large door-to-door salesforces, often recruited on a commission basis, can achieve a broad competence in all of the products they sell. It is worth remembering in this context the criticism that the financial institutions have received in the debate over mortgage defaults, where they have been attacked for 'heavy selling' and over the lack of awareness by some consumers of the implications of the mortgage packages to which they committed themselves (Potter and Drevermann, 1988).

West German financial institutions have been active in forging international retail banking links as well as reordering their domestic ones, particularly with institutions in other countries of the European Community. After 1992, each country in the European Community will have to open its financial markets to the products of the financial intermediaries of other Community countries. German banks have extended their domestic practice of intercompany agreements to the European level, particularly in France and Spain which have rapidly growing, but currently protected, financial services markets. Part of the reason is defensive as West Germany's protections will be eroded after 1992 as well.

Weak price competition is one factor that may help to explain German financial institutions' concern with gaining positions across a wide range of product markets, and the way they all seem to develop large branching and sales networks and giant organisational pyramids in order to achieve them. Furthermore, they tend to emphasise the quality of their service in contrast to that of their competitors.

A key area in which price competition is limited is in deposit-taking. This is especially important in Germany as so much financial intermediation is directed towards the collection of deposits from the personal sector for subsequently lending on. The spreads the financial institutions achieve in this process is consequently the major determinant of their profitability and of the way in which they develop.

Table 8.11 shows a selection of retail and wholesale interest rates in West Germany at the beginning of 1989. It can be seen that the difference between the rates offered on retail deposits and on wholesale money market and capital market interest rates is considerable. Furthermore, to earn more than a desultory real interest rate retail deposits have to be tied up for a number of years. The options for the small investor are limited. Equities in particular offer low yields, even before brokerage commissions.

Table 8.11 Selected average retail interest rates, December 1988

	Average (%)	Spread (%)
Short-term borrowing		
Current account credit	8.75	7.25–10.25
Instalment credit	10.04	9.09–11.24
Mortgages		
Variable interest rate	6.69	6.06–7.82
Fixed interest rate		
For 2 yr	6.93	6.38–7.82
For 5 yr	7.07	6.66–7.51
For 10 yr	7.58	7.39–8.02
Savings		
Savings deposits		
Statutory notice	2.01	2.00–2.50
12 months' notice	2.77	2.50–3.50
4 years' notice	3.97	3.75–4.50
Time deposits (1–3 months)		
Less than DM 100,000	3.71	3.00–4.35
DM 100,000–1 million	4.25	3.50–4.80
Bank savings bonds (4 yr maturity)	5.48	5.00–5.75
Special savings facilities		
1 yr lump sum contract	4.19	3.75–4.75
7 yr instalment with one-off bonus	5.06	5.03–5.43

Note:
Annual rate of inflation: 1.3%
Money market rates (3 month funds): 5.65% (ave.) 5.35–6.00% (spread)
Mortgage bond yield: 6.5%
Dividend yield on equities:
  Excluding tax credit: 2.23%
  Including tax credit: 3.48%

Source: *Monthly Report of the Deutsche Bundesbank.*

Interest rate leap-frogging on retail deposits and the competing away of restrictions on access to them, which occurred both in the USA and Britain during the 1980s, has not taken place in West Germany. Instead the profitability of financial intermediation via the collection of retail deposits has never been in question. As banks lend most of the money deposited with them on a long-term basis, the profitability of their operations is affected by shifts in the yield curve. Profits grow as long rates rise above short ones and decline as the yield gap narrows. But banks are partly shielded against these adverse consequences of shifts in the yield curve because their retail customers rarely, if ever, receive a rate equivalent to wholesale money market rates. So losses are rare for the banks, unless they make disastrous investment mistakes, which some of the smaller ones have done. In contrast to the US banks, German ones experienced an upward trend in their interest rate margins and their profitability (as measured by the return earned on their assets) from the late 1960s through to the mid-1980s (OECD, 1986). The same OECD report then goes on to imply that substantial competitive pressure does exist in German banking but counter-evidence can also be easily mustered as the following points indicate.

One reason that the rates on retail savings are relatively poor is that the Bundesbank does not allow certain financial instruments to be marketed, including securities of less than one year's duration which would be close substitutes for bank deposits. Such instruments would be similar to US money market funds, and open competition would force them to be priced at wholesale money market rates or even higher. The justification for the ban is the effect of them on monetary control, and since 1980 there has been an informal agreement under which a list of financial instruments is proscribed (OECD, 1986). Another factor is the practice of fixing interest rates by the savings and co-operative banks. Even if the rates are not strongly adhered to, they send out a signal to competitors and they dampen interest rate leap-frogging in a similar way to the consequences of the British building societies' cartel prior to the early 1980s.

The low returns offered on personal bank deposits and the ability to sell a wide variety of retail financial products means that retail customers are vital to banking profitability. Estimates have suggested that the commercial banks derive three-quarters of their profits from individual account-holders (management consultants McKinsey, quoted in *Financial Times*, 7 May 1989). The profitability of retail deposit-taking and limited price competition over it helps to explain the enormous number of branch offices in the German banking system. Such a large number does not indicate an efficient retail banking structure, yet in the battle for markets where non-price competition is the rule, each of the financial majors has to maintain a strong presence for fear of losing market share. The smaller companies that cannot do so find their position squeezed.

The Bundesbank and the West Germany government presumably accept the limited price competition, the interlocking marketing arrangements and the expansion of the major banking groups as the price to be paid for easy monetary control and the stability of the financial system. Some political parties like the liberal FDP, however, have started campaigns against the power of the banks in the German economy. It might also be the case that the West German economy has experienced lower interest rates because of the structure and operation of the retail financial system. In a country with such high personal sector savings, the low interest rates paid to most savers imply a major redistribution of income away from them in favour of borrowers and the banks that act as intermediaries and price-makers in the process. Although the ultimate consequences have to be qualified if savers subsequently gain from second-round effects because lower borrowing costs induce higher investment and greater long-term growth. The ability of the banks to collect cheap retail deposits and channel them through to industry may have been of far greater benefit to West German companies in the post-war era than the much discussed and more visible existence of bankers on their boards of directors and the large shareholdings they control (Cable, 1985; Mayer, 1988).

It is interesting to speculate that the development of a European Communitywide financial market will have profound effects on the way in which the West German retail banking system operates. As yet, though, there is insufficient information about the structure of that market and the regulatory rules under which it will operate to enable any considered judgement of the effects to be made. The other big imponderable for the West German financial system is, of course, current developments in relations between East and West Germany. The consequences of greater integration are likely to be profound, but at the time of writing the outcomes are unclear.

9

The consequences of the mortgage finance revolution

This concluding chapter will draw together some of the features of the retail finance systems of the three countries surveyed in order to provide an assessment of the consequences of the gradual merging of mortgage finance with other aspects of retail finance. No attempt will be made to cover all the issues, instead some of the recurrent themes of earlier chapters will be addressed. In particular the question was raised in the first chapter of whether the new competitive structures were universally beneficial. The answer must be a mixed one.

9.1 An overview of the changes in mortgage and other retail finance

The disappearance of the traditional specialist mortgage institution

All three countries surveyed used to have at least one type of specialist mortgage finance institution through which mortgage finance was channelled. The overall framework of retail banking was also distinct in each country, as was its relative importance in the country's financial system and in the institutional linkages it had with the money and capital markets. The old frameworks began to dissolve at some time during the 1970s. The process of dissolution was speeded up in the 1980s by a variety of additional factors — including widespread deregulation of retail finance (except in West Germany).

Much of the impetus for change came from external forces. New information technology was one factor, but it facilitated rather than determined the precise direction of the transformations that have occurred. Important causes have been economic factors. Inflation, housing market booms and recessions, fluctuations in economic growth and a greater volatility of interest rates in general, and of the spread between short- and long-term rates in particular, have all had significant impacts on the restructuring process. None of the traditional forms of mortgage finance could cope with the changing economic environment, but few were prepared to retrench in the face of adversity either. At the same time, other institutions were encouraged to expand into the mortgage business.

Profitability and increased size are frequently poorly correlated, yet there is a near universal desire on the part of financial institutions to grow. Expansion has usually been justified by well-worn phrases like 'the competitive threat', 'getting ahead in the financial supermarket race', 'the importance of diversification' and 'new profit opportunities'. Sometimes legitimate business practices have not been followed, with 'moral hazard' and criminal practices, for instance, found amongst ambitious thrifts in the USA. For some other institutions, expansion was a high-risk gamble for survival. But for many others the speed of expansion can be understood only in terms of managerial aggrandisement. The outcome not only engenders internal inefficiencies, but if many managements adopt the same strategy whilst oblivious to the actions of others the result is over-capacity in retail financial services.

Crisis as the motor of change

Change in the US financial system has often been crisis-induced and the savings and loans associations have been a major source of those crises. They faced three major threats to their viability between the mid-1960s and the late 1980s and some near misses in between. Over a twenty-five year period they and the state institutions and laws that regulate them have been unable to resolve fully the conflicting pressures they face. Legislative change in US banking as a whole has been forced by those S&L crises. Yet liberalisation has failed to produce the hoped-for stable conditions under which a more efficient banking system can exist. Instead it created frameworks which allowed greater freedom for opportunistic and/or over-optimistic managements to indulge in interest rate leap-frogging and poorly judged investments. Other competitors then had to respond, weakening their own situations.

It is unclear whether the reforms of the late 1980s — aimed at tightening up the deposit insurance system, regulatory supervision and capital reserves — will be sufficient to create the desired stabilising environment. Nor is it obvious that they will improve the efficiency of retail banking. The reforms attempt artificially to divorce the likelihood of insolvency (which they try to reduce) from the competitive processes that generate the behaviour that may lead to insolvency (which apart from fraud and new limits on thrift lending they ignore). Players in US retail financial services now have to put up higher stakes and cheating is more difficult but the game they play is essentially the same as that set up in the early 1980s. It is questionable whether simply giving thrifts a higher handicap will solve the problems.

In western Europe the process of change has been different. Not only because of regulatory differences, but also because the retail finance institutions offering mortgages have had greater control over their own destinies in a number of important respects. A major factor has been their ability to influence the interest rates set, either through overt cartels or through the impact of their size and the potential threat it implies to competitors. On the deposit side, this has meant that interest rates have not settled down to oscillate around equivalent wholesale rates in a steady manner. On the mortgage side, in the UK, interest rates have been manipulated in response to threatening competition rather than to rates which reflect efficient intermediation spreads.

The impact of large financial institutions on the trend towards the relaxation of regulation is less clear. Dominant political ideologies in the 1980s made deregulation a popular way of describing the changes going on, even if some moves involved reformulation as much as relaxation of regulatory control. Others, like the late 1980s' US thrift measures, were a tightening up of previous laxity. The USA exhibited aspects of pressure group lobbying (often by unequal contestants). In it the thrifts were said to have had much influence on the early 1980s' legislation but, not surprisingly, little on that agreed in 1989. In the two western European countries surveyed, little similar political jockeying occurred as interests were less in conflict. There has been neither widespread general political suspicion of the role of retail finance institutions nor particular countervailing responses from other parts of the financial structure to the demands of particular types of institution. Some worries about the role of the big banks were surfacing in West Germany at the end of the decade. But, in Britain, criticism of particular financial institution's domestic behaviour was usually subdued. The government rather than the financial institutions was blamed for the mid-1980s' credit boom, for instance; whilst both the clearing banks and the building societies supported the deregulation process implied in the Building Societies Act, 1986.

The absence of political confrontation in western Europe may have contributed to the smooth process of transformation and absence of crisis-induced measures as no effective political coalition was blocking them. This point, of course, refers to the processes of change not to their outcomes. Just because financial crises were avoided does not of itself make the final outcome a better one. It is more likely anyway that the size of British and German financial institutions relative to American ones made it possible for them to ride some fairly disastrous investment mistakes, rather than the absence of crises having to be explained by resort to the political plane. West European governments in the 1980s were passive reactors rather than positive actors in the world of retail financial services.

Housing market instability and regressive subsidies.

Another feature of all three countries is that property markets have been highly volatile during the 1970s and 1980s. The effect may be regional — as with US and West German housing markets — or it may arise in only one type of market, such as office building. But the volatility has imposed costs on mortgage finance institutions. Over-optimism during property market upturns may lead to over-investment in mortgage retailing facilities and/or to poorly judged mortgage and related property investments. The late 1980s US thrift crisis is a classic illustration of a cycle of over-expansion followed by excess capacity and bad debt.

In all three countries housing subsidies are biased towards owner-occupation, with higher income households tending to benefit most. In Britain and the USA the subsidies are also predominantly tied to mortgage borrowing and so encourage the use of this financial instrument by the personal sector. West German subsidies are less tied to the mortgage market but the subsidies are still extensive, and, in addition, some savings subsidies are specifically earmarked for contracts that involve lending by specific types of institution (Bausparkassen).

In all three countries the front-loading effect of inflation on the real cost of mortgage finance to homeowners exists. The absences of taxes on the increases in house prices enjoyed by existing homeowners, especially during market booms, has also contributed to substantial shifts in personal sector wealth, to greater price volatility, and to further recourse to borrowing.

Retail versus wholesale finance

No clear advantage has emerged for either retail or wholesale market funds to be the preferred form of mortgage finance. The role of wholesale funds has increased substantially in Britain and the USA, but it has complemented rather than eclipsed retail sources. The type of wholesale funding also varies. In Britain, money market funds have predominantly been used, whereas in the USA the capital market has been the prime source; although brokeraged accounts in the US come close to a wholesale money market for retail finance institutions. In West Germany, the opposite has happened, with the bond market declining in importance whilst the role of retail funding has grown.

The reasons for the distinct roles in mortgage finance played by the various parts of countries' financial systems relates to the unique institutional and regulatory structures of each country, and to the new competitive forms that have emerged in them over the past two decades. Another element has been differences nationally in the spreads between short- and long-term interest rates on wholesale funds and between them and those pertaining in retail deposit-taking. In the USA the yield curve has generally favoured capital market sources — outside of a limited number of 'crisis' years. In Britain, conversely, the difference has been far less marked and frequently to the advantage of short-term rates. In West Germany, deposit-taking institutions have managed to keep the rates on retail funds low enough to create problems for institutions, like the mortgage banks, that rely on the capital markets.

Is the future one of giant multi-function financial institutions?

In terms of the types of institutional structure that now exist in retail banking, no ideal form seems apparent. Many institutions have opted for the giant financial supermarket/Allfinanz strategy. The success or the desirability of this financial form, however, is still uncertain. Some of the most profitable retail finance institutions in Britain and the USA, after all, have been those that limit their activities to a narrow range of functions by acting as specialist financial institutions. Good examples are money market funds and mortgage bankers in the USA, and the wholesale mortgage finance companies that have grown up in the UK. Such institutions have taken advantage of computerisation and the flexibility that their specialisms give them to make major inroads into other, overhead-encumbered institutions' traditional markets. The qualification has to be made here that many of those specialists are subsidiaries of wider financial conglomerates. But that point itself needs to be qualified by noting that ownership forms do not seem to influence how they operate (apart from giving ready access to start-up capital and to an image that inspires consumer confidence).

Another interesting aspect of the current divides in retail financial services is the division between banking, insurance and pensions. Some of the clearest separations that still remain in retail financial services are between institutions that are banks, or ones that adopt some of their functions, and those that act primarily as insurance companies or pension funds. Trends towards a merging of these previously separate spheres are apparent in both Britain and West Germany, but so far only in West Germany are major head-on collisions beginning to occur between the large insurance companies and banks in the battle over Allfinanz.

A variety of factors may account for the remaining major divisions in retail finance. Regulatory limitations are important in the USA and West Germany and until the mid-1980s they have been so in the UK. Ownership patterns are also of significance in all three countries because insurance companies and pension funds are often mutually or publicly owned. But, ownership and regulatory barriers apart, it may simply be true that there is no overwhelming reason why these financial services are better offered by one giant financial institution than by smaller concerns or specialists.

Change has not ended

Discussion of the banking, insurance and pensions divisions highlights the fact that in none of the three countries has a stable institutional structure in retail finance been reached. How it will develop in the future is still uncertain, but the scales at present seem tipped in favour of large financial conglomerates. This is not necessarily because they are the most efficient type of financial intermediary but because they have one overriding advantage — they survive.

In the European Community in particular it seems likely that major changes in retail finance will take place over the next decade as regulatory barriers are brought down with the introduction of the single European market after 1992 and the greater movement towards economic and monetary union. Some British commentators have suggested little major change will result (Bank of England, 1989) but such views are derived from the perspective of a weakly regulated financial system and little detailed understanding of European practice. Many other EC countries may find major changes occur to their financial systems. Moreover, even for Britain, once exchange rate risks are limited it seems unlikely that the sources of retail funds for investment in British financial products will remain purely domestic rather than pan-European. Earlier chapters indicated that, at present, if exchange rate risks were eliminated and regulation permitted it, the arbitrage profits that could be made from cross-European retail funding are currently huge. Moves towards monetary union will undoubtedly narrow these spreads. That narrowing, however, will be part of a competitive process that could lead to a substantial restructuring of EC-based retail financial institutions. Given current uncertainty over EC policy towards the future development of retail finance and only initial opening moves in cross-European integration of financial institutions, it is difficult at present to form a clear impression of the likely structure of retail finance in the EC over the next decade.

9.2 Benefits of the transformation of retail and mortgage finance

A number of general gains for consumers have occurred as a result of the merging of mortgage and other retail finance, although some of the benefits come with negative consequences as well.

Credit is more freely available, with mortgage demand now rationed more by price than by queue. There were several occasions when mortgages were severely rationed in the 1970s whereas, apart from the first few years, the 1980s were a period when mortgage credit was much easier to find for most households. There is, in addition, greater choice over mortgage instruments. American consumers can choose between fixed and variable interest mortgages, whilst British homeowners now have a wide variety of possibilities — including fixed or variable interest rates or a rate linked to an external marker like LIBOR; and the mortgage can be denominated in currencies other than sterling, especially ECUs, the European Community currency. In practice, however, most British households still opt for the traditional mortgage instrument. In West Germany, households and landlords can also contemplate a wider range of mortgage packages than used to be possible. Mortgage advances everywhere can be linked with insurance and pension schemes, if desired.

Some of the most substantial changes have been on the deposit side. Savers in Britain and the USA have benefited from intense competition for their deposits. New deposit conditions have raised interest rates considerably and improved the conditions of access to accounts. It is now possible to obtain interest on current/checking accounts, so a major subsidy by the public to the banking system has finally been breached. West German households have not enjoyed the same benefits, but financial liberalisation after 1992 may force improvements there as well. In all three countries, furthermore, there is easier access to personal deposit accounts because of investments by financial institutions in information technology. Banks also now court personal customers in a style undreamt of even a decade ago.

None of these consumer gains are insubstantial, and they have been used to justify the benefits of the new competition in retail finance. Moves to reinstate earlier styles of financial regulation and functional separation would be highly unpopular as a result. But associated with these benefits have been some substantial costs, as can be seen from the individual country analyses in the foregoing chapters. Whether the costs outweigh the benefits is a question that cannot easily be answered. There are too many imponderables for accurate evaluation, whilst the distributional incidence of costs and benefits varies considerably across individuals and between them and specific institutions. One of the greatest imponderables is the possibility that instability in the financial system has been increased. Another is that interest rates as a whole may have been pushed up in the UK and the USA by the mortgage credit explosion, over-capacity and failures. Problems in mortgage markets through their effect on general interest rates also spill over into the general world economy.

To a great extent, however, trying to calculate all the costs and benefits of the change is unnecessary when considering whether some developments are undesirable, because it might be possible to alter particular contexts in which the new financial competition operates so that some, at least, of the costs and potential risks are ameliorated.

9.3 Drawbacks of the new frameworks for financial services

One feature that has come out strongly in this analysis of retail financial systems is that none approximates to the ideal of efficiency generally associated with competitive markets. This is not simply because of the murkiness of the real world in relation to the purity of abstract models, but because of certain systematic processes that currently operate in retail financial service provision. Most of the effects cannot precisely be quantified, yet each of them raises serious concerns about the nature of the transformation of retail finance.

One commentator has suggested that true innovations either offer extra efficiency by reducing intermediaries' spreads or extend market completeness by covering a greater number of the contingencies that exist in the world (van Horne, 1985). Many aspects of the new retail financial competition meet neither of these criteria.

Interest rate distortions

In Britain and the USA, where deregulation has encouraged widespread interest rate competition, interest rates in the retail sphere have not settled down to approximate those in equivalent wholesale markets (with a slightly increased spread for the greater administrative costs and risks of retail borrowing and lending).

Rather than corresponding to such a pure competitive model — with low intermediation costs and retail and wholesale spreads brought into equivalence by rational profit-seeking actors looking for arbitrage possibilities — traditional features of institutional power and constraint are still significant in the process of interest rate determination. In particular, the fortunes (or their lack) of the large traditional mortgage lenders still exert a strong influence on the level of mortgage interest rates relative to others. One example is the impact in the USA of the late 1980s' thrift crisis on interest rates in the secondary mortgage market (see Chapter 6). In Britain, even after the demise of their interest-fixing cartel, the building societies are still able to affect the position of mortgage interest rates relative to those in the money markets, as Chapter 7 describes. By doing so, they end up having a degree of control over the profitability of their competitiors' operations. It is also not simply a question of identifying one type of institution which, individually or collectively, can be regarded as having monopoly characteristics. Strategic responses by different types of institution may be just as significant and less easy to affect via legislation. The limits of price competition within such oligopolistic structures can be seen on occasions in 1980s' mortgage markets. In Britain, for example, there were large potential arbitrage profits in the spread between wholesale funds and mortgage interest rates in the mid-1980s but they remained there for a number of years despite a significant erosion by new competitors of the building societies' market share.

With regard to interest rates on retail deposits, it is apparent that they are influenced by contemporary competitive strategies as well as by levels in other markets. Retail deposit interest rates have in a number of instances been bid up to what were generally recognised as unrealistic levels. The notorious 'Texas premium' of the mid-1980s is one of the most extreme examples (Chapter 4) but other cases exist. British building society complaints of 'expensive retail funds' in 1987 arose because they pushed retail deposit rates well above wholesale money market rates, and were saved from chronic losses only because their competitors did not then force mortgage interest rates down to money market levels. Another example is the interest rates now available on current/checking accounts. In many instances in both the UK and USA they have been used as loss leaders to attract customers for other products. In West Germany, conversely, the institutions have managed systematically to keep retail deposit rates well below wholesale short-term rates.

Cross-subsidised inefficiencies

High retail deposit account interest rates and free banking services have to be paid for by someone, and generally, it is the user of another service. Financial institutions, in particular, may load the costs onto the parts of their business where the demand is less elastic.

Borrowers often bear the cost. Relatively high interest rates on building society deposits in the mid-1980s led to higher mortgage interest rates, for instance. The interest-free credit offered by credit card companies until the billing date are borne by higher interest charges for those who do not repay promptly, and by retail outlets and their non-credit card customers. The effect is heightened if, as in Britain, credit card companies could until 1990 require shops to charge uniform prices whether their cards or another payment medium is used. (Alternatively when shops can charge differential prices they may do so in a discriminatory way.) With British current accounts, interest and free banking are offset by higher overdraft rates and incidental charges, and many of the latter, as the Consumers' Association has complained, are unknown to the customer (*Which?*, June 1989). Users of other financial products are also likely to face higher and often unknown margins in the commissions that institutions earn on selling those products to them.

So what is wrong with cross-subsidies? Financial institutions could even claim that in a multi-product business like their own, it is difficult to price individual products accurately, so that some overheads must be assigned arbitrarily to different parts of their business. A little more profit here and a little loss elsewhere is anyhow balanced out for many consumers. Economic theorists might also add that economic efficiency is only achieved when financial services are priced at long-run marginal costs, rather than average ones considered here. But, in practice, the two types of cost are similar if there are constant returns to scale and limited economies of scope in retail banking, as the evidence presented in Chapter 4 suggests is the case.

The intuitive appeal of the 'it-all-comes-out-in-the-wash' type of argument in support of cross-subsidisation is that it ignores three major problems. They are particularly important if institutions can actually identify the costs of providing particular services and are able to respond to that information. So they are especially relevant if the extreme claims about banks not knowing the costs of individual parts of their businesses are discounted.

The first problem is one of the structure of a financial services industry with extensive cross-subsidisation. Use of the services that are subsidised will be encouraged, whilst use of those that pay for the subsidies will be discouraged. This in aggregate could lead to substantial inefficiencies in resource allocation. Two examples illustrate the point. 'Costless' credit cards lead to the squeezing out of other payment media and a reluctance to invest in new technology which would threaten the ascendency of the credit card; and free banking with easy account access leads to far more transactions than if people had to pay transaction charges, with customers paying part of the cost in greater queuing time for the use of the free facilities.

The second problem is that cross-subsidisation is likely to be systematic between social groups and frequently regressive in its incidence. Large deposits, for instance, are likely to be the most price sensitive and so will get the best interest terms, and the depositors of large sums are generally the better off. Net borrowers, conversely, tend to be at a younger stage in their life cycle than net depositors. If the cross-subsidies are frequently from borrowers to depositors then they lead to intergenerational income transfers.

The third difficulty is that the cross-subsidisation is taking place in an industry where market profiles are important and information imperfect. As a result competition may be stifled. Existing multi-product financial institutions can use cross-subsidies to push down the price of their products which face particularly severe competition from a new entrant. This negative response for the innovator may be compounded by consumer information deficiencies. Competitors offering a cheaper version of the same product may suffer from an inability to gain consumer awareness and acceptance, particularly if marketing techniques create the illusion of spurious product differentiation associated with the financial packages on offer in favour of large, multi-product institutions.

Excess capacity

All three countries surveyed show evidence of growing excess capacity in retail financial services. The excess capacity is unsurprising because specialist financial groups have all diversified into each other's fields, setting up new subsidiaries, opening new branches and waiting for the customers to roll in. As each type of institution feels it must offer more facilities to surpass competitors, overall capacity snowballs.

The financial institutions themselves frequently lose out in the long run from the excess capacity as the resultant higher operating costs depress their profits. Customers bear the costs as well in the greater spreads required by institutions to finance their facilities. The extra capacity may also be a substitute for price competition, as was shown in West Germany and in the behaviour of the cartel-constrained UK building societies prior to the early 1980s. Because excess capacity lowers the profitability of financial institutions it may also pose problems for the financial system as a whole or for governments when institutions fail. The regulatory authorities may even have to subsidise loss-makers if their failure is seen to impose too great a threat to the financial system as a whole (as with the thrifts in the 1980s).

The effect of excess capacity, furthermore, may be indirect. Reduced profitability may induce some institutions to take on higher-risk investments. When many of those investments subsequently fail the problems begin to mount.

Macroeconomic effects

There has been considerable concern, particularly in Britain, over certain effects of the new structure of retail finance on the macroeconomy, as Chapter 2 notes. A greater availability of consumer finance has helped to fuel consumer booms, which have subsequently sucked in imports and created balance of payments problems. Mortgage liberalisation, when it has gone hand-in-hand with rising house prices, is said to have encouraged regional and wealth inequalities and to have fuelled inflation both directly through the impact of extra credit and indirectly through the effects on house prices. The extra demand for funds by the financial institutions for their expanded consumer lending may also have pushed up general interest rates; the enhanced rates offered on retail deposits may have had an additional effect.

Each of these claims are controversial hypotheses but they do raise the point that both retail financial services and the housing market are major components in an advanced economy and that structural changes in either are as a result likely to have substantial macroeconomic implications.

9.4 Does the bad squeeze out the good?

The efficient market theory (EMT) approach to financial markets (see Chapter 3) suggests that in the competitive process more efficient producers squeeze out the less efficient ones or, at least, they force them to improve their operations. For EMT, in other words, the good drives out the bad. But in a number of respects the foregoing analysis of the American, British and German retail financial markets could be cited as evidence for the opposite proposition: that the practices of particular types of inefficient producer make it difficult for the more efficient to survive, especially if the efficient are recent entrants. Less starkly, it could be said that there is little evidence that competition is a force overwhelmingly in favour of the efficient. (Efficiency here is defined in terms of the criteria used by Tobin and discussed in Chapter 3.) This seeming paradox has a number of aspects which are considered below. But theoretically it arises because efficient market theory fails to recognise some of the consequences of the limited information open to market agents.

Five key information deficiencies in retail finance are highlighted in Chapter 4. They are: (1) limited knowledge of the creditworthiness of personal borrowers; (2) limited knowledge of the soundness of financial institutions; (3) restricted consumer knowledge of financial alternatives; (4) constraints on the ability of financial institutions to cost their own sources of funds, and (5) limits on the information that financial institutions have when contemplating their investment strategies. Together these constraints are argued in Chapter 4 to generate the widespread existence of business strategies based on misplaced hunches about future market trends and competitor responses, plus opportunistic and over-optimistic behaviour, and so lead to situations where the most efficient producers are not the market leaders. Market profiles are what seem to count and, within limits, those with the best market profiles need not necessarily be the most efficient deliverers of retail financial services. Greater size was suggested to be an advantage in creating and sustaining a successful market profile. But greater size does not automatically lead to a cheaper provision of retail financial services because there seems to be an absence of significant economies of scale and scope in retail banking.

Size had another great advantage — survival. It enables firms to cope with the limited information on investment opportunities so that horrendous investment mistakes tend to depress profits severely for a few years rather than lead to insolvency. In addition, size gives retail finance giants a depth of resources with which to ride out a competitive battle. They may not be the cheapest providers of particular financial services but lower-cost smaller producers may lack the resources for a long-term battle of survival against better endowed and aggressive competitors.

Associated with survival is the ability of giant firms to influence, within limits, the parameters affecting their destiny. They have a significant presence in the markets in which they operate. They may take advantage of this through explicit cartels or other monopolistic practices or through oligopolistic 'games' with competitors to influence the spread between their borrowing and lending rates and the commissions they achieve on their off-balance sheet activities. Size enables diversification to be combined with financial strength so that cross-subsidisation and market profiles can be manipulated in attempts to see off threatening competition.

The overall conclusion of this argument is that information limitations in retail finance lead to considerable advantages for larger institutions, *even though they may not be the most efficient*. Governments and regulatory bodies, furthermore, may also prefer larger institutions precisely because they are less likely to fail than smaller ones. They may, as the US authorities seem to have done, opt for a financial structure whose regulations favour the larger enterprise and generate competitive weaknesses for smaller ones. The perceived threat to the financial system is then claimed to be the reason for condoning the growth of giant financial conglomerates.

It may not be true that large institutions exist simply because they can use their size to fend off competition and survive in the ways just described. The current framework of competition in retail financial services, however, encourages such responses. Yet, the regulatory environment could be changed in ways that limit some competitive practices without necessarily threatening the beneficial effects of competition, as is sketched out in the final section.

There are other ways, not associated with size as such, in which it can be postulated that the bad may drive out the good in retail financial services. Many of the factors listed in the previous section were of that form, such as interest rate leap-frogging forcing every institution to take greater risks; the gains from cross-subsidisation squeezing out lower cost providers of financial services; and the industrywide impact of excess capacity. There are reasons to believe that these features, moreover, are cyclical in nature.

9.5 The cyclical incidence of over-optimism, opportunism and excess capacity

The new patterns of competition in retail markets are often too recent to be able to identify accurately any cyclical patterns in institutional behaviour. Yet it is possible to hypothesise some characteristics of institutions' behaviour from the available evidence in different countries to suggest the potential for such a cyclical pattern. The fact that times when institutions are in severe crisis are infrequent may generate the belief that each set of problems is unique and passes with time and government attention, whereas it might actually be the case that there are more systematic tendencies at work.

A medium-term cycle in retail financial services may take the following form.

During an expansion of the economy, market conditions in general will strongly favour investment in retail finance. Real incomes are likely to be rising, so that consumers are more prepared to take on large financial commitments, including pensions and insurance and mortgages. Residential property markets are probably expanding and prices slowly edging upwards; other property markets may also offer good investment opportunities. Expectations about the economy will be good – low inflation, incomes set to rise and growth prospects good. Added to these factors, retail financial institutions are likely to find the yield gap especially advantageous for them with long-term interest rates (which govern many investment opportunities for them) considerably above short-term ones.

The stage is set for the ascendency of the optimists and expansionists in retail finance. The pace and content of investment, retail deposit interest rates and additions to capacity will then be set by them; others will feel forced to follow suit which in the prevailing state of euphoria may not cause them too much concern. The rapid expansion of credit and the facilities for lending it will help to stimulate the boom in the economy as a whole.

The next stage of the cycle is where competition between financial institutions begins to squeeze retail margins. Some institutions, in addition, may feel they have lost out by not responding quickly enough and adopt rapid expansion strategies to catch up; whilst the super-optimists may still make the running and push retail deposit interest rates up relative to money market rates or depress the yields in previously attractive investment areas through bidding up prices or pushing down interest rate spreads. The expansion of facilities will force up operating costs, reducing margins even further.

The underlying weaknesses in retail finance may not become apparent until the wider economy begins to slow down or faces a sudden external shock. Then the beneficial characteristics of the initial growth phase go into reverse. Inflation may rise or growth falter, or fears may grow of either of them occurring, which will tend to narrow or reverse the yield gap. Demand for retail credit may fall as the growth of disposable income falters. The investment strategies of the optimists may come unstuck leading to several insolvencies and/or concern about the viability of some major institutions. Stagnation will follow, and chronic excess capacity during it and low profits on normal business may encourage some institutions to be even more optimistic and adventurous the next time the market picks up.

Each phase could have effects on the firm-size structure of the retail financial services industry. During an upswing, new entrants are encouraged and they may grow rapidly at the expense of established firms. During the period of crisis and subsequent stagnation, conversely, insolvencies and takeovers may strengthen the position of the larger enterprises. The effect may also be ratchet-like with the larger firms getting progressively bigger over the cycles.

What has been described is obviously a crude 'story'. It is broadly based on the analyses of earlier chapters but takes no account of institutional and legislative differences between countries and the changing contexts in which each successive cyclical phase exists. The world does not regularly repeat itself. Yet the story seems just as valid as that propagated under the name of efficient markets, and deserves as much concern in policy discussions as arguments that financial markets should be as unconstrained as possible to let 'competition' dictate that what exists is what is best.

9.6 Policy review

The argument of this book has not been that competition in financial markets is bad and should be constrained as much as possible. The frameworks of the 1930s, 1940s and 1950s should not be revived. Similarly, strict regulation of interest rates, financial products and capital flows by the state are also likely to be doomed to failure in the modern world. It seems, however, that financial markets have developed faster than the theories which purport to provide the analytical frameworks on which legislation is based. Competition and the merging of retail financial services can provide considerable benefits, but only if attempts are made to limit the worst of the battles between financial institutions.

No simple blueprint can be devised, but perhaps the frequently voiced enthusiasm of policy makers for the financial services supermarket and its variants should be questioned. Policy might be better directed at protecting consumers and economies from some of the more undesirable outcomes of contemporary financial market competition than being directed towards achieving ends whose benefits may be limited or non-existent but whose costs may be large.

Policy could be redirected in a number of ways, none of which are simple reversals to an older order. This is not the place for detailed policy proposals but several suggestions stem from the conclusions reached above. A stronger policy towards large financial conglomerates seems in order. Rather than using criteria like market share, the onus should be on financial institutions to demonstrate the benefits to regulators of newly acquired or developed businesses, rather than simply having rules that ban certain combinations of financial services and/or firm sizes. The taxation biases amongst retail financial products also require urgent attention, especially mortgage interest subsidies. The process of adjustment may be painful, but so are the potential consequences for the economy, the financial services industry and distributional equity if nothing is done.

One of the features on which great emphasis has been put in this book is limits on information in financial services. Attempts should be made to improve the information available in retail finance, especially to consumers. Many wholesale markets would not exist in their present forms without the battery of financial information rapidly available in them, from credit rating agencies to detailed expert advice. Retail financial markets in terms of employment have even more intermediary advisers, but consumers do not necessarily benefit as much as do players in wholesale markets because of the ways in which retail advisers earn their income through commissions. Advisers, consequently, are likely to be biased towards particular institutions and products when they are giving advice. Half-hearted attempts have been made to get around this problem by forcing independent agents to reveal their commissions and other devices. But as long as their income is commission-dependent it is difficult to see how biases can be totally removed. As a result it would seem important for public agencies and governments to investigate and finance means of extending the independent advice and information available to consumers.

If the arguments about a tendency towards chronic excess capacity in retail financial services are valid, and the excess capacity creates the problems suggested, it might be prudent for governments and the regulatory authorities to think of means of containing it. The options are considerable. In the case of the proliferation of branch networks, for instance, limitations could be imposed in a variety of ways ranging from planning controls over the siting of branch offices to efficiency taxes linked to factors like unit administrative costs or throughput of branches, with offsetting allowances for innovatory investments.

Cross-subsidisation could similarly be constrained. For instance, customers could be required to receive audited margins on the financial products they are contemplating prior to their decision to proceed. Regulatory limits could be put on the extent of 'loss leaders'. Turnover taxes could be imposed on transactions.

One final reform could be added. Limits could be put on the spreads around wholesale market indicators that institutions are able to offer on their lending and borrowing interest rates. If handled sensitively, this would eliminate over-optimistic interest rates on retail deposits, loss leaders on borrowing rates, and attempts to remove competitors though the joint manipulation of retail lending and borrowing interest rates. The interest controls of the 1930s and later tried to take interest rate fixing out of the marketplace, whereas constraints on spreads would keep it there. The more efficient would benefit from making a larger profit out of the potential spread available or be able to trim their spread within the set limits forcing others to become more efficient or go out of business.

One thing is certain. The retail financial services industry is continuing to change dramatically. As a result, policy discussion cannot remain within the confines of theories and debates outlined one or two decades ago. They, after all, existed to consider the deregulation of a financial system that is now a part of history. And history is never repeated.

References

Aaron, H. 1972. *Shelter and Subsidies*. Washington DC: Brookings Institute.

Anderson, G. and Hendry, D. 1984. 'An econometric model of UK building societies', *Oxford Bulletin of Economics and Statistics*, vol. 46 pp. 185−211.

Arrow, K. 1982. 'Risk perception in psychology and economics', *Economic Inquiry*, vol. 20, pp. 1−9.

Ball, M. 1983. *Housing Policy and Economic Power: The Political Economy of Owner Occupation*. London: Methuen.

Ball, M. and Kirwan, R. 1976. 'Urban housing demand: some evidence from cross-sectional data', *Applied Economics*, vol. 9, pp. 343−66.

Ball, M. 1988. 'The international restructuring of housing production', in Ball *et al.* (1988), *op. cit.*

Ball, M., Harloe, M. and Martens, M. 1984. 'Comments on *Building Societies: A New Framework*', mimeo.

Ball, M., Martens, M. and Harloe, M. 1986. 'Mortgage finance and owner occupation in Britain and West Germany', *Progress and Planning*, vol. 26(3), pp. 185−260.

Ball, M., Harloe, M. and Martens, M. 1990. *Housing and Social Change in Europe and the USA*. London: Routledge.

Bank of England. 1989. 'The housing market', *Bank of England Quarterly Bulletin*, vol. 19, pp. 66−77.

Barnes, P. 1984. *Building Societies. The Myth of Mutuality*. London: Pluto Press.

Baumol, W., Panzar, J. and Willig, R. 1982. *Contestable Markets and the Theory of Industrial Structure*. New York: Harcourt Brace Jovanovich.

Benston, G., Hanweek, G. and Humphrey, D. 1982. 'Scale economies in banking: a restructuring and reassessment', *Journal of Money, Credit and Banking*, vol. 14, pp. 435−56.

Boddy, M. 1989. 'Financial deregulation and UK housing finance: government−building society relations and the Building Societies Act, 1986', *Housing Studies*, vol. 4, pp. 92−104.

Boleat, M. 1985. *National Housing Finance Systems: A Comparative Study*. London: Croom Helm.

Boleat, M. and Kaye, J. 1989. 'Building societies and wholesale funding', *Housing Finance*, vol. 1, pp. 26−34.

Bover, O., Muellbauer, J. and Murphy, A. 1988. 'Housing, Wages and Labour Markets', Discussion Paper 268, Centre for Economic Policy Research, London.

Brambring, G., Drevermann, M., Franken, H., Hardt, K.-E., Hentzsch, S. and Nordalm, V. 1983. *Ursachen- und Wirkungsanalyse von Zwansversteigerrungen Öffentlich Geforderter Eigentumsmassnahmen in NRW, Ergebnisbericht.* Bochum: AWOS GmbH.

Brumbaugh, R. and Carron, A. 1987. 'Thrift industry crisis: causes and solutions', *Brookings Papers in Economic Activity*, vol. 2, pp. 349–88.

Brumbaugh, R., Carron, A. and Litan, R. 1989. 'Cleaning up the depository institutions mess', *Brookings Papers in Economic Activity*, vol. 1, pp. 243–96.

BSA. 1981. *The Determination and Control of House Prices.* London: Building Societies Association.

Cable, J. 1985. 'Capital market information and industrial performance: the role of West German banks', *Economic Journal*, vol. 95, pp. 118–32.

Campbell, T. and Horovitz, P. 1984. 'Reform of the deposit insurance system: an appraisal of the FHLBB and FDIC studies', *Contemporary Policy Issues*, vol. 6, pp. 56–68 (May).

Canner, G. 1982. 'Redlining: research and federal legislative response', Staff Paper 121, Board of Governors of the Federal Reserve System, Washington DC.

Carron, A. 1982a. *The Plight of the Thrift Industry.* Washington DC: Brookings Institution.

Carron, A. 1982b. 'Financial crises: recent experience in the US and international markets', *Brookings Papers in Economic Activity*, pp. 395–422.

Carron, A. 1983. 'The political economy of financial regulation', in Noll, R. and Owen, B. (eds), *The Political Economy of Deregulation.* Washington DC: American Enterprise Institute.

CDP. 1976. *Profits Against Houses.* London: Community Development Projects Information and Intelligence Unit.

Checkoway, B. 1980. 'Large builders, federal housing programmes and postwar suburbanization', *International Journal of Urban and Regional Research*, vol. 4, pp. 21–45.

Clark, J. 1984. 'Economies of scale in banking using a generalised functional form', *Journal of Money, Credit and Banking*, vol. 16, pp. 53–68.

Clarke, R. and McGuiness, T. 1987. *The Economics of the Firm.* Oxford: Basil Blackwell.

Cleary, E. 1965. *The Building Society Movement.* London: Elek.

Copeland, L. 1989. 'Market efficiency before and after the crash', *Fiscal Studies*, vol. 10, pp. 13–33.

Daunton, M. 1988. 'Homeloans versus council houses: the formation of American and British housing policy 1900–20', *Housing Studies*, vol. 3, pp. 220–32.

DB. 1984. *Statistische Beihefte.* Frankfurt am Main: Deutsche Bundesbank.

DB. 1989. *Monthly Report of the Deutsche Bundesbank.* Frankfurt am Main: Deutsche Bundesbank (March).

de Bondt, W. and Thaler, R. 1989. 'A mean-reverting walk down Wall Street', *Journal of Economic Perspectives*, vol. 3, pp. 189–202.

Dhillon, U., Shilling, J. and Sirmans, C. 1987. 'Choosing between fixed and adjustable mortgages', *Journal of Money, Credit and Banking*, vol. 19, pp. 260–7.

Dicks, M. 1989. 'The housing market', *Bank of England Quarterly Bulletin*, pp. 66–71 (February).

Downs, A. 1980. 'Too much capital for housing?', *The Brookings Bulletin*, vol. 17, pp. 1–5.

Duesenberry, J. 1987. Comment on Brumbaugh and Carron (1987), *Brookings Papers in Economic Activity*, pp. 386–8.

Duke of Edinburgh's Report. 1985. *Enquiry into British Housing*. London: National Federation of Housing Associations.

EAG. 1981. *The British and German Banking Systems: A Comparative Study*. London: Economists Advisory Group, Anglo-German Foundation.

Esaki, H. and Wachtenheim, J. 1984/5. 'Explaining the recent level of single-family starts', *Federal Reserve Bank of New York*, pp. 31–7 (winter).

Fama, E. 1965. 'The behaviour of stock market prices', *Journal of Business*, vol. 38, pp. 34–105.

Fama, E. 1976. *Foundations of Finance*. New York: Basic Books.

Fama, E. and French, K. 1988. 'Permanent and temporary components of stock prices', *Journal of Political Economy*, vol. 98, pp. 246–74.

FDIC. 1983. *Deposit Insurance in a Changed Environment*. Washington DC: Federal Deposit Insurance Corporation.

Fforde, F. 1983. 'Competition, innovation and regulation in British banking', *Bank of England Quarterly Bulletin*, pp. 363–70.

FHLBB. 1985. *Savings and Home Financing Source Book*. Washington DC: Federal Home Loan Bank Board.

Fisher, F. 1989. 'Games economists play: a noncooperative view', *RAND Journal of Economics*, vol. 20, pp. 113–24.

Florida, R. 1986. 'The political economy of financial deregulation and the reorganization of housing finance in the United States', *International Journal of Urban and Regional Research*, vol. 10, pp. 207–31.

Foster, C. and van Order, R. 1984. 'An option-based model of mortgage default', *Housing Finance Review*, vol. 3, pp. 351–71.

Francis, A., Turk, J. and Williams, P. (eds). 1983. *Power, Efficiency and Institutions*. London: Heinemann.

Francke, H.-H. and Hudson, M. 1984. *Banking and Finance in West Germany*, London: Croom Helm.

FRB. 1987. 'The recent growth of consumer credit', *Federal Reserve Bulletin*, pp. 130–41 (August).

FRB. 1988. 'Home equity lines of credit', *Federal Reserve Bulletin*, pp. 361–73 (June).

FRB. 1989. 'Trends in banking structure since the mid-1970s', *Federal Reserve Bulletin*, pp. 120–33 (March).

FRBNY. 1987a. 'Bankers on pricing consumer deposits', *Federal Reserve Bank of New York Quarterly Review*, pp. 6–13 (winter).

FRBNY. 1987b. 'The pricing of consumer deposit products: the non-interest rate dimensions', *Federal Reserve Bank of New York Quarterly Review*, (winter).

Gabriel, S. 1987. 'Housing and mortgage markets: the post-1982 expansion', *Federal Reserve Bulletin*, vol. 73, pp. 893–903 (December).

Gates, J. 1988. 'The big battalions still marching in', *Housing Finance*. London: Building Societies Association.

Gilbert, R. 1981. 'Will the removal of Regulation Q raise mortgage interest rates?' *Federal Reserve Bank of St Louis Review*, vol. 63, pp. 3–12.

Gilbert, R. 1986. 'Requiem for Regulation Q: what it did and why it passed away', *Federal Reserve Bank of St Louis Review*, vol. 68, pp. 2–37.

Gilbert, R. 1989. 'The role of potential competition in industrial organization', *Journal of Economic Perspectives*, vol. 3, pp. 107–27.

Gilbert, R. and Holland, A. 1983. 'Has the deregulation of deposit interest rates raised mortgage rates?' *Federal Reserve Bank of St Louis Review*, vol. 66, pp. 5–15.

Gilligan, T., Smirlock, M. and Marshall, W. 1984. 'Scale and scope economies in the multi-product banking firm', *Journal of Monetary Economics*, vol. 13, pp. 393–405.

Goodman, J. 1985. 'Adjustable rate home mortgages and the demand for mortgage credit', Working Paper 41, Board of Governors of the Federal Reserve System, Washington DC.

Gough, T. 1982. *The Economics of Building Societies*. Basingstoke: Macmillan.

Gough, T. and Taylor, T. 1979 'The Building Society Price Cartel', Hobart Paper no. 83, Institute of Economic Affairs, London.

Gravelle, J. 1983. 'Tax subsidies to housing, 1953−83', in *Housing: a Reader*, Congressional Research Service, Library of Congress, Committee Print 98−5, Washington DC.

Grebler, L. 1983. 'Housing credit versus monetary policy', in *The Business Cycle and Public Policy*. Washington DC: US Congress, Joint Economic Committee.

Green, J. and Shoven, J. 1986. 'The effect of interest rates on mortgage prepayments', *Journal of Money, Credit and Banking*, vol. 18, pp. 41−59.

Hadjimatheou, G. 1976. *Housing and Mortgage Markets: The UK Experience*, Farnborough: Saxon House.

Harvey, D. 1984. *The Limits to Capital*. Oxford: Blackwell.

Hendry, D. 1984. 'Econometric modelling of house prices in the United Kingdom' in Hendry, D. and Wallis, K. (eds) *Econometrics and Quantitative Economics*. Oxford: Basil Blackwell.

Hess, A. 1987. 'Could thrifts be profitable? Theoretical and empirical evidence', *Carnegie−Rochester Conference Series on Public Policy*, vol. 26, pp. 223−82.

Hilferding, R. 1981. *Finance Capital. A Study of the Latest Phase of Capitalist Development*. London: Routledge and Kegan Paul.

HMSO. 1984. *Building Societies: A New Framework*. Cmnd 9316, London: HMSO.

Horovitz, P. 1983. 'The case against risk-related deposit insurance premiums', vol. 2, *Housing Finance Review*, pp. 253−63.

HPR. 1977. *Housing Policy*. Technical Volumes, Parts I−III. London: HMSO.

Hunt Commission. 1971. *Report of the President's Commission on Financial Structure and Regulation*, Washington DC.

Jaffee, D. 1987. Comment on Brumbaugh and Carron (1987), *Brookings Papers in Economic Activity*, pp. 378−81.

Kane, E. 1983. 'A six-point program for deposit insurance reform', *Housing Finance Review*, vol. 2, pp. 269−78.

Kane, E. 1984. 'Technological and regulatory forces in the developing fusion of financial services competition', *Journal of Finance*, vol. 39, pp. 759−72.

Kane, E. 1985. *The Gathering Crises in Federal Deposit Insurance*. Cambridge, Mass.: Ballinger.

Kareken, J. and Wallace, N. 1978. 'Deposit insurance and bank regulation: a partial equilibrium exposition', *Journal of Business*, vol. 51, pp. 413−38.

Kaufman, G. 1984. 'The role of traditional mortgage lenders in future mortgage lending: problems and prospects'. Paper presented at the Conference on Housing Finance, HUD, Washington, March 1984.

Kaufman, G. 1987. Comment on Hess (1987), *Carnegie−Rochester Conference Series on Public Policy*, vol. 26, pp. 283−88.

Kaufman, G., Mote, J. and Rosenblum, H. 1984. 'Consequences of deregulation for commercial banking', *Journal of Finance*, vol. 39, pp. 789−803.

Kaufman, G. and Kormendi, R. 1986. *Deregulating Financial Services. Public Policy in Flux*. Cambridge, Mass.: Ballinger.

Keynes, J. 1936. *The General Theory of Employment, Interest and Money*. London: Macmillan.

Kindleberger, C. 1978. *Manias, Panics and Crashes*. Basingstoke: Macmillan.

Kindleberger, C. 1987. *The World in Depression*. Harmondsworth: Penguin.

King, B. 1983. 'Interstate expansion and bank costs', *Federal Reserve Bank of Atlanta Review*, pp. 40–5 (May).

Köster, J. and Mezler, J. 1979. 'Wohnungseigentumsquote, Bestimmungsgründe der Wohnungseigentumsquote in den Ländern Belgein, Dänemark, Frankreich, Grossbritannien, USA, Bundes Republik Deutschland', *Schriftenreihe Wohnungsmarkt and Wohnungspolitik 07.005*. Bonn: Der Bundesminister für Raumordnung und Städtebau.

Kuroda, M. and Kaneko, T. 1986. 'Economies of scale and lending behaviour in the banking industry', *Bank of Japan Monetary and Economic Studies*, vol. 4, pp. 1–40.

Lawrence, C. and Shay,R. 1986. 'Technology and financial intermediation in multiproduct banking firms', in Lawrence, C. and Shay, R. (eds), *Technological Innovation, Regulation and the Monetary Economy*. New York: Ballinger.

Litan, R. 1987. *What Should Banks Do?* Washington DC: Brookings Institution.

McCall, A. 1980. 'Economies of scale, operating efficiencies and the organizational structure of commercial banks', *Journal of Bank Research*, pp. 95–100 (summer).

Mahoney, P., White, A., O'Brien, P. and McLaughlin, M. 1987. 'Responses to deregulation: retail deposit pricing from 1983 to 1985', Staff Study 151, Board of Governors of the Federal Reserve System, Washington DC.

Martens, M. 1985. 'Owner occupied housing in Europe: postwar developments and current dilemmas', *Environment and Planning*, vol. 17, pp. 605–24.

Martens, M. 1988. 'The revolution in mortage finance', in Ball *et al.* (1988), *op. cit.*

Mayer, C. 1988. 'The assessment: financial systems and corporate investment', *Oxford Review of Economic Policy*, vol. 3(4), pp. i–xvi.

Mayer, T. and Nathan, H. 1983. 'Mortgage rates and Regulation Q', *Journal of Money, Credit and Banking*, vol. 14, pp. 107–15.

Mayes, D. 1979. *The Property Boom*. Oxford: Martin Robertson.

Meyerson, A. 1986. 'The changing structure of housing finance in the United States', *International Journal of Urban and Regional Research*, vol. 10, pp. 465–96.

Minsky, H. 1980. 'Capitalist financial processes and the instability of capitalism', *Journal of Economic Issues*, vol. 11, pp. 505–23.

Minsky, H. 1986. *Stabilizing an Unstable Economy: A Twentieth Century Fund Report*. New Haven: Yale University Press.

Mishkin, F. 1986. *Money, Banking and Financial Markets*. Boston: Little, Brown.

Morgan Grenfell. 1989. *Building Societies: Buy or Be Bought?*, London: Morgan Grenfell.

Nationwide Building Society. 1987. 'House prices in Europe', *Nationwide Building Society Background Bulletin*. London: Nationwide BS.

NBPI. 1966. *Rate of Interest on Building Society Mortgages*, National Board for Prices and Incomes, Report no. 2, cmnd 3136. London: HMSO.

Nevitt, A. 1966. *Housing, Taxation and Subsidies*. London: Nelson.

OECD. 1986. *OECD Economic Surveys: West Germany, 1985/86*. Paris: OECD.

OECD. 1987. *OECD Economic Surveys: Netherlands, 1986/87*. Paris: OECD.

OECD. 1988a. *OECD Economic Surveys: United Kingdom, 1987/88*. Paris: OECD.

OECD. 1988b. *OECD Economic Surveys: United States, 1987/88*. Paris: OECD.

OECD. 1988c. *OECD Economic Surveys: West Germany, 1987/88*. Paris: OECD.

OECD. 1988d. *OECD Economic Surveys: Denmark, 1987/88*. Paris: OECD.

OECD. 1988e. *OECD Economic Outlook*, vol. 44 (December). Paris: OECD.

Ornstein, F. 1985. *Savings Banking: An Industry in Change*. Reston, Va.: Reston.

Pleyer, K. and Bellinger, D. 1981. *Das Recht der Hypothekenbanken in Europa*. Munich: C.H. Beck'sche Verlagsbuchhandlung.

Poole, W. 1987. Comment on Brumbaugh and Carron (1987), *Brookings Papers on*

Economic Activity, vol. 2, pp. 381–6.

Potter, P. and Drevermann, M. 1988. 'Homeownership, foreclosure and compulsory auction in the Federal Republic of Germany', *Housing Studies*, vol. 3, pp. 94–104.

Pyle, D. 1984. 'Deregulation and deposit insurance reform', *Economic Review of the Federal Reserve Bank of San Francisco*. pp. 5–15.

Radcliffe Committee. 1959. *Report of the Committee on the Working of the Monetary System*, Cmnd 827. London: HMSO.

Rhoades, S. 1982. 'Structure–performance studies in banking', Staff Study 119, Board of Governors of the Federal Reserve System, Washington DC.

Rhoades, S. 1986. 'The operating performance of acquired firms in banking before and after acquisition', Satff Study 149, Board of Governors of the Federal Reserve System, Washington DC.

Roistacher, E. 1987. 'The rise of competitive mortgage markets in the United States and Britain', in van Vliet, W. (ed.), *Housing Markets and Policies under Fiscal Authority*. New York: Greenwood Press.

Schäfer, O., Seuferle, W. and Wocher, C. 1986. 'Tradition und Perspektive — Wüstenrot im Wandel' in Hahn, G. and Otto, K-F. (eds), *Ein Zuhause für Menschen*. Frankfurt am Main: Helmut Richardi Verlag.

Scherer, F. 1980. *Industrial Market Structure and Economic Performance*, Boston: Houghton Mifflin.

Schnitzer, M. 1972. *East and West Germany: A Comparative Economic Analysis*. New York: Praeger.

Shaffer, S. 1984. 'Scale economies in multiproduct firms', *Bulletin of Economic Research*, vol. 36, pp. 51–8.

Shapiro, C. 1989. 'The theory of business strategy', *RAND Journal of Economics*, vol. 20, pp. 125–37.

Shepherd, W. 1979. *The Economics of Industrial Organization*. Englewood Cliffs, NJ: Prentice Hall.

Shepherd, W. 1984. '"Contestability" vs competition', *American Economic Review*, vol. 74, pp. 572–87.

Shiller, R. 1981. 'Do stock prices move too much to be justified by subsequent changes in dividends?' *American Economic Review*, vol. 71, pp. 421–36.

Siedman, W. 1986. 'The American experience: bank supervision in the United States', in Dale, R. (ed.), *Financial Deregulation*. Cambridge: Woodhead-Faulkner.

Sinai, A. 1976. 'Credit crunches: an analysis of the post-war experience', in Eckstein, O. (ed.), *Parameters and Policies in the US Economy*. Amsterdam: North-Holland.

Smirlock, M. 1985. 'Evidence on the (non) relationship between concentration and profitability in banking', *Journal of Money, Credit and Banking*, vol. 17, pp. 69–83.

Soros, G. 1987. *The Alchemy of Finance*. New York: Simon and Schuster.

Stiglitz, J. and Weiss, A. 1981. 'Credit rationing in markets with imperfect information', *American Economic Review*, vol. 71, pp. 393–410.

Stoughton-Harris, T. 1988. 'Building societies in the new environment', *Housing Finance, 1988*. London: Building Societies Association.

Stow Report. 1979. *Mortgage Finance in the 1980s*. London: Building Societies Association.

Strange, S. 1986. *Casino Capitalism*. Basingstoke: Macmillan.

Stuzer, M. and Roberts, W. 1985. 'Adjustable rate mortgages: increasing efficiency more than housing activity', *Federal Reserve Bank of Minneapolis Quarterly Review*, pp. 10–20.

Summers, L. 1986. 'Does the stock market rationally reflect fundamental values?' *Journal of Finance*, vol. 41, pp. 591–601.

Tobin, J. 1984. 'On the efficiency of financial system', *Lloyds Bank Review*, vol. 153, pp. 1–15 (July).

Topalov, C. 1988. 'Regulation publique du capitalisme et propriété de masse du logement: la "revolution hypothecaire" des années 1930 aux Etats-Unis', *Economies et Sociétés*, vol. 51, pp. 51–99.

Tucillo, J. with Goodman, J. 1983. *Housing Finance: A Changing System in the Reagan Era*. Washington DC: Urban Institute.

van Horne, J.C. 1985. 'Of financial innovations and excesses', *Journal of Finance*, vol. 40 (3), pp. 621–35.

Weiss, M. 1987. *The Rise of the Community Builders*. New York: Colombia University Press.

Weissbarth, R. and Hundt, B. 1983. 'Die eigentumsbilding im wohnungsbau', *Schriftenreihe Wohnungsmarkt und Wohnungspolitik 07.014*. Bonn: Der Bundesminister für Raumordung, Bauwesen und Städtebau.

Whitehead, C. and Kleinman, M. 1988. 'British housing since 1979: Has the system changed?' *Housing Studies*, vol. 3, pp. 3–19.

Whitehead, C. and Kleinman, M. 1989. 'Back to the future', *Roof*, pp. 35–6 (March/April).

Wilson Committee. 1980. *Report of the Committee to Review the Functioning of the Financial Institutions*, cmnd. 7937. London: HMSO.

Wojnilower, A. 1980. 'The central role of credit crunches in recent financial history', *Brookings Papers on Economic Activity*, vol. 2, pp. 277–326.

Yanelle, M-O. 1989. 'The strategic analysis of intermediation', *European Economic Review*, vol. 33, pp. 294–301.

Index